Fighting
Parkinson's...
and Winning

Fighting Parkinson's... and Winning

A memoir of my recovery from Parkinson's Disease

Howard Shifke

ISBN-13: 978-1979354028
ISBN-10: 1979354022

Printed and bound in USA by CreateSpace
First Printing, 2017

Book interior and cover design by Script + Vine
www.scriptandvine.com

Fighting Parkinson's Drug Free
58395 Lindsay Lane
Warren, OR 97053

www.fightingparkinsonsdrugfree.com

For Sally
my partner through eternity

and

our children,
Steven, Genevieve, and Victoria
the other three-fifths of my
Parkinson's recovery team

CONTENTS

IMPORTANT INFORMATION TO KNOW PRIOR TO READING THIS BOOK

This book is my story of having Parkinson's Disease and recovering from Parkinson's Disease. I am not advocating that anybody endeavor to do my Parkinson's Recipe for Recovery. I am telling my story, and nothing in this book should be construed as medical advice.

I am not a doctor. If somebody reading this book wishes to do any, or all, of my Parkinson's Recipe for Recovery® (Recipe), I do not recommend that anybody do anything that I did for my recovery without first receiving approval from his or her doctor(s), including mental health doctors, and from his or her religious and spiritual advisors.

I did not take any medications, nor did I take herbal supplements, herbal formulas, or Ayurvedic formulas. My recovery was a combination of soul, mind, and body healing.

The title of my website and blog is Fighting Parkinson's Drug Free. It is named this because I began my blog when I had Parkinson's, and this is an accurate description of what I was doing for my recovery.

Special note for those on medications: please do not stop taking your medications cold turkey (all at once). I feel it would be dangerous to your health. If you wish to do the Parkinson's Recipe for Recovery and have cleared it with all of the appropriate professionals listed above, many people over the years have started the Recipe while on medications. You would not be excluded from doing the Recipe just because you are taking medications.

INTRODUCTION

You are about to embark on a journey of my recovery from Parkinson's Disease. As your guide, I feel it would be helpful to learn a little bit about me before you begin the journey.

I was born in Miami, Florida, in 1961. I have an older brother by two years and a sister six and a half years younger. When I was young, I was a good student, played sports, played trumpet in the junior high school band, and felt that I was a well-adjusted child.

I did have one particular behavior that followed me through life, and I see it as something that helped me get Parkinson's. It was perfectionism. My level of perfectionism put me in a perpetual state of wanting to control everything and never feeling that my best was good enough.

As a result, I physically and mentally pushed myself to unhealthy limits. I did not know that this would one day contribute to me having Parkinson's because I was just living life the way I understood life was supposed to be lived. And, perfectionism, the adrenaline-mode, had its benefits.

One of the benefits that the need for perfection provided was that I was a good student and made exceptional grades. This assisted me in getting an academic scholarship to university and helped me get into law school.

After law school, I moved to Tampa, Florida, and practiced law for thirteen years. Another benefit that the need for perfection provided was that I was an excellent attorney.

A little over a year after I arrived in Tampa, I met Sally. Less than ten months later, we got married.

We have three children; two are graduated from university and married, and one still is in university and living away from home.

In the autumn of 2009, I got Parkinson's Disease. I developed a soul, mind, and body alternative recovery program, and on June 12, 2010, nine months later, I had my full recovery.

I saw my neurologist in August of 2010 and again in December of 2011, and both times he notated in my medical records that I did not have the signs and symptoms of Parkinson's Disease. He is the same neurologist who diagnosed me with Parkinson's, and he did not take away his diagnosis.

I am grateful that you are here and allowing me to take you on my journey through Parkinson's all the way to my recovery and what has been going on since then. Enjoy the journey.

—*Howard*

Part One

Parkinson's Disease:
Where it all began for me

September 21, 2009. This is the day that everything changed. The day started out just like any other day. Busy family, busy morning, everybody off to work and school and then the house to myself. I worked from home.

In the middle of the afternoon as I sat in front of my computer reading an email, I suddenly felt that the whole world was shaking. I soon realized that it was me who was shaking. The strange thing was that although I felt vigorous shaking from my head to my toes, I looked down at my arms on the chair's armrests and they looked calm.

Since I was in front of the computer, I went to Google and typed my query: "internal shaking." Google, of course, must have known that I meant "internal tremors," and everything that came up was about Parkinson's Disease.

I thought, "I don't shake like mom did, so it can't be Parkinson's Disease. Maybe it will be gone by tomorrow." I had watched my mother deal with Parkinson's for twenty-four years before she died two and a half years before my tremors appeared this day, and she had severe dyskinesia

3

shaking, which at the time I thought was Parkinson's tremors.

So, the fact that I did not shake like she did was comforting and it helped me not worry about the situation. Also, many things had been going wrong with me physically that I had been ignoring for the previous few years, so I was filled with a good bit of denial at that time as well.

That night as I was getting into bed, the tremors never having stopped, I was anxious as to whether or not I would be shaking the whole bed and have to explain to my wife, Sally, what was going on. Fortunately, the shaking inside me did not translate into visible or physical shaking outside of me. I was in the clear, so I thought.

The next day, I was more serious about my research. Everything I researched said Parkinson's Disease. I kept denying it, going to more websites, looking for long lists of symptoms so that I could continue to say to myself, "No, you do not have it."

But I had tremors, and I had been walking hunched over, and I was slowing down even though I was only 48 years old, and occasionally I was shuffling my feet, and my balance had become poor, and I had pain and discomfort, and I had very stiff and rigid muscles, and I had urgent and frequent urination, and I was constipated, and I was fatigued. Oh yes, and I was in denial.

Looking back now, it is clear that I had been suffering from some of these issues but kept shrugging them off. In 2009, I started seeing these symptoms in harsher manners.

In February of 2009, I went to the gas station and was unable to squeeze the pump with my left hand (my stronger hand). A day or two later, I had terrible pain in my arm as I went to lift the water pitcher off of the kitchen counter.

I told Sally and the children that I must have hurt my arm or had it bent too long on phone calls, but there was a terrible pain and a weakness in my left arm and hand. I decided I would rest my left arm and do more things with my right arm.

When I was young, as I would endeavor to do things like eating and writing with my left hand, I was told, "Put that in your other hand." So, I ate and wrote with my right hand, and I played sports and did everything else with my left.

In late March, three mornings in a row, when I put the dog food in the bowl and removed the bowl from the counter to put it on the floor, I dropped the bowl. Our dog was seven pounds, so it was not a large or heavy bowl.

On the third morning, as I was sitting on the floor picking up the dog food, I thought, "Mom got Parkinson's when she was 48, you just turned 48. Mom used to drop things, you are dropping things." Then, I remember pausing for a moment and thinking, "no, that's not it."

In April of 2009, I had such severe pain in my arms when doing my morning brocade of Qigong exercises that I had been doing every day for tens years, that I just stopped.

None of this got me to go to a doctor and have myself checked out. My denial was very powerful. Of course, my denial was just another name for fear. My fearful, over-thinking, adrenaline-driven mind would not allow me to face the truth that my body was broken terribly and no longer functioning properly.

What was I afraid of? The potentially bad news a doctor would give me when I arrived at his or her office in a body that was broken terribly and no longer was functioning properly. This fear of learning from a professional that something dreadful was wrong with me was so strong that I suppressed the entire thing for as long as was humanly possible.

My over-thinking mind kept telling me this story: if I did not see a doctor, then no doctor could tell me that something was wrong with me. Then, I could continue to pretend that I was doing things perfectly and that I was in control of my body. Also, I would not have to take responsibility to do something about whatever it is that was wrong with me because nobody was officially telling me there was something wrong with me.

This is what I mean when I say that my denial was powerful. It allowed me to lie to the one person who absolutely knew the story I was telling myself was a lie…me. And, I was willing to accept me lying to me about how bad I was because I was afraid of what it might be, and my life was too busy to stop for one moment to take care of me; I needed to be taking care of everybody else, so I thought.

The tremors on September 21, 2009, WOKE ME UP! Like getting whacked in the back of the head by a 2x4" piece of wood, they woke me up. Denial was weakened and fear was strengthened. What now?

So, there I was on September 22, 2009, with symptoms I had been denying and suppressing for months, and full-blown tremors that were making me crazy on only the second day, and I knew I needed to tell Sally. That night, we sat down and I broke the news to her. She asked me how I came to my conclusion. I outlined for her the research and experiences that I have written above, and I showed her a list I put together off of the Internet that had fourteen listed symptoms for Parkinson's.

I then commented to her that I drank lots of water, so I crossed frequent urination off of the list because I felt it could be attributed to my drinking a lot of water. She just stared at me. Apparently, denial did not wear well on my face. She said that crossing one off of the list didn't really change things. And we cried.

One of the things that was weighing heavily on our minds was my mother. My mother had Parkinson's for twenty-four years. She had died two and a half years prior to my tremors showing up. Mom had denied for twenty-four years that anything was wrong; Parkinson's was not a conversation that was allowed in our family.

However, just because Parkinson's was not a conversation that was allowed in our family did not mean that my mom's Parkinson's was not in our faces. We were just expected to deny along with her that anything was wrong.

From an outsider son looking in at his mother, here is what I saw over the twenty-four years. In the beginning, my dad told me, "Your mother has a condition where her nervous system is not working well, but she manages it with L-dopa and there is nothing to worry about. She does not want to discuss it, so if you notice anything erratic with her movement, do not say anything."

My mother was a wonderful woman, a mom's mom. She loved her children dearly and never would want to worry us. So, what my dad said fit my mom's character and her outlook of life...if you do not like something happening with you, pretend it isn't happening.

There are some instances that stand out in my mind regarding my mother's experience with Parkinson's that I need to write about so there is a better understanding of why I did not take Parkinson's medications.

Mom's neurologist had moved from Miami to Tampa and she did not want to change neurologists. Plus, Sally and I, and our children, lived in Tampa, so a neurologist's visit also meant seeing the grandchildren.

On one visit, I met my parents for lunch at a restaurant near my office in downtown Tampa. My mom was really shaky and had a hard time walking and standing. Then, in the middle of lunch, her uncontrolled shaking caused her arm to swing across the table sending plates of food and glasses of water crashing to the floor.

This scared me. And my mom sat there crying. And my dad simply said, "That was caused by your mother's medications. We are here for a neurologist's visit to have her medications adjusted." End of discussion.

After the neurologist's visit, I was told that the medications had been adjusted and that everything was fine. Fine is such an interesting word. In my family it meant, "Mind your own business, do not ask any questions, and pretend like nothing is wrong." I was a "pleaser," had been that way since childhood. I bit my tongue and said nothing further.

Then there was the time my parents arrived at our home and when I opened the door, mom's arms were bruised and she had a black eye. Privately, my father told me that there was an issue with the medications; when mom stood up, it made her lightheaded and she would fall down. Recently, she had hit her face on a piece of furniture before hitting the floor. And she would be receiving a medication adjustment at her neurologist's visit.

Fast-forwarding twenty years into the disease and medications saw my mother's mind beginning to slip. On one occasion, my parents were at our home and Sally went out to pick up a couple ingredients for that evening's dinner.

I was in the kitchen gathering the utensils to set the table, and my mother approached me to ask me who was going to be at dinner because she wanted to make certain she knew everybody's name at the table. I said it was just Sally, the children, her, dad, and me. She asked me if the people in the other room would be at the dinner table, and if so, what were their names. In the other room were my dad and my children.

Needless to say, this was a very strange encounter with my mother, especially since nothing of mental slippage had been mentioned and, of course, I was told that mom's neurologist said everything was fine.

As time went on, the scenarios looked more like this: My mother would say something that barely resembled words, then she would close her mouth as the tears would well up in her eyes, and very clearly would say, "Howard, nothing that just came out of my mouth made any sense, did it?" My saddened reply was, "No mom, it didn't."

I pressed my father on this issue. According to my father, my mother's neurologist had explained that after a couple of decades of Parkinson's medications, the medications simply wore out my mother thinking processes in her brain. She ended up with Alzheimer's and Dementia along with her crippled Parkinson's body.

Within a few years after that, she died.

So, fresh in our minds were mom's complete debilitation and the fact that the medications had overtaken her mind about three years before she died. This was scary now that I was facing the same disease.

In the first week or so after my tremors appeared, my body went through some dramatically disturbing debilitation. I learned three major things in those early days:

1. I could no longer get out of a chair without upper body assistance;
2. I could no longer go up the stairs without holding the hand railing and using upper body strength to help pull me up the stairs; and,
3. I had to struggle to get food to my mouth when using a utensil.

I remember Sally saying, "Isn't this supposed to be a slowly degenerative disease? I am watching you falling apart in front of my eyes in a matter of days." The only explanation that seemed plausible was that I had been doing a morning brocade of Qigong exercises for ten years and it had held off the onset of the Parkinson's. I surmised that the Parkinson's had built up extra strength below the surface to overtake me even with the ten years of basic Qigong, and once it overtook me physically, my body all but collapsed.

However, it was fortunate for me that during those ten years of doing my morning brocade of Qigong exercises, I had taken an interest in alternative healing and Traditional Chinese Medicine. I had accumulated many books, and we had practiced various forms of alternative healing in our home over those ten years.

There were three important things I had learned about alternative healing from those experiences in our home: 1. It works; 2. It takes time; and 3. There will be times when feeling worse is part of getting better.

I spent the next week at the library doing research. I read whatever I could get my hands on regarding Parkinson's from Western Medicine and Eastern Medicine perspectives.

I learned many things, including that the external, uncontrolled shaking that my mom had was dyskinesia caused by her medication called levodopa. It then made sense to me that my physical appearance with Parkinson's did not resemble what had been my mom's physical appearance.

Also, I learned that Western Medicine did not identify a cause of Parkinson's, viewed it as incurable, and was practicing disease management with medications to help with the symptoms. The view was that the dopamine was depleted and that the brain cells were dying and dead.

Traditional Chinese Medicine had a different viewpoint. What I learned was that for centuries Traditional Chinese Medicine discussed the symptoms, but the disease was not referred to as Parkinson's Disease because Dr. James Parkinson did not write "An Essay on the Shaking Palsy" until 1817.

In the years leading up to my getting Parkinson's, in my studying Traditional Chinese Medicine, authors constantly kept referring to *The Yellow Emperor's Classic of Medicine* by Maoshing Ni as the beginning of Traditional Chinese Medicine.

I had been able to get a paperback copy some years prior to getting Parkinson's, but the book was very complicated and I put it on the shelf after having read only a few pages. There is nothing like facing Parkinson's to have motivated me to pull the book off of the shelf and figure it out, no matter how complicated…excuse time was over.

I began reading *The Yellow Emperor's Classic of Medicine*, and I came upon a section that described the symptoms I was experiencing. However, there was a cause listed. The liver. The liver had become weakened, so the body had become too toxic, and the weakened liver had become invaded by external wind…wind is what makes things shake…tremors. This made sense to me.

Also, I researched Parkinson's medications. What I found was very interesting to me, and I shared it with Sally this way, "The medications are to help with symptoms only and they do not heal a person from the disease. Plus the side effects include tremors, stiffness, slowness, and constipation; I already have all four of those things. I do not need them more."

Additionally, since the liver already was overworked and not cleaning toxins efficiently, medications would be the last thing I would want to take, as they would burden the weakened liver even more.

It seemed to me that everything in Western Medicine that was written about Parkinson's Disease was actually written about "Parkinson's Disease on medications." I decided I was going to endeavor to recover from the disease itself, not just hide the symptoms, and that I would learn exactly what was Parkinson's Disease because I was going to experience it raw and unaltered by medications.

So I sat down with Sally and I outlined my treatment plan, which is described in brief below and in great detail in Part Two of this book. It now is called the Parkinson's Recipe for Recovery; back then it did not have a name, but was "just what I was doing to have my recovery from Parkinson's."

I told Sally I knew I would fully recover from Parkinson's. However, I did add this to the conversation: "Even though I have complete faith and I know in my heart I will recover some day, if I am wrong and the doctors are right, then at the end of the path, I think I will be completely paralyzed." Sally's response was instant, and it was simple: "It is just a body. You won't lose your mind like your mother, so I won't lose you. If you can tolerate what the disease dishes out to you, I am all in."

And off the cliff we went into the abyss of unchartered territory of actually fighting Parkinson's Disease and moving toward a Parkinson's recovery.

I share this so that my story of fighting Parkinson's drug free will make more sense. Doing my methodology of recovery and eventually having a full recovery from Parkinson's was my Plan A, and I had no Plan B. With Plan A only, I was forced to see the silver lining in every cloud, something that was incredibly new to me.

Emotionally, this was a difficult journey. I spent a lot of time in the beginning wondering why I had the disease and feeling that I had let down my family once again.

When I say, "let down my family once again," I am referring to the ten years leading up to the onset of the Parkinson's. In the mental/emotional/spiritual part of my recovery, which is explained in Part Two of this book, I go into great detail explaining the difficulties and stress of the ten years leading up to me getting Parkinson's.

As a result of the events that are explained in Part Two, these had been difficult years financially, and I felt it all was my fault. My children having to leave private school because we no longer could afford it. My fault. Our electricity getting turned off a few times over those ten years. My fault. Our house falling into a state of disrepair over those ten years. My fault. Living in Florida and having no air conditioning for a couple of years. My fault. This book would be too long to read if I tried to list here everything unpleasant that had happened to our family over those ten years, all of which I had considered my fault.

I saw myself with distain, no longer a "good provider," not worthy as a person, and it all was my fault. I was filled with self-judgment, self-criticism, a large amount of "would have, should have, could have" reflections of the past, and then, Parkinson's.

Parkinson's, as if my family already had not been through enough. Parkinson's. Talk about kicking a guy when he already is down. Parkinson's.

However, there was a special place in my heart for Sally and our children called love. I loved them so much, and my having Parkinson's was so unfair to them, I simply needed to solve the disease and have a full recovery. I saw no other way out.

So, every day, out of love for them and sheer determination to get better for them, I dragged myself out of bed at 4:00am and did my recovery program. It was the least I could do for them since I felt I had let them down again.

In the beginning of doing my program for my recovery, I kept a Parkinson's Daily Journal. My intention was to document what I was doing and how I was doing. Since I had not been to a neurologist for a formal diagnosis at that time (I received a formal diagnosis five weeks later), I felt it was important to detail as much as possible what my symptoms were like and what I was doing each day in my furtherance of my Parkinson's recovery.

Moreover, since I felt confident I would be having a recovery some day, I wanted to document how I was each day and what I was doing each day to enable me to share my methodology with others in the future.

My Parkinson's Daily Journal contains entries of the first 51 days of working on my recovery. After that, my handwriting was so poor and it hurt so much to write, I stopped writing in my journal.

The excerpts from those first 51 days are contained in Appendix One of this book. However, below is the first entry as it lays out my philosophy of Parkinson's and my methodology for recovery.

09/28/09. Last Tuesday, I sat down with Sally to explain that I have Parkinson's. I have tried denying this for a little while, but the internal tremors were very strong that day and no telling when they might appear as external tremors.

Sally and I have been through everything, and she is the strong one and I needed a plan.

We talked things through and agreed to explore every option and jointly make a decision.

After much research and much discussion, the plan is to move forward with a Traditional Chinese Medicine (TCM) approach. There are three main causes of Parkinson's from a TCM viewpoint:

1. Qi and Blood Deficiency, which is caused by emotional stress, anger, frustration, and resentment.
2. Phlegm-Fire Agitating Wind, which is caused by dietary considerations such as consumption of too much greasy, fried or sweet foods.
3. Kidney and Liver Wind; Deficiency, which is caused by overwork and insufficient rest which unbalances the body's natural rhythm.

The healing approach will change as the disease changes. However, the starting point is to keep a strict diet in place, perform Qigong (Chi Kung) for elevating the Qi and Blood Deficiency, elevating the Kidney and Liver Yin Deficiency, and acupressure for stimulating the brain and spinal column. [In layman's terms, here is what I was getting at: The liver was overworked and not cleaning the blood well (Blood Deficiency). As a result of the blood being deficient, it was not bringing the body the proper nutrients and oxygen, thus causing the body to be weak and fatigued (Qi, life energy, Deficiency). The physical part of the healing methodology was to heal the organs and bring the body back into balance so blood and Qi would no longer be deficient and the body again would be vibrant].

Reference Materials:

1. *The Yellow Emperor's Classic of Medicine* by Maoshing Ni, Ph.D.
2. *Chinese Health Care Secrets* by Henry B. Lin
3. *Qigong Empowerment* by Master Shou-Yu Liang
4. *Soul Mind Body Medicine* by Dr./Master Zhi Gang

Sha
5. *Integrative Acupressure* by Sam McClellan
6. "Degenerative Diseases, Interpretation and Treatment with Chinese Medicine" by Subhuti Dharmananda (http://www.itmonline.org/arts/degenerative.htm)
7. *What Your Doctor May NOT Tell You About Parkinson's Disease* by Jill Marjama-Lyons, M.D.
8. *Teach Yourself Chi Kung* by Robert Parry

What I am experiencing:

1. Internal tremors when my body is at rest. When I move, they seem to go away, although it just may be that my attention is elsewhere because I am moving rather than being stationary.
2. Rigidity. My left arm is very tight in the muscles, particularly my forearm. I am in constant pain in my left arm and although it is my stronger arm as I played all sports left-handed, I have no strength. I have a hard time lifting the water pitcher and cannot squeeze the pump at the gas station.
3. Bradykinesia. My movements are slow and my balance is horrible, particularly when I first get out of bed. Example: I cannot hold my shorts and lift one foot to step into them. I have to hold onto something, hold my shorts in one hand at floor level, step into them and finally pull them up. My walking is very slow and if I am not consciously paying careful attention, I walked hunched over while shuffling my feet. I need to use the chair arms or the table to stand from my sitting position. I need to focus before walking up the stairs holding the railing. It is painful, but I can walk up the steps. I must hold on and focus on my

balance because I go backwards when I lift either leg. Sometimes I have to go one step at a time where the second leg moves up only to the step where the first leg is located and I progress a step at a time in this manner. When I turn around to go back in the other direction (regular walking, not stairs) I go in a semi-circle almost like walking around a marker.

Treatment: [Note to reader: Much of this may be new to you. It is not critical to understand all of the terms now. They will be explained in great detail later in the book, particularly in Part Two, which is an in-depth explanation of the Parkinson's Recipe for Recovery].

1. Dietary—fruits, vegetables, whole wheat (bread, rice, barley), oatmeal. No preservatives, no alcohol, no fried foods. Focus is to dispel the Phlegm-Fire Agitating Wind. (reference: Chinese Health Care Secrets).
2. Qigong—Medical Qigong focused on elevating the Kidney and Liver Deficiencies. Buddhist Qigong for elevating the Qi and Blood Deficiency. (reference: Qigong Empowerment).
3. Acupressure focused on the Governing Vessel, GV, and Conception Vessel, CV. (reference: Integrative Acupressure).
4. Sound, Vibration, Energy elevation, near hand-far hand healing techniques (reference: Soul Mind Body Medicine).
5. Exercise for Qi circulation in the same channels as #3 above. (reference: Teach Yourself Chi Kung).
6. Smile more, be more patient with my situation, think before moving. Try to be a nicer person. Take each moment as it occurs and deal with it in the best

possible manner. No fear allowed. Let my family know every day how much I love them.

I learned today that if I want to try to walk normally, I need to focus on standing up straight, extending my leg and getting my foot off the ground, and, swinging my arms. Apparently, as I have been hunched and shuffling my feet, my arms have stopped swinging. Consciously swinging my arms helps a lot with balance.

I learned another very important thing: when I am walking, I need to be really focused. I got the mail and on the way back up the driveway, I started looking through a magazine; the next thing I knew is that I was completely off balance and I fell down. I read an article last week where the author, a Parkinson's sufferer, said that the days of walking and chewing gum were over. I laughed. Today, I learned it wasn't funny.

And off I went to work on my recovery. I was careful about my walking and balance after the fall in the driveway. It is hard to explain how it happened. One moment I was walking up the driveway and looking in the magazine, just like I had been doing for the over 15 years we had lived in that home, and the next moment I was down on the driveway...no notice, no wobbling, no trying to catch my balance...just down.

Parkinson's had such an unpleasant way of getting my attention. I found myself often thinking, "the strangest thing happened today." I would wonder, "what made the symptom change?" or "why did I fall in the driveway?" or "why do I get these spaced-out-and-don't-feel-like-doing-anything feelings overtaking me sometimes for hours at a time?"

My body was not doing what I wanted it to do and I was over-thinking everything that was happening with me. At the beginning of my recovery journey, I had a lot of questions and I had no rational explanations for answers.

But then again, Parkinson's Disease for me had no rational explanation.

I knew I had it. I knew I did not want it. I knew mostly everybody said I could not have a recovery. I knew I wanted a recovery. I put a treatment plan together to have a recovery. To most people, this, too, was completely irrational.

In the beginning of my journey to recovery, I was excited to be doing something positive in furtherance of my recovery. However, there were some functional issues that were plaguing me and required immediate attention.

One of these was eating. When I went to eat with a fork or spoon, my arm and hand would get the food on the fork or spoon and lift it up from the plate or bowl. Then, it would freeze, mid-air, hovering a couple of inches above the food. I would have to think about moving the utensil and food to my mouth.

Initially, I tried concentrating on the fluid motion of picking up the food and going directly to my mouth, but I was not being successful. Sometimes, I could force my hand, and with a tight, painful, cogwheel motion, I could force the food to my mouth with about 6–8 clicks of my elbow joint. Sometimes all of the food would be on the utensil, sometimes not.

However, I realized at some point that I did not have a problem getting chips or finger-food directly to my mouth. So, I sat in a chair in front of my bathroom mirror and picked up my toothbrush as if it was an eating utensil. With repeatedly examining the picking up of food with a utensil versus the picking up finger food, I discovered the problem and created a solution.

When using a utensil, my hand came in from the side of the food, and my shoulder and elbow got involved in the movement as my elbow came away from my body. The problem was that my shoulder and elbow froze and locked once the utensil was lifted a bit above the food.

When eating finger food, my shoulder and elbow remained close to my body and the movement of my hand moving the food to my mouth was a simple bending of the elbow similar to a "curl" with a dumbbell weight.

After much practice, I arrived at my solution, that is, the one I used when eating at home with my family or by myself. I put my elbow on the table (sorry Miss Manners) directly next to my plate or bowl, positioned where I could lay my arm, from elbow to hand, flat on the table next to the plate with the palm of my hand facing upward.

I placed the utensil in my palm where the part that was going to pick up the food came out of the pinky side of my hand. From there, I could approach the food from the back of the plate, get the food on the utensil, and with a simple bend of the elbow like doing a dumbbell curl, the utensil came straight up to my mouth. My shoulder and elbow did not interfere with this process because they were not being used, except for the bend of the elbow, which did not freeze.

When this elbow-on-the-table was not appropriate, I tried to eat finger food whenever possible because I could easily get it to my mouth. When neither of these was available, I did what I had to do. I was hunched forward anyhow, so once I would get my food hovering above the plate, I would lean forward and bring my mouth to the food.

Nobody ever said anything about this. I would imagine that nothing was said because I had Parkinson's and was doing the best I could, but sometimes I felt that the others were so appalled, it simply left them speechless.

One additional important thing I learned in doing this special eating routine was that I was doing the best I could, and that I could not do better than my best. Part of getting the Parkinson's was a lifetime of never thinking that my best was good enough, followed by self-judgment and self-criticism. I had to learn to accept that I had Parkinson's and was doing the best I could, and it was good enough.

I had come up in life with a feeling that I needed to be perfect and do everything perfectly. I feel that this created an enormous conflict inside me. On the one hand, I felt I needed to do things perfectly, and on the other hand, I knew I never had done anything perfectly.

This was a constant emotional struggle in my recovery. Accepting that my best was actually the best I could do and that it was good enough was a difficult lesson. However, it was a necessary lesson.

I finally gave in that it was okay to give myself an emotional break because I had Parkinson's and could not do things the way I used to. I

figured that once I recovered, I would be able to do things the way I u
to. I can tell you after all of these years subsequent to my full recovery, that
this is a correct assessment. Not only can I do things "the way I used to"
pre-Parkinson's, but I do them with a far greater appreciation than I ever
had in the past.

Another issue I had to face in the beginning, and mostly throughout
my recovery, was a lack of energy. When I began doing my recovery Qigong
exercises, Medical Qigong for the Liver gave me a big surprise. When I got
to the 4th repetition, I broke out in a sweat, got lightheaded, and had to
lie down on the floor.

As I was lying on the carpet in my bedroom and completely saturating
it with sweat, I remember thinking that I was way more toxic than I had
imagined. This reaction also showed me that I had selected the correct
Medical Qigong, but I wondered how on Earth was I ever going to get to
the 10 repetitions listed in the Qigong instructions. Eventually, I slowly
worked my way to 10 repetitions.

Getting out of a chair was another issue I realized was a new and
difficult part of my daily existence. I could not get out of a chair without
using my upper body to push down on the chair arms or to push down on
my desk or a table to initiate getting up from a chair.

There was something not functioning in the initiating movement to
get out of a chair. Once my bottom was lifted from the chair and I leaned
forward, I could straighten my knees and stand the rest of the way up.

Then there were the stairs. When I had Parkinson's, we lived in a two-
story home. One day I was walking from the kitchen down the hallway
and turned to go up the stairs. My feet froze at the bottom of the stairs. No
matter how much I tried to lift my foot, my body refused.

I then reached out and grabbed the railing. Then, and only then, would
my foot release. I got up to the first step and felt myself falling backwards, so
I held the railing with both hands and used whatever upper body strength I
had to pull myself up the stair as my legs labored in the process.

It occurred to me that it made completely good sense that I needed to
hold the railing to go up the stairs. My balance was so poor that if I were
not holding on, I would have fallen backwards onto the tile floor. That

: been pleasant.

le me realize that my freezing was directly related to my

ng mind never had to move my body prior to the onset of

ior to Parkinson's, my body just moved when I went to do

something; thinking was not involved.

When I got Parkinson's, and my body stopped doing what I wanted, I looked to my mind to solve the problem. This was a necessary, but unfortunate, thing to have to do. Essentially, I had given my mind a promotion well beyond its experience and abilities.

The thinking mind does not know how to move a body. However, the Parkinson's demanded it. If I could not move a certain way, I mentally tried to work out how to move the way I wanted to move. My mind, though, did not know how to move me in a consistent and smooth manner; it did its best, but my movement was slow and awkward.

Prior to Parkinson's, if I was sitting in the living room and the phone rang in the kitchen, without thinking, I got up, walked down the hallway and answered the phone. When I had Parkinson's, it was a completely different scenario.

With Parkinson's, if I was sitting in the living room and the phone rang in the kitchen, my first thought would have been, "They will have to leave a voice mail because I never will make it to the kitchen in five rings." Then, I would endeavor to get to the kitchen to see who called.

It would look something like this: First, I would get out of the chair in the way described earlier. Next, I would take a number of "baby" steps in place to turn myself a quarter of a turn to face the kitchen. Then, I would start shuffling or walking (depending on my abilities that day) toward the kitchen.

That involved a lot of thinking. However, I realized over time that my thinking mind did not know much about movement, so my movement was slow with jerking motions, inconsistent in speed and balance, and unreliable as to whether I would be taking steps or shuffling.

Also, I realized I had no choice except to rely on this over-thinking mind because movement with Parkinson's would have been dangerous if careful attention had not been given to the details. Emotionally, it was difficult to have to think about moving, as it was a constant reminder of how difficult it was to move.

Plus, I shook. I shook and shook and shook, but nobody could see it. Trying to describe internal tremors was nearly impossible. Without an external tremor, many people presumed I had hurt my back because I shuffled or walked slowly, was hunched forward, and I was in obvious pain.

And then came the worst of it: *"Did you hurt your back?"*

"No, I have Parkinson's Disease."

"You can't have Parkinson's Disease because you don't shake like Michael J. Fox and Muhammad Ali."

"They shake like that from their medications."

"No they don't; you don't know what you are talking about. You must have something else."

Although I desperately was trying to get anger and frustration out of my life because I saw them as two of the top things that cause Parkinson's to come to the surface, I would walk away from these encounters carrying my old companions, anger and frustration. It was hard to remain calm when I felt like nobody except a small handful of people understood me.

Fortunately, one of those people was Sally, and every night she performed Governing Vessel Acupressure from my tailbone, up my spine, to the top middle of my head. It was the one and only time in the day when my tremors would cease momentarily.

However, momentarily was all I needed to say, "Thank you, I love you, good night," and off to sleep I went. Governing Vessel Acupressure had been mentioned in our acupressure book as something to do for assistance with Parkinson's tremors, and I am grateful to this day that the information was accurate.

Prior to Parkinson's, I had been an early-morning riser. We had a busy household, so in the early morning hours, usually 4:00am, sometimes 3:00am, I would awaken and begin my day. It was a wonderfully quiet and peaceful time of the day where I could exercise, read, and do spiritual work.

4:00am became my "do the Recipe" time of day. The Recipe had exercises, reading was good for calming the mind (and I added in meditation) and spiritual work was there as well. It fit my morning schedule nicely.

Of course, my morning schedule included Parkinson's. There were days when the alarm went off and I opened my eyes rather peacefully. Then I would get off of the bed, or endeavor to get off of the bed. There were some mornings when I thought, "Wow, this wasn't just a bad dream. I actually have Parkinson's."

Getting off of the bed was a challenge, plus I was concerned about waking Sally. So, I would do the 6-8 bounces into the mattress to get myself onto my back. Then I would take a few deep breaths.

Next, in a somewhat simultaneous movement, I would slide my feet and lower legs off of the side of the bed while pushing my elbow into the mattress in hope of getting enough momentum that I would then find myself sitting on the edge of the bed with my lower legs and feet hanging off of the edge. Whew! There were many days that this effort was so difficult, I just wanted to lie back down and go back to sleep.

Of course, there were those days when my body wanted no part of this, so I simply had to get enough momentum to roll off of the bed onto the floor. It was a start because it got me out of bed. On those days, I would crawl out of the bedroom. This was an exhausting and humiliating process.

Even though I was the only one who knew this was going on, I still was mortified. And, on the mornings when my legs would not cooperate at all, I went down the stairs on my bottom, one step at a time. Once I reached the foyer on the steps, I would assess my legs to see if they were able to support me.

Then I would head into the bathroom, empty my bladder, put on my contact lenses, and go to the kitchen and turn on my espresso machine. In Appendix One of this book, you can see that I had become obsessed with how long this took me each day. Ultimately, it was just another opportunity to assess my symptoms and criticize my slowness.

Eventually, I needed to quiet my mind and become more accepting of my symptoms, my slowness, and my other shortcomings. However, in the beginning of my recovery, I documented my demise and criticized myself for it along the way.

There is another reason I got out of bed at 4:00am each day to do the

Recipe: I did not want to worry Sally and our children with my terrible symptoms in the morning. I knew my mother's situation was fresh in all of their minds, and by the time I finished doing the Recipe in the morning, I looked and moved the best I was going to look and move all day—excellent time for seeing the family.

Although this allowed me to "put my best foot forward" when seeing the family in the morning, it had not prevented me from judging and criticizing myself on a regular basis. Since my get-out-of-bed routine was the same each day, I looked to the kitchen clock to decide how much slower I was on any particular day.

This was not a joyful way to begin the day. I remember thinking (and then writing in my Parkinson's Daily Journal) how much slower I had become in getting to the kitchen in the morning. I could not get out of my self-criticizing mind (e.g. "Oh, I took 8 minutes to get to the kitchen when it used to take me 4 or 5 minutes.").

When I look at it now, I realize how much my adrenaline-mode mind was just sitting around waiting for me to be less than perfect so it could call me out on the issue, criticize me, and then tell me how much worse I was doing. It got to the point that it seemed like I was looking for reasons to criticize myself, and then self-criticism became a self-fulfilling prophecy.

At some level, I was really lost. I had announced to Sally and myself that I would be having a Parkinson's recovery, I had put the tools in place to get there, but I still was sailing in uncharted seas…nobody had put together a recovery plan like the one I had put together for myself, so there was no point of reference to determine how I was doing.

At no time did I doubt that I would have a recovery in the future by doing the Recipe. The part I had to figure out was how could I keep a positive attitude about what I was doing when my symptoms were changing in what looked like unfavorable ways.

One day in the middle of severe leg pain, the answer came to me regarding the question, "what does everything that looks unfavorable going on with my body actually mean?"

"It means I am getting better." That is what I decided. It occurred to me in middle of the severe leg pain that it had been a while since I had felt anything in my right leg, specifically the outer part of my thigh. The fact that I was feeling something meant the communication between my leg and my brain was functioning well.

If the communication between my leg and my brain was not functioning well, then I would have felt nothing. With a smile, I thought, "Since I am the only person doing my recovery program then I get to interpret what everything that occurs means."

And with that thought, I decided that no matter what was happening, it meant that I was getting better. Yes, this may sound crazy, but to me, there was a logical method to my madness.

I was working on my recovery, and everything I was doing in my recovery program was designed to heal me. I knew from previous holistic healing at home over the previous ten years, that almost all of the time, there was a period or two of feeling worse on my way to getting better.

Plus, since the Recipe was my Plan A, and I had no Plan B, being afraid I was getting worse was a luxury I could not afford. Negative thinking about if I was being successful in my recovery would do nothing to assist me.

So I did something I never before had done. I decided that I was going to find a silver lining in every cloud…I was going to find a positive reason for every single thing that was occurring with my symptoms. This was a way of acting, thinking, and feeling like I never before had done.

However, the way I normally had been acting, thinking, and feeling is what I was doing when I got Parkinson's, so doing something different would probably work. It would have to work. That is how I felt.

In the beginning of my recovery, Sally and I kept the Parkinson's to us. We did not see any point in discussing it with anybody until such time as we had a better idea of what it was all about. I was okay with this idea because I knew how hard it was going to be to tell our children that I had Parkinson's.

As we were heading into the first couple of weeks of October of 2009, Sally and I discussed when and how we were going to tell our children, Sally's mom, my dad, my brother and sister, and our friends Mary and Jerry.

By mid-October, I had been doing my recovery program for a few weeks and kept watching myself getting physically worse, which brought up our time frame in telling all of them. October 16th was Sally and my twenty-first wedding anniversary. I was sad that day, feeling completely awful about myself. "Happy Anniversary, all I have to offer you is a husband with Parkinson's Disease."

With my increasing symptoms, we realized that we owed it to our children to tell them what was going on. We saw Sally's mom regularly, and we saw Mary and Jerry fairly regularly, plus my dad and my sister and her now-husband were coming to our home in November for Thanksgiving, and my brother needed to hear it from me, not our dad. We prepared for the "Big Tell."

First was our children. We had to wait for a weekend where we could get Steven to come home from college so we could tell them all at once. That day got scheduled for October 17th.

My tremors were on the inside; it had not been an issue to "hide" the Parkinson's until then. The stiffness, slowness, and pain...I just told our daughters Genevieve and Victoria, who were living in our home at the time, that I had hurt myself, end of discussion.

Sally and I have discussed what occurred that day and our memories are solid on how it went. First, when I told our children I had Parkinson's Disease, everybody cried...a lot. I would like to put this into perspective.

My mother died in 2007. The medications had taken her mind three years before that. In 2004, my children were 13, 11, and 7, and for the next three years, their interactions with their grandmother included trying to talk to a person crippled in a wheelchair with Alzheimer's and Dementia and holding their ear to her mouth as she tried to utter words.

As you can imagine, it paints a rather unpleasant picture when coupled with the fact that their dad now had the same disease.

I then explained to them that I was not going to end up like grandma. I told them that the medications had taken her mind and that I was not going to take the medications. I told them that the current theory of Parkinson's was incorrect, and that I had put together a holistic healing program that would lead to my recovery.

Please know that these are the same children who for the previous 10 years did Dr. Sha near hand far hand chanting for congestion, had us do acupressure and Jin Shin Jyutsu on them for colds, sore throats, and injuries, and who knew that this type of healing worked.

I told them that they were intelligent children and that they could go on the Internet and verify that Parkinson's did not lead to Alzheimer's and Dementia, but instead, that it was the long-term usage of the medications that lead to Alzheimer's and Dementia.

They were satisfied. The crying stopped, the mood changed, and the day went on. None of us were afraid of Parkinson's.

I was blessed with a loving family. Each one stepped up and helped in areas where I needed help. The Parkinson's brought us closer.

Steven was a freshman in college and lived in the dormitory about a 30-minute drive from our home. He would come home every few weekends and assist with some household work I could not do anymore at that time such as climbing the ladder to put food in the bird feeder.

Genevieve was a junior in high school. She was my nighttime driver. I realized early on that driving at night was too difficult for me. The darkness and bright lights caused a sensory overload that made driving at night a near impossibility for me.

Victoria was in seventh grade in middle school. She approached me one day and asked what she could do to help me get better from Parkinson's. I told her that I needed to keep my brain active, so it would be a big help if she would do the daily crossword puzzle in the newspaper with me.

Sally, the love of my life, is the glue that held us all together. She was a wife, mother, full-time employee who also had to work every seventh Saturday, family cook, and Governing Vessel acupressure practitioner for my tremor relief every evening. And, she was my all-in 100% partner in life and Parkinson's recovery. She knew I would have a full recovery every bit as much as I knew it.

Sally has expressed that two things brought her the most sadness in my recovery. First was that I could no longer take our evening walk together with our dog. Second was that I was struggling to the breaking point physically as I was trying to learn that I was a precious being, one worthy of forgiveness, compassion, and love, especially my own.

She stood back and watched me painfully struggle through the end of my recovery, constantly battling myself and criticizing myself, without forgiveness or compassion for myself, because she knew I needed to make this breakthrough myself…nobody else could do it for me.

Next to tell were our friends Mary and Jerry. Mary and Jerry knew Sally before I met her. They were long-time friends, the friends who our children called Aunt Mary and Uncle Jerry, those kind of close friends…family.

Sally and I scheduled to go to Mary and Jerry's house for a visit on October 20, 2009. After dinner, when we were making certain our children were settled in at home with what they were going to be doing that evening, Sally and I prepared to go over to see Mary and Jerry. And then came the pain.

I started experiencing excruciating pain on the right side of my abdomen. I told Sally I could not go, and she offered to stay home. Ultimately we agreed that she would go and tell them without me there. It turns out that I was in the beginning of a gallstone attack.

I remember this situation well. I lost 8 pounds in one day. It began with the pain on the evening of the 20th. Then, the chills, the sweats, the bathroom visits, the curling up on the floor, the getting in a hot bath… nothing could relieve the pain.

I was in so much pain, I thought I was going to die. I remember thinking, *here I am and I will be remembered as a guy with Parkinson's who died sitting on the toilet in the middle of a gallstone attack.* My mind was interesting in how quickly it could paint the worst possible picture of what was occurring in my life. There are some adventures that make a strong mark in one's life and this was one of them for me.

At 12:45am on October 21st, the stone finished passing through the duct and the pain went down in half. I was able to fall asleep. At 2:00am, I woke up and went downstairs to have a glass of water.

As soon as I finished the eight ounces, I broke out in a sweat and began having chills again, so I headed back upstairs to get in bed. As I was going through the bedroom doorway, I skipped the bed and headed directly for the bathroom to throw up. Five minutes later, I threw up again.

Sally told me that this was good because the articles she had read about passing a gallstone said that after the gallstone successfully passed, I should throw up. Apparently I was still an over-achiever...threw up again in the morning after a glass of water and a cup of peppermint tea.

Sally explained that she spared me the "success meant throwing up" news earlier when I was in such agony and it was not something I really needed to look forward to. Generally "success" was incredibly more pleasant.

In assessing the situation, this is what I concluded: my gallbladder had been in such bad shape that after three weeks of Medical Qigong for the Liver, I had a breakthrough—so much bile released into my terribly weakened and dry gallbladder that it lifted the stones to the top and one of them went into a very dry common bile duct. Over 6.5 hours later, it made it's way to the other side and passed.

This type of assessment was an integral part of keeping my positive attitude. It was how I approached my Parkinson's recovery; whatever was occurring with my body, it was a sign that I was getting better. I then would look for a positive attitude reasonable explanation for why anything had occurred, accepted it, and moved on. It was my new way of surviving.

In the category of "everything happens for a reason," this ordeal, as I called it, brought to my attention issues with my Large Intestine meridian, and I was able to make a little more sense of my Parkinson's. What I mean by this is that I received a real awareness that my Large Intestine was not functioning properly. It helped me learn that my body was a remarkable organism in taking care of itself as long as I continued to provide it the proper tools and materials to support its healing processes.

Generally, when my body would give me experiences I did not like, I would want to squash the experiences. This is what I did on the way to getting Parkinson's; I suppressed and ignored the unpleasant physical experiences.

However, with this gallstone attack, I learned a completely different lesson. My body was so remarkable that many times an "unpleasant thing" going on actually was a solution to an unknown problem. It was pointing out a previously unknown problem that needed to be solved that was unrelated to the unpleasant experience.

During the gallstone episode, periodically I headed to the bathroom for bowel movements. I went approximately seven times and passed probably ten feet or more of stools.

I had no idea that my body was holding so much "matter" in my intestines. Clearly, this was a major problem and was making me more ill with my Parkinson's. As unpleasant as the gallstone situation was, it opened my eyes to an additional issue instead of just closing my eyes in misery.

It helped me fully embrace and explore all that was going on with my Parkinson's, which ultimately assisted me in solving the disease.

That was part of the journey…each day making a little more sense out of my Parkinson's…each day making a little more sense out of my life.

As a result of the gallstone attack, I had two days in a row where I did not do the physical part of the Recipe, and I was not fearful that it would have any negative impact on my recovery. Instead, it reinforced the necessity of knowing that my best was good enough.

This gallstone ordeal also served as a reminder to me about a deeper view of the Recipe and what was occurring to bring about my recovery:

The body. The physical part of the Recipe was healing my organs.
The mind. The mental part of the Recipe was calming my mind. This was going to lead to improvement of symptoms.
The soul. The spiritual part of the Recipe was opening the natural dopamine flow. This would lead to finishing my full recovery.

I feel that it was the ability to transcend the physical misery, to take myself to a happier place mentally and spiritually, especially when my body was in physical misery, that helped transform my life and my recovery. It began to bring me back into balance to the clear understanding that I am my soul, my essence, my spark that lights me up as uniquely me. I am not my body. I am not my mind.

At the worst of physical misery and at the worst of mental self-judgment and self-criticism, I did my best to open my heart and find joy in my life.

Next up to tell about the Parkinson's was my dad. I called him November

1, 2009, and told him that I had Parkinson's Disease. He asked me if I had been to a neurologist and I said no.

My dad immediately jumped down my throat about "self-diagnosing." I explained my reasoning to him about what I was going through as well as what I was going to do and not going to do about the Parkinson's; it fell on deaf ears.

At the end of the call, I agreed to call Marcie at the neurologist's office the next day. This was the same Parkinson's specialist who had been my mother's neurologist up until the time she died two and a half years before I got Parkinson's.

In agreeing to call the neurologist's office, I had not yet realized that I was still suffering from my life-long issue of making other people happy and avoiding conflict.

All in all, it was a good thing that I went to the neurologist. Even though I knew I had Parkinson's, some people only feel you have a disease if a doctor says you have the disease.

After I got diagnosed with Parkinson's and told these same people that I was going to have a recovery, they told me I was in denial because I was refusing the treatment plan of taking medications.

I learned that doing something different made many people, including family and friends, uncomfortable. However, not taking medications was one area where I had no flexibility and did not care if it created conflict with others or made them uncomfortable...it was important for taking care of my health and me.

In response, I was very clear on this point:

I fully accepted that I had Parkinson's.

I was in denial that I could not get better!

Accepting that I had Parkinson's disease was the first step in fighting the disease. Acceptance went something like this: "I accept that I have Parkinson's Disease...what am I going to do about it to recover?" The "what am I going to do about it to recover" was the difficult part because it presumed something that required me to discard conventional protocol for Parkinson's—it presumed that I could do something about it to recover.

And, it also meant that I had to take responsibility to heal myself.

Acceptance.

I accepted that I had Parkinson's Disease.

I accepted that I could do something about it.

I accepted responsibility to do something about it.

I accepted that doing the Recipe put me on my path toward recovery.

I accepted that I would do the Recipe and stay on my recovery path until I fully recovered.

I accepted that I had the power to heal myself and that I was healing myself.

I accepted that I was recovering every day that I was doing something positive in furtherance of my recovery.

I accepted that I was worth it.

Denial.

I denied that Parkinson's was incurable.

I denied that there was nothing I could do to recover from Parkinson's.

I denied that unless I was taking medications or having brain surgery, that I was doing nothing for my Parkinson's.

I denied that the Recipe would not work for me.

I denied that I was not worth it.

On the days when symptoms seemed worse and fear crept in, it was difficult to keep these acceptance and denial positive thinking, good attitudes in the forefront of my feelings.

I needed to focus on the fact that the journey I was on was life, not Parkinson's. Parkinson's was just something happening in my journey called life, so I dealt with it while I was living my life to its fullest.

Every road had bumps. It was how I viewed the bumps that mattered. Some people see the bumps as roadblocks to life; I preferred to see the bumps as nuisances that made me slow down and caused me to navigate more carefully, which brought me more awareness.

And lo and behold, while I was slowing down and navigating my life more carefully with greater awareness of my Parkinson's bumps, I noticed so many beautiful things I had been missing. Over time, my Parkinson's bumps in the road became a blessing. They became mere signs to follow that I needed to pay more attention to healing my life. And, when I finished healing my life, my soul, mind, and body, I did not need any more messages or signs, and they left.

However, back in November of 2009, when I called Marcie at Dr. Sanchez-Ramos' office, she gave me a January 28, 2010, appointment to see him. I was happy when I couldn't get in to see the neurologist until January 28, 2010, nearly three months from my call, because I was not looking forward to seeing a neurologist who did not believe I could get better from Parkinson's.

I called my dad and let him know that my appointment was January 28, 2010, and his response was, "I can't wait that long." Later, I got a call from Marcie that there had been an opening on November 5th, and would I be available to see Dr. Sanchez-Ramos then. I presumed my dad must

---

Morsani Neurology #2
13330 USF Laurel Dr, Tampa, FL 33612
813-974-2201

Juan Sanchez-Ramos M.D.
FLME47064
NPI:1205859352

Name **HOWARD SHIFKE**   MRN   1743331

Address 2714 CHAMBRAY LANE, TAMPA, FL 33611   DOB   03/23/1961

Azilect 1 MG Oral Tablet #**30**

Quantity: (thirty tablet)

TAKE ONE TABLET BY MOUTH EVERY DAY

Signature of Prescriber

Rx VOID unless printed on blue background safety paper
Back of the paper has "Secure RX" repeated all over
The front of this paper has safety feature that reads VOID
when copied - Printed in ink that resists erasure

Written: November 05, 2009   **Refills Authorized 5 Times**   Rx: 45749876

UBS0905066:

Morsani Neurology #2
13330 USF Laurel Dr, Tampa, FL 33612
813-974-2201

Juan Sanchez-Ramos M.D.
FLME47064
NPI:1205859352

Name **HOWARD SHIFKE**   MRN   1743331

Address 2714 CHAMBRAY LANE, TAMPA, FL 33611   DOB   03/23/1961

Amantadine HCl 100 MG Oral Capsule #**90**

Quantity: (ninety capsule)

one po tid MDD:300 TDD:300

Signature of Prescriber

Rx VC   on blue background safety
Back of the paper has "Secure RX" repeated all over
The front of this paper has safety feature that reads VOID
when copied - Printed in ink that resists erasure

Written: November 05, 2009   **Refills Authorized 3 Times**   Rx: 45750963

UBS09050662

---

have called her and worked something out.

Of course, I was still in adrenaline-mind mode, abundantly caring what everybody else was thinking, from my dad all the way to the neurologist I had yet to meet. However, the one thing I was certain I never would do "just to make the other people happy" was to take Parkinson's medications. They were not the right choice for me.

On November 5, 2009, I went to see Dr. Sanchez-Ramos at USF Health. At my neurologist visit, Dr. Sanchez-Ramos put me through 30-45 minutes of physical tests.

Three tests in particular stuck out in my mind: 1. A repetitive motion test where the repetitive motion of one hand tapping on my thigh caused my other shoulder to become stiff and then my other arm to fly around uncontrollably; 2. A "follow the pen with your eyes" test where he told me he could detect cogwheel rigidity in my eyes; and 3. After the walk and turn test in the hallway, he told me to wait there for a moment as he needed to get something—he then went behind me and grabbed my shoulder and shook it and let go—I fell backwards and he and the assistant had to catch me.

In the end, he wrote me two prescriptions, Azilect and Amantadine. I never filled them. In fact, here they are:

He told me that everybody who had Parkinson's needed to be on medications. I told him that I was not going to be taking these medications as as I had explained earlier during the appointment. As a result of my telling him that, he scheduled me to come back in three months instead of six months.

As I was leaving, he called my name as I reached the door, and I turned around. He came over to me, looked me straight in the eyes and said that I would fall because my balance was so poor. Then, he highly recommended I at least fill the Amantadine prescription because "when you fall, you will want to have that at home ready to take."

Fortunately for me on this one point, I was still in my stubborn, adrenaline-driven, perfectionist mode, and oh yes, did I mention angry about his words. I thought, "I refuse to fall." And, after that day, I NEVER fell.

I realized in my recovery that I did not need to fall. In fact, I did not need to do anything that anybody told me would happen with my Parkinson's. I looked at it like this: I am not following what Western Medicine is telling me to do, so Western Medicine has no idea what I will and will not experience with my Parkinson's.

I felt in my core that I was so much more than a bunch of Parkinson's symptoms. It bothered me that Western Medicine felt that it could control my life by saying "oh, now that you have Parkinson's, all of these terrible things will occur."

It is why acceptance and denial were critical continuing lessons in my recovery.

I accepted that I had Parkinson's, and then had received a diagnosis to prove it. This was healthy acceptance.

I continued to deny that I could not get better. This was healthy denial.

What I decided my life would be like in between "You have Parkinson's" and "You don't have Parkinson's anymore" was up to me. It was my life, and I wanted to live it to the fullest! This was healthy living.

Although I disagreed with my neurologist's prognosis that I could not recover from Parkinson's, I did learn some valuable information from my visit with him and the tests he performed.

Part of what I learned from the tests at the neurologist's office was that repetitive movement on one side of the body set off rigidity and uncontrolled movement on the other side of the body. This was the reason I added Awareness of Neural Impulses and re-training my brain in the Recipe.

I felt that I needed to have a better understanding of how my electrical impulses were flowing, and I decided the electrical flows would work better if the left side of my brain was flowing down to the left side of my body and the right side of my brain was flowing down to the right side of my body.

I remembered when I was young having learned about people who had a brain injury to one side of their brain leaving the opposite side of their body paralyzed, and that these people eventually were able to move their entire body. This told me that the non-injured part of their brain was able to move the same side of the body it was on, which at the time was paralyzed.

I felt that if I could re-train my brain to move the side of the body it was on, then I would not suffer from the crossover issues experienced at the neurologist's office. When I did the awareness of neural impulses (explained in depth in Appendix Two, p. 259), each time I moved a limb, I then closed my eyes and the only impulses I felt were on the opposite side of the body.

I knew I needed to fix this, and I worked on visualizing the energy flowing from one side of my brain down the same side of my body. This is explained in great detail in Part Two of this book.

After my diagnosis, I called my brother and my sister to let them know about the Parkinson's diagnosis. My brother, Mark, asked a lot of questions, many of them focusing on how I felt about his children being at risk rather than worrying about himself. I told him that I did not see a problem for his children, and probably not for him either.

My sister, Allison, lived in Miami, and she had seen our mom on a fairly regular basis in the last years prior to our mom's death. I told her what I had been doing for the previous five weeks working on my recovery, and that I had no intention of taking the Parkinson's medications.

She responded that the only thing she was going to ask of me was to please not take the medications if I thought it would be possible to forego them. She had seen what the medications had done to mom's mind, and she could not picture me that way. She also told me that she and Rick would make a point to visit more often when they could because we never knew where this would be heading, so let's make a point to see each other more.

As I made my way through November of 2009, I saw my symptoms worsening, but I took what I felt was a realistic attitude toward the Parkinson's. My physical body had been declining for a number of years and I was doing nothing about it except denying it and making excuses.

My tremors showed up in September of 2009 and my official diagnosis was in November of 2009. I did not get Parkinson's the day of my diagnosis. I did not get Parkinson's the day my tremors showed up.

Clearly, I had Parkinson's at least a few years prior to the tremors and diagnosis, so I was not going to be slowing or halting the progression within a few weeks of starting my recovery program. To me, that was a realistic outlook.

When I started my recovery program, I felt that I probably would have to do the Recipe every day for two or three years before I would see a benefit from it; not a full recovery in two or three years, but just a benefit in slowing or halting the disease in two or three years.

I had no idea at the time how much of a psychological advantage this gave me over the disease. Psychologically, it completely diminished the importance of the symptoms and what they might be doing on any particular day. I was expecting that the symptoms probably would be getting worse for two or three more years before I physically caught up with the disease, so why worry what they looked like on any day?

As I was making my way through November of 2009, my symptoms continued to escalate, but I really saw it as part of what I needed to experience in my recovery. I felt that at some point I would hit the bottom, and then up would be the only direction I would go from there.

However, during that time I was keeping my Parkinson's Daily Journal, and this kept me looking at my symptoms on a daily basis even though I was doing my best to not give them much importance.

Finally, on November 17, 2009, I wrote my final entry in my Parkinson's daily journal:

> **11/17/09.** Up at 4:00am. Eight hours in bed. Got up a few times to use the bathroom, but no problem going back to sleep.
>
> I feel rested and stiff...slow moving, but the weighted feeling of yesterday is gone. Got to the kitchen at 4:09am. Expecting a great day today.

The entry was short and to the point, and barely legible in handwritten form. Writing was at a temporary end for me. The pain from the rigidity of holding the pen and trying to make letters happen had made writing nearly impossible to perform and nearly impossible to read, so I stopped.

Hindsight tells me that it was a blessing that I could no longer write in my daily journal. When I read through it, yes, there is a lot of hope and faith, and there is a lot of love for my wife and children. However, I will have to admit that there was a whole lot of being consumed with living Parkinson's instead of living life.

Looking at it now, I see that I was measuring my deterioration, from how long it took me to get to the kitchen each morning to how stiff I was or how painful my rigidity had become.

I had yet to let go of my perfectionism. Since I was documenting my Parkinson's recovery, my perfectionism told me that I needed to document everything "perfectly," right down to each thing I could no longer do each day that I could do the day before, including a full and complete analysis of my symptoms right down to the comparison of "are my symptoms better or worse today than they were yesterday."

When I could no longer write in the daily journal, I stopped paying attention to the minutiae of the symptoms, and I stopped comparing each day to the day before. Since I was not documenting these things on a daily basis, my need to be perfect about what was going on with my symptoms disappeared, and my ability to be in the moment of what I was doing grew. My symptoms became nothing more than a reminder that I had more work to do in my recovery.

I know I had been measuring those things so I would know when I was recovering. How foolish was I. I had overlooked the fact that every day when I woke up, got out of bed, made my coffee, and did my Recipe, I was recovering. That's right, recovering…moment by moment…recovering just in the doing!

I did my Recipe because I had faith that I would have a full recovery one day. If I had lacked faith in my recovery, I would have stayed in bed or slept so much that I would not have known if it was day or night. But I had faith in my life and my recovery; I did the hard work every day.

Faith is an interesting thing. When one is experiencing wonderful things in life, faith in one's self and in one's life are easy and natural. When one is experiencing difficulties in life, faith in one's self and in one's life are difficult and unnatural. Progress in life takes place when one is experiencing difficulties in life and still can find faith.

Thanksgiving of 2009 arrived, and my dad, Allison, and Rick came up from Miami. Facing them was difficult. One thing about internal tremors is that nobody could see when I was anxious and shaking more. But as they were pulling up the driveway, I stepped outside to greet them.

I shook and shook and shook, which made my movement substantially impaired. They could not see my shaking, but they could see my tentativeness as I greeted them. There was very little to say at that moment.

As the weekend visit progressed and I relaxed a bit, I was able to explain to them my recovery program and what I had learned from my research about Parkinson's. It felt good to talk about it, and my ears needed to hear my confidence in my recovery.

We made it through the rest of the holiday season with family and friends, and each visit was a little easier than the one before. As I was struggling with Parkinson's, we were struggling financially.

However, my dad; Sally's mom; my brother Mark and his wife Pat; Allison and Rick; Sally's siblings; and our friends, Mary and Jerry, opened their hearts and wallets to our children so our children were well taken care of with gifts throughout the holiday season. For all of you, Sally and I are abundantly grateful.

As 2009 came to an end, I was happy to see it go. I looked toward 2010 with a smile on my face anticipating good things to come. And then, things came crashing in…overwhelmingly severe constipation.

I became extremely miserable with the constipation. I was so miserable that I felt it was worse than the Parkinson's. Plus, the electrical impulses in my body were flowing so incorrectly that I felt the urge to have a bowel movement twenty-four hours a day every day.

I would sit in the bathroom for twenty minutes five or six times a day, and nothing, nothing but frustration. I began doing research about the large intestine, constipation, and all things that people do not discuss in life as relates to having a proper bowel movement on a regular basis.

I remember how saddened I was, thinking, *Wow, I am 48 years old, and my days have been reduced to wondering whether or not I will be having a bowel movement.* Clearly, my positive attitude and acceptance of what was happening in the moment went straight out the door with the constipation.

My research taught me that one of the main culprits in getting this problem was me. I had lost 35 pounds in the first few months after getting tremors. Since Parkinson's provided few pleasures in life, and I needed to eat more just to not lose more weight, I over-indulged during the holidays.

The turkey sandwiches and meat dishes were a delight. I ate and ate and ate, and did not gain any weight back. I thought it was remarkable. My research explained that animal protein took a lot of energy to digest and that it stayed in the body a fairly long time compared to non-animal protein, greens, grains, fruits, and vegetables.

Since I was working hard to build my internal energy, and since I knew everything inside my Parkinson's body was moving slowly just like my limbs were moving slowly, I knew I needed to make a change.

And then, while upstairs researching constipation and large intestine function, Sally was downstairs cooking one of my favorite meals, ropa vieja, which is a meat dish filled with wonderful spices. As the aroma was arriving in my room, instead of my usual salivating, it turned my stomach. At the conclusion of my research, I went downstairs to deliver the news. I needed to switch my diet to vegetarian.

After explaining my situation and that I would not be eating the ropa vieja, Sally looked at me with empathy and said, "Okay."

I switched to a vegetarian diet, just like that. Sally joined me. She took it on as an adventure, an expansion of her culinary skills, and she shined. It truly helped my recovery as it cleared up the constipation issue and improved my energy.

As January was coming to a close and bowel function was resuming itself to a more normal daily process, I realized what an impact the shifting of energy had taken on my symptoms. I felt cleaner and healthier on the inside, but I felt weaker with worse looking symptoms on the outside.

Normally in my recovery, this would not have bothered me. However, I had an upcoming neurologist visit on February 4, 2010. I was dreadfully afraid that if my neurologist looked at my symptoms the way I felt they were exhibiting themselves, he would put pressure on me to take the medications.

My fear got the best of me and I asked Sally to take the time off of work to come to my neurologist appointment for moral support.

At the conclusion of the appointment, which included the 30-45 minutes of physical tests, my neurologist told us that he could not explain it, but that I had improved in three areas: my walking was improved, my balance was improved, and the rigidity in my right shoulder was improved. As a result of this, he was not as anxious as at the conclusion of my first visit and he told me to come back in six months.

As I continued working on my recovery, most days were the same physically. I called it "my Parkinson's normal."

It was what I reasonably could expect each day to be based on the way I moved through the day; slow, stiff, hunching, painful, tremoring, shuffling, me, as I was at that time.

However, all along, I knew things were changing on the inside; that is, that my organs were healing. This is a really important point. The physical part of the Recipe was for healing my body on the inside. It was not exercises to help with my symptoms.

I knew I needed to experience the symptoms to solve them. The Recipe was not developed for my "disease management," like the Western Medicine approach to Parkinson's. The Recipe was developed for my disease recovery!

When I say I knew things were changing on the inside, it is because I got my sense of smell back; my fingernails were growing fast, strong, and healthy looking; the whites of my eyes were clear and white rather yellow and milky. All of these were signs that my liver was healing.

I was getting rid of indigestion and acid reflux, and my urinary urgency went away. These were signs of healing my stomach and spleen, and my kidneys and bladder. And the constipation was under control, a clear sign of healing my intestines.

When people looked at me on the outside and judged me by the way my symptoms looked, they had no idea of all of the improvements I was having on the inside. I needed to learn that there was no reason to care what others thought when they looked at my symptoms. I struggled with that lesson.

Having compassion for those who were negative to me because of what my symptoms looked like was a monumental task! Even though I knew I was healing my body on the inside, the healing of my mind and my soul still were struggling.

By mid-March of 2010, I felt that I had stopped the disease from progressing. Except for little fluctuations that might last a day or two, physically my symptoms had not changed in a number of weeks, and I felt that my internal organs were healed.

Although this was an incredible thing, stopping the progression of the disease, it was confusing to me that I was not having any large, recognizable symptom relief. I told Sally that I had reached a point where my symptoms had not changed, and my condition was livable.

I explained that even though I knew I would be having a recovery some day, if I had to live the rest of my life with how my symptoms were at that time, I could do it. I would not be thrilled about it, but just in the knowing that I would not be getting physically worse, I would manage.

Part of why I was confused is that I had looked at my recovery as a soul, mind, and body recovery. I felt that by having unwavering faith in my recovery that I had accomplished the soul healing. I felt that by getting anger and frustration out of my life that I had accomplished the mind healing. I felt that by healing my internal organs that I had accomplished the body healing.

If that was accurate, then I should have been sitting in a full recovery. I realized that I must have missed something. And, I knew what I must have missed was in the soul and mind healing because I was quite certain that my internal body was healed.

At that point, I decided to get on the Internet and research Parkinson's again, which was something that I had not done in six months. My goal was to see if I could figure out what I had missed.

I was searching for people who were doing alternative things. All I kept coming up with was people who were taking Parkinson's medications and talking about alternative remedies for the side effects of the medications. I became frustrated. Apparently, I had not fully extricated frustration from my being; I complained to Sally and our children.

They suggested that I start a blog. Me, the guy who lost writing ability four months earlier and was down to one finger typing, to write a blog. I learned some valuable lessons that day, one of which was "don't complain too much or your family will tell you to start a blog."

I said okay. I did not do this to please Sally and our children. I did it because what they said made sense to me. They said that if I wrote a blog and discussed what I was doing, then other like-minded people would have the opportunity to find me and we could help each other.

First, I needed a name for my blog. I remembered an article I had read months earlier when researching Parkinson's where the author wrote that he noticed that if he spoke to somebody with cancer, they would refer to their condition as "I'm fighting cancer."

The author went on to write that people with Parkinson's would respond, "I have Parkinson's Disease." It struck a nerve with me when he concluded that cancer sufferers were fighters and expected to prevail over their disease, and that Parkinson's sufferers accepted the fact that they had an incurable disease and did not expect to prevail, so why fight it.

I said a few choice words under my breath to that author, and I decided to call my blog, "Fighting Parkinson's Drug Free." "Fighting Parkinson's" because that is what I was doing. "Drug Free" because that is how I was doing it.

I was very timid in the beginning of the process. On March 25, 2010, I began my blog with my first blog post entitled, "Recently diagnosed with Parkinson's Disease." Here is what I had to say:

Hi.

I turned 49 years old two days ago. In November of 2009, I was diagnosed with Parkinson's Disease. My mother had Parkinson's for 24 years before she died, and a couple of months before receiving my official diagnosis, I was pretty much certain I had it.

My mother was not diagnosed with Parkinson's right

42

away, and she had been put on drug treatments prior to her Parkinson's diagnosis. She responded well to the initial Parkinson's medications, and hence received her diagnosis. She fought a long and valiant fight, but in the end, it seemed like the drugs took their toll and played as much a part in her passing as did the disease itself.

I am fortunate to have learned from her experiences and her courage, and I am fortunate that her Parkinson's specialist is located in my city—he is my Parkinson's specialist now.

I am doing my best to fight this drug free. Admittedly, my movements are slow, my balance is not good, I have regular nagging pain, and I tire much more easily than before. However, I have decided to listen to these messages my body is sending me and work toward a long-term solution from a holistic perspective. I am interested in sharing my experiences to help others and I am interested in hearing others' experiences to help me and anybody else who reads this blog.

All I can do is share what I am doing...what works and what does not. Everybody who suffers from Parkinson's suffers in a different way. Obviously, if something I am doing looks like it would be worth you giving it a try, let your doctor know what you are thinking about doing. I am not a doctor, and I am not advocating you do anything that you and your doctor have not discussed. My doctor is fantastic and has given me the green light to explore the approaches I will be describing in later posts.

I would not be able to fight this fight if it were not for the love of my wonderful wife and children, as well as my extended family and friends. I have many blessings in this life, and I feel that Parkinson's is just a roadblock...not an immoveable object.

I look forward to a meaningful dialogue.

All my best,
Howard

Starting the blog was cathartic. Some days when I was particularly miserable in my physical being, I would write a post. There was something about clicking the "publish" button and sending my post out to the Internet and the Universe that was liberating.

In the beginning, except for a few family and friends, I had nobody following my blog. I was okay with that because I realized that I was writing the blog for me as much as for anybody else. I started re-connecting with my inner voice.

I realized that my extended family, none of which lived in Tampa, should know that I had Parkinson's if they had not heard yet, especially since I had started a blog. I imagined that at some point in time I would see some of them at holiday events, weddings, or funerals in the future.

I put together an email and sent it to family groups of aunts, uncles, and cousins. This is what I sent in emails with the subject, "Hello from Howard Shifke:"

Hi All,

I hope you are doing well. I do not know how news travels, and I would like to let you know what is going on with me.
I am fighting Parkinson's Disease. I realized I had Parkinson's in September of 2009, and was officially diagnosed with it in November. The doctor took my history and said my first diagnosable symptoms were in February of 2009. According to the experts, it is an incurable, progressively degenerative disease that attacks the motor skills and that 60-80% of the neurons controlling motor skills have died before the patient ever realizes they have the disease. The medications and surgeries do not help make one better, they only make one more comfortable while the body deteriorates. The experts do not leave a lot of wiggle room for having a happy outlook, and I have way

too many blessings in life to accept their opinions at face value. I have been studying Chinese Medicine and Holistic Medicine for nearly a decade, and I am fighting Parkinson's with non-conventional methods—why use the conventional methods—they do not work, and we know from Mother's experience with Parkinson's before she died, they destroy your brain as well.

I have been unable to locate anybody who is attempting to fight Parkinson's with a completely holistic approach such as mine, so Sally and the children suggested I start a blog to see if I can help others and to see if there are others out there who may be able to assist me. Even people who are taking medications may benefit from some of the things I have learned. My blog is very new, and I put 4 entries in there to get it started and I will be adding much more information as time goes on. Here is the link to my blog http://fightingparkinsonsdrugfree.blogspot. com/. The entries are in chronological order starting at the bottom. If you wish to follow the blog, you can click the follow button and set up a quick Google account using your own email address. Feel free to forward the link to anybody you wish.

By the way, I feel pretty good, and I do not look different, except that I have lost 35 pounds (Parkinson's is not the way I would recommend losing weight; the internal tremors apparently burn a lot of calories). The external shaking that most people associate with Parkinson's is actually a side-effect of the medications. It is called Dyskinesia, and since I am taking no medications, I have no external shaking.

Anyhow, thank you for reading my long-winded email. I hope you will take a look at my blog and pass along the information to anybody who you think it may benefit. Also, if you have any questions, comments, suggestions, please let me know. I am an open book and very willing to hear what anybody else has to say.

> *Love,*
> *Howard*

I received many well wishes from extended family members, and some of my cousins started following my blog. It was nice to be able to re-connect with many relatives after so many years of not being connected.

In the beginning of writing my blog, I did my best to let readers know what I had been up to the previous six months working on my recovery, and I wrote about topics such as sleep, coffee and caffeine, and the food I was eating (fourth month as a vegetarian).

During that time, my symptoms were pretty much the same as they had become in March. In doing more research, I sensed that the soul healing would involve a deeper understanding of myself and a releasing of life's traumas. Also, I sensed that the mind healing would require learning to meditate and calm my mind.

I was resistant to both of these notions. How was I supposed to meditate and calm my mind? My over-thinking, always-worrying, brilliant, precious mind was supposed to turn into a calm, non-thinking, non-worry mind? Preposterous. I wanted nothing to do with it.

How was I supposed to heal my soul by solving life's traumas with forgiveness and compassion? My mind (the precious one in the paragraph above) was telling me that some people did not deserve to be forgiven. And, loving myself? Preposterous. I wanted nothing to do with it, either.

Then came May of 2010, the month of overwhelming misery. In May of 2010, my symptoms took a decided turn for the worse. And, I knew exactly why it was happening.

It was a result of me having the internal battle I was having with myself regarding the need to calm my mind and the need to open my heart. The more I struggled with learning to like and love myself, the worse my symptoms got.

At that time, I had not written too much about symptoms on my blog. However, after having breakfast with an old friend who cried when I told him I had Parkinson's and asked me to explain rigidity, here is an excerpt of what I posted on May 10, 2010:

I have rigidity in my arms, legs, and upper back into my shoulders. Last week, a friend asked me to explain my rigidity so he could get a better sense of what I am experiencing.

1. My arms—the next time you sit down to eat, pick up some food with your utensil, and while holding your utensil just above the plate or bowl, flex and tighten every muscle in your arm from your shoulder to the grip on the utensil. While maintaining this, try to get the utensil with the food to your mouth. My arms are tight like this all the time.
2. My legs—stand as straight as you can and then put a little bend in your knees. Next, flex your calves and thighs. Now, try to walk. Or do this in front of the stairs and see if you can walk up the stairs without holding on. When you add the symptom of very poor balance to the formula, you can see why leaning forward when walking and holding on when going up the stairs are commonplace among those fighting Parkinson's. My legs are tight like this all the time.
3. My upper back—it is tight and hurts all the time. I really do not have a good example for you to emulate.

Having a positive attitude is the key to everything. My mind and body have accepted the pain, so I am not consumed by it every waking moment. Deciding every day that fighting Parkinson's drug free is a fight worth fighting is what keeps me going. Quite frankly, getting to spend time with Sally and the children to celebrate Mother's Day yesterday is really what keeps me going.

All my best,
Howard

May was the month where people were looking at my symptoms and telling Sally and me that whatever I was doing was not working. My symptoms were really terrible, but as is written in this blog post, I was starting to really open up my heart, "getting to spend time with Sally and the children to celebrate Mother's Day yesterday is really what keeps me going."

During May, I also discovered a group in Santa Cruz called the Parkinson's Recovery Project. At the time, they had been doing Parkinson's research for about a dozen years.

There was a 690-page pdf on their site that I downloaded and read. Two main things were meaningful to me from the pdf. First, somebody else agreed with me that one could recover from Parkinson's, and it would involve some calming of the mind and opening of the heart.

This was a very positive reinforcement of the feeling I was having and had recently stopped resisting. Second was Yin Tua Na (Forceless Spontaneous Release). Essentially, their research found a large amount of people with Parkinson's had a reverse flowing stomach meridian that was a result of an old ankle or foot injury and the Yin Tua Na was a foot holding technique to help fix the flow.

Had I identified earlier that there might have been a stomach meridian backward flow issue when I started the Recipe, I would have performed stomach meridian acupressure instead of Yin Tua Na or FSR.

However, since they wrote about this technique being successful for getting the stomach meridian flowing in the correct direction, I asked Sally to hold my foot. I felt an energy release in my leg on one of the days, so I felt I had derived a benefit, which is why it is listed in the Recipe.

This was a small part of the Recipe (total of 2.5 hours, or 30 minutes per day for 5 days), particularly when compared to everything else in the Recipe (performed daily for nine months). As far as I saw it, every benefit I received was a welcomed benefit, and each thing I did that showed me any level of a positive physical reaction was a welcomed part of a greater whole in my healing and recovery.

However, I knew that it was my emotional and spiritual struggles that were holding me back. I did not have a problem having forgiveness and compassion for others, but I did have a problem having forgiveness and compassion for myself.

My mind was beating me up on a regular basis. I had spent my life feeling like I needed to be in control and do things perfectly. As a result, my mind had saved, categorized for easy retrieval, and continuously dumped on me a lifetime of not being perfect enough.

When I first was attempting to calm my mind and find forgiveness for myself, my mind let me know that I was unforgivable: "What about the 98% on the math test in second grade; you should have gotten 100%." "What about the day you walked in the winning run in the seventh grade softball district championship." "What about when your timing was off and you came in late for the trio in 'Bugler's Holiday' in ninth grade band."

This is the tip of the iceberg. This list of what I now look at and see as mistakes, missteps, errors…life…no big deal…were an enormous deal to me, and my Parkinson's mind knew it. It was relentless.

Eventually, I learned to meditate, and it helped me immensely to calm my over-thinking judgmental mind. I started seeing life through calmer, non-judgmental eyes, even in how I viewed myself.

Then came the bigger challenge, loving myself. I was completely uncomfortable with the entire notion that I needed to love myself. At the time, I was just starting to have breakthroughs where I thought it was permissible to like myself and forgive myself.

Ultimately, I decided that it was okay to love the seed of God inside, my soul; I would nurture my soul. I felt that as my soul healed and grew back into its radiance, it would transform into love for me.

Sally noticed me changing as a person. She mentioned that I needed to write on my blog what I was doing because I would not have credibility if I went from completely miserable to full recovery without some posts in-between explaining what was going on.

I was hesitant to do this. The negativity about me not taking medications, self-treating, and looking physically miserable was overwhelming. I was not excited to write on my blog about calming my mind and opening my heart in self-love. I saw it as another way for people to be unpleasant to me.

Sally responded by saying that hadn't I told her that I needed to not worry what people were thinking about me and to just be the best me I could be. She was correct.

Here is an excerpt from what I posted on May 31, 2010:

> Adrenaline—you are walking through the jungle and a lion jumps out and starts chasing you. When your survival mode adrenaline kicks in and you start running, other things are required of your body. Your stomach gets the message from the brain that says, "eating is of minor importance right now so do not send me hunger pangs." The bladder and the large intestine get the message from the brain that says, "no time to evacuate, so I need you to shut down temporarily." The body gets the message from the brain that says, "you are being pushed to your physical limits, but I do not want to hear about your pain—shut it off." The heart gets the message from the brain that says, "no time for joyful emotions, so do not release dopamine, just store it for later."
>
> What I have had to come to terms with over these last couple of weeks is that I ran from the lion for ten consecutive years [this is explained in-depth in Part Two of this book] and he only stopped chasing me on a rare occasion or two for very brief moments. Shortly after the lion stopped chasing me, my tremors began and my Parkinson's symptoms became apparent and debilitating. My home life, Sally and the children, was, and is, loving and supportive. However, external factors resulted in ten years of stress filled with fear, anger, frustration and resentment.
>
> Although the stress and those emotions have been put to the side, my subconscious brain still has me functioning in adrenaline mode. After ten years of functioning in this emotional survival mode, my physical body and organs have forgotten how to be normal. I need to get out of adrenaline mode and re-train my organs and body. I have been hesitant to write about this because, from a

conventional mind-set, this theory is "out there" and there may be some who read this blog and feel I have lost my mind. To them, all I can say is what Socrates told a young Dan in Dan Millman's book *Way of the Peaceful Warrior*, "Sometimes you have to lose your mind before you come to your senses."

I needed to lose my mind. My mind was an adrenaline-driven, self-judging, self-criticizing mind. It told me that I was not worthy and deserving—not as a person, and not for a Parkinson's recovery. Yes, I absolutely needed to lose that mind.

As I spent more time getting out of the house and seeing people, I spent less time thinking about the Parkinson's. Also, I was becoming more comfortable in my own skin. I was learning to love myself and that I was a worthy and deserving person…everybody was.

I went from my judgmental mind into my compassionate heart. I started looking at everybody, myself included, as a suffering being. I felt that everybody was suffering from something, physically, mentally, and/or spiritually, including me.

Instead of looking at somebody's words or actions and making judgments with my mind, I started looking at the suffering behind the words and actions. This changed me forever.

I found acceptance, for myself and others.

I found forgiveness, for myself and others.

I found compassion, for myself and others.

I found love, for myself and others.

On June 9, 2010, I had a big break in my symptoms; most symptoms took a 50% decrease and some went away altogether. I was very excited and thought that was it, my full recovery any day. Two days later, I found myself with no further change.

After some quiet meditation, it came to me, and I announced my realization to Sally at breakfast on June 11, 2010, like this: First I told her I knew what I needed to do to complete my recovery and what I was about to tell her might sound like the most selfish thing ever to come out of my mouth, but it was not selfish, and then I said, "There is no person on this planet worth me continuing to have Parkinson's Disease just to make them happy."

After I made my announcement to Sally, and she agreed with me that I needed to be happy, I then announced this to her: "And, after the dust settles and I am cured from Parkinson's, if nobody talks to me, I still will be the happiest guy in the world because I will no longer have Parkinson's. Plus, I know you will still be talking to me, and I am okay with that."

Sally seemed puzzled and asked why would people not be talking to me. I explained that nobody knew the real me except her so I knew she would still talk to me. However, maybe nobody would accept the real me, and maybe nobody would like the real me, and thus, maybe nobody would talk to the real me.

The fear of being the real me is what had been holding me up. The more I resisted being absolutely vulnerable, being genuinely me, the more physically miserable I had become in the last month leading up to my full recovery. And through that physical misery, I let go.

I surrendered.

I realized that I needed to clear my shelf of my annual Academy Award for Best Actor in the part of Howard Shifke, and I threw them all in the trash along with the script I had been acting from for the previous 45 years or so.

I realized that the script from which I had been acting the Howard Shifke part all those years had been written by others (parents, siblings, teachers, coaches, relatives, friends, etc.); the script had not been written by me, and it had little to do with who I really was, the real me. I decided that my script of life going forward would have to be whatever rolled out in front of me, trusting and accepting that if it was rolling out in front of me then it was necessary in my life...accept it and deal with it in the moment, moment after moment. That's it.

That night, I let go of the remaining fear of being me.

That night, when Sally came to do the Governing Vessel Acupressure as she had every night for nine months, I told her things were okay and it would not be necessary.

As explained in the Recipe, after my usual meditations, affirmations, and prayers, I added the following that night before going to bed:

> *Dear God, I surrender my ego to you. I surrender my attachment to my Parkinson's Disease to you. I am not afraid anymore. I no longer fear Parkinson's. I no longer fear the scorn I may face by being cured from a disease the experts say there is no cure. I no longer fear the people who may say I was misdiagnosed or that I faked having the disease. I am surrendering my ego to you, that part of me that felt I needed to remain attached to Parkinson's because the experts say once you have Parkinson's you always have Parkinson's. I am forgetting about my old self (Parkinson's) and stepping into my new self (No Parkinson's)."*

I awoke the following morning with my remaining symptoms gone.

You see, I had found me again. That silly, funny, joyful little 5 year-old boy who had never left me, but who clung so tightly to fear of being his real self. Yes, that little boy whose teacher wrote in his report card in 1966, "Howard also has a sense of humor, which is **not** common in a kindergarten class."

In the vulnerability of my recovery, I had found him, me, my essence of who I had been since the beginning, but who I had become too afraid to show to anybody except Sally. I am grateful that she has put up with my silliness all of these years.

In writing this book, I share my vulnerability with you. How much more vulnerable can I be than to share my story of recovery from Parkinson's when the conventional viewpoint still is that what I am saying I did, what I know I did, and what is medically documented that I did is not possible?

By working hard on my recovery, and in the end, by being vulnerable and casting my fear of being me to the side, I am symptom free from Parkinson's, and I have been living a very joyful life.

Part Two

Parkinson's Recipe for Recovery®:
My methodology of recovery

The Parkinson's Recipe for Recovery (Recipe) is the methodology I developed, and it is what I did to fully recover from Parkinson's Disease.

Here is an example of how I see the recovery process:

A 10-year-old child falls and breaks his arm. His mother takes him to the doctor. The doctor says, "No problem. I am going to set your arm in place, put a cast on it, and when you come back here for your next visit, I am going to remove the cast and your arm will be better, 100% as good as new."

Let's look at what happens in the healing process:

1. The child has faith in the doctor (soul).
2. Because he has faith in the doctor, he does not worry that his arm is not going to heal (mind).
3. As a result of 1 and 2, he does not obsess about his arm, and then, his body heals his arm (body).

Applying this to my Parkinson's recovery:

1. I had complete faith I would recover (soul).
2. I never, not for one moment, worried that I would not recover (mind).
3. I listened to my body's signals and messages, and I exercised and ate properly (body).

I also prayed and meditated, and I was quite miserable for a number of months before I recovered, but I am providing a simple example to make a point on a complex topic. Sally and I discussed that someday there was the possibility of having to use a walker, or of being in a wheelchair, or of being paralyzed. The critical component here was that I did not worry about those things because I knew I would recover. Instead of being afraid of them, I accepted that they might be things I would have to experience in order to recover.

The issue of not taking medications is a difficult issue to address. I fought Parkinson's without medications. Here is my opinion: Parkinson's is an electrical problem, not a chemical imbalance. If it was a chemical imbalance, then chemicals would get it back into balance with medication, and life would be wonderful.

I feel that Parkinson's is an electrical problem because that is how it felt inside. It was not a feeling I had felt in the past when I had an illness such as a virus or a flu. The tremors felt like electrical currents that were not flowing correctly inside me.

When my movement changed, the tremors changed. It was like the electricity was getting redirected. During regular movement, the tremors were barely noticeable. However, when I was standing, sitting still, or lying down, my entire body shook on the inside with tremors.

I could feel the changing electrical current inside me. Movement and changing emotions changed the electrical flow. Those were feelings I never had experienced in my life until I had Parkinson's.

Plus, I felt that my organs were not functioning well, particularly my liver and kidneys, because they were not getting the correct amount of electricity from my brain. My Parkinson's brain was low on energy, and my organs and my limbs were not receiving enough electrical energy.

Moreover, since Parkinson's was considered incurable, it made no sense to me to follow the Western Medicine treatment plans, including taking medications, when those treatment plans had been around for 200 years and had not cured a single person of the disease.

The official position was that the treatments could not even slow or halt the disease. I felt that these chemical solutions did not work against the disease, and treated symptoms only, because Parkinson's was caused by an electrical problem.

Moreover, I did not believe that the dopamine was depleted or gone. I believed that the body had been working in adrenaline mode (physically and mentally), and that the dopamine had taken a back seat; essentially, it had mostly closed the faucet, and was not flowing at full capacity.

It is why I believe the medications cause Dyskinesia; the body is being given artificial dopamine replacements that are not able to fully assimilate into the system and thus cause uncontrollable movement instead of controllable movement.

Here is the Recipe for my recovery. I call it my "Recipe" because a recipe for a meal in a book or magazine might look very appealing. However, if I do not use the ingredients in the manner that the recipe prescribes, I diminish my opportunity to get the meal in the picture.

I wanted to maximize my opportunity for recovery, so I treated my recovery protocol the same way, just like the recipe in the book or magazine.

Ingredients (Discussed in detail below and in Appendix Two; the times listed are the approximate amount of time it took me to perform these ingredients):

Exercise: Medical Qigong for the Liver. (15 minutes in morning and 15 minutes in evening)

Exercise: Medical Qigong for the Kidneys. (10 minutes in morning and 10 minutes in evening)

Exercise: Qigong for Clearing Liver Wind. (5 minutes in the morning)

Exercise: Neck exercises. (5 minutes in the morning)

Exercise: Standing and Balance. (5 minutes in the morning)

Exercise: Awareness of Neural (electrical) Impulses. (15 minutes in the morning)

Exercise: Near hand-far hand Exercise for Kidney and Brain. (10 minutes in the afternoon)

Acupressure for Tremors: Governing Vessel, GV2-20. (5 minutes in the evening)

Jin Shin Jyutsu for Balancing Energy Flows. (12 minutes in the morning)

Brain Vibration Chanting. (5 minutes each of morning, afternoon and evening)

Sitting Zazen. (10 minutes in the morning)

Vegetarian diet.

Yin Tui Na (Forceless Spontaneous Release). (30 minutes in the evening for 5 days)

Mediations, affirmations, prayers. (Varied throughout the day)

It is rare that you will see the words Parkinson's Disease in any of the ingredients. I worked on the organs I felt were impacted by the disease and I used the modalities that I felt would work on the parts of the body impacted by the disease. Other than the Acupressure for GV2-20 and the Yin Tua Na, nobody in the past had advocated any of the other things I did as being something to do for Parkinson's specifically.

Based upon what I saw as the three main causes of what brought Parkinson's symptoms to the diagnosable surface, my focus on the physical body was not about the symptoms; my focus was about the causes.

After ten years of doing regular Qigong and still getting Parkinson's, I needed Medical Qigong for healing my organs and increasing my energy to address the physical causes of Parkinson's.

Qigong, in general, is considered a soft exercise. It is a slow moving, deep breathing way to stretch the body and stimulate the lymph system to cleanse toxins from the body. In simplest of terms, the heart pumps the blood, and movement stimulates the lymph system.

I knew that my liver and gallbladder were not functioning well and my blood was not being cleansed well of toxins. As a result of blood deficiency and my liver being overworked and weakened, my kidneys were being overworked for cleansing toxins as well.

This meant that my kidneys became weakened and could not provide the proper flow of energy to my brain. So, I needed to strengthen my liver and my kidneys. This is why the Recipe has Medical Qigong for the Liver, Medical Qigong for Calming the Liver, Medical Qigong for the Kidneys, and Medical Qigong Healing Sound for the Kidneys.

I started doing the Recipe.

The changing of my diet and the physical part of the Recipe healed my body on the inside. However, there was so much more to this recovery than just healing my body on the inside. I knew I could not exercise my way out of Parkinson's.

Parkinson's attacks the body. It absolutely is a physical disease. However, I realized that to heal from the physical disease, I needed to heal myself as a whole being. I needed to heal my body, heal my mind, and heal my soul. I had become completely out of balance.

Ultimately, I grew to see Parkinson's as a symptom instead of a disease. It became a very large symptom that my life had become out of balance. The Recipe brought balance back into my life, physically, mentally, and spiritually.

My new outlook became: Parkinson's…the symptom reflecting a life out of balance.

Physically, I was out of balance. I moved slowly and cautiously, often looking down instead of forward. What did that do? It put my body in a posture that made it virtually impossible to walk balanced. My neck was bent, my spine was bent, the fluid in my semicircular canals was shifted, and my visual frame of reference (important for balance) was my legs or the floor, and I acquired what is often referred to as a Parkinson's gait, and mostly a Parkinson's shuffle.

Mentally, I then become out of balance because I was afraid of falling or freezing, and initially, I was afraid of the future dealing with Parkinson's as I worked on my recovery. I knew I would recovery one day, but did I have it in me to actually see it through to the full recovery? Was I worthy and deserving of having my full recovery? This is right where Parkinson's wanted me...not living in the moment, but instead living in the past (getting Parkinson's) and being fearful of the future (dealing with Parkinson's).

Spiritually, I had days where I just broke down because of feeling so overwhelmed by the disease. At that point, Parkinson's was winning.

Essentially, when I was staring at my legs and feeling unbalanced, I was looking at the past. When I lived with the unbalanced body, I feared the future. I realized that it was going to be impossible to move forward in life in a balanced manner if I continued staring backwards and being fearful of moving forward. Ultimately, with a lot of soul-searching, this experience increased my faith.

Faith was critical in my recovery. Faith in myself that I was my own cure to Parkinson's, and that I would be able to see my recovery through to the end. Although that carried a lot of responsibility, I also had faith that the Recipe was the correct methodology to bring me to my full recovery. The Recipe was my road map for bringing my soul, mind, and body back into balance.

In the end, it turned out that the physical healing of the organs on the inside was much easier than calming my mind and opening my heart. Here is how I went about healing my mind and my soul, thus bringing myself back into balance and having my full recovery. In the Recipe, these are listed under the headings Sitting Zazen, and Meditations, Affirmations, and Prayers. The physical organ healing comes after.

CALMING MY MIND

When I had Parkinson's, there were some things that I needed to explore to understand my mind's function in getting Parkinson's and in getting recovered:

1. What were my mental/emotional attitudes that negatively impacted my health?
2. How did my Adrenaline-mind-mode-over-thinking negatively impact my health?
3. What would I need to do to free my mind from my habitual

negative mental/emotional trappings, such as anger, stress, fear, and anxiety, as well as Adrenaline-mind-mode-over-thinking?

4. How could I calm my mind to live a fearless life?

In my Parkinson's Recipe for Recovery I discuss what I see as the main causes of Parkinson's, and it is important to review them again to see how my mind played a role in me getting the disease.

There are underlying factors (genetics, heavy metals, environmental toxins, etc.) that make a person susceptible to getting Parkinson's. However, I feel that there are three main causes that bring Parkinson's to the surface as diagnosable symptoms:

1. Qi and Blood Deficiency, which is caused by emotional stress, anger, frustration, and resentment.
2. Phlegm-Fire Agitating Wind, which is caused by dietary considerations such as consumption of too much greasy, fried or sweet foods.
3. Kidney and Liver Wind; deficiency that is caused by overwork and insufficient rest which unbalances the body's natural rhythm.

When I looked at numbers 1 and 3, I realized that at some level, the way I had lived my life emotionally had helped my symptoms rise to the surface of my body.

I remembered instances when I was young and had a big test at school for which I was unprepared. My emotional stress caused by fear of my unpreparedness and my not wanting to get a bad grade caused me to have an upset stomach, or a headache, or a fever, or all of the above.

And, those maladies were not in my mind, but instead, they were a physical manifestation of stress and fear. The physical symptoms were real, they were measurable, and I was not faking; I stayed home from school because I was physically ill that day.

Shifting to Parkinson's, there were underlying factors that made me susceptible to getting the disease. However, the constant negative emotional manner in which I was living my life and responding to life's events with anger, frustration, stress, and anxiety, were the things that caused the underlying factors of the Parkinson's to raise themselves to the surface as diagnosable symptoms.

I had worn down my own immunities with toxic emotions and my body lost its ability to cleanse at an efficient rate. When I added in cause number 3—the thinking and over-thinking, constantly striving to have every answer and be the best at everything, my fear-driven adrenaline-mode mind that never rested—I realized I had worn down my mind.

As a result, my internal electricity and my brain could no longer get the messages to my limbs and organs with the strength and vitality it took to have them functioning correctly. This caused my dopamine faucet to close down to a trickle.

There were habits and tendencies I realized existed pre-Parkinson's that I needed to review in order to better understand how my body would have a physical reaction to the people and events in life.

When I had been under pressure, and I felt stress, anxiety, and fear, did my body ever feel a little shaky, kind of like tremors? *Yes.*

When I had been faced with difficult choices in life and I analyzed them and analyzed them and analyzed them until I was paralyzed in my thinking, was I able to act upon my issues with fluidity? *No.* Or, did my decisions seem rigid? *Yes.*

When my mind had been completely cluttered with toxic junk and I felt I could not think clearly, did my constipated mind exacerbate an already constipated body? *Yes.*

As a result, I knew I had to change my dis-eased way of thinking and responding to life's events so I could feel ease. I will discuss this more in depth later.

I want to reiterate a very important point. I am not saying that Parkinson's is a disease of the mind. It absolutely is a disease of the body. However, I had to acknowledge that "dis-ease" of my mind assisted me in having my symptoms rise to the surface.

Once I acknowledged this, I could better understand how "ease" of my mind would help remove the "dis" from the "dis-ease" of my mind, which could have an enormous impact on my physical symptoms. My liver was not functioning well, so my blood was overrun with toxins. Having blood overrun with toxins made my blood deficient in delivering oxygen and other essentials to my body…blood deficiency. As a result of this, my kidneys were overworked and could not deliver enough energy to my brain, which lead to overall lack of energy or fatigue…Qi (life energy) deficiency.

I realized that there were no Parkinson's symptoms when I was sleeping. This is not just because I was not experiencing them so they appeared to go away. It was because when I was sleeping, my mind was calm and my physical body was not making any demands on my brain except for breathing and heart beating.

If it is possible to have no symptoms when sleeping, what if I could achieve in my waking hours a state of calmness of mind and openness of heart that I achieved when I was sleeping? I sensed that the Recipe would get me there.

Calming my mind to transform and eliminate negative emotions became very important to me in my recovery. It began with one simple word: Acceptance.

ACCEPTANCE

I realized in my recovery that my habitual response to things that occurred in life that I did not like was anger. This anger was followed by the frustration I faced by not being able to un-change what already had occurred, and that made me more angry, which was followed by even more anger at myself for not foreseeing the event and not preventing it.

It had become my habit to go through this cycle again and again and again. I tried to break this habit by doing my best to eliminate anger from being. I learned that the anger was so deeply ingrained that it surfaced whether I wanted it to or not. Essentially an anger-impulse, automatic negative reactivity had become my bad habit.

Eventually, I realized that the only way for me to break a really bad habit was to create a more powerful habit from the other end of the spectrum… acceptance…of everything!

This was EXTREMELY DIFFICULT!

I began by exploring why the negative emotions surfaced from inside me all the time, and, quite frankly, it was hard to pinpoint. They were just there, all the time. There was no reasonable explanation for how I could be in my tomato garden and feel anger or anxiety as an underlying current in my being. This had been going on for as long as I could remember in my adult life. The negative emotions were just there.

In my recovery, I learned that I was not strong enough to just stop the negative emotions. They were relentless. So I had to develop a positive habitual response to everything, and I became relentless! It was the only way to battle this internal turmoil and to create my new habit. I fought negativity with positivity, or acceptance. I used one word: OKAY!

My new-habit habitual response to life became "okay." I literally forced myself to think and say okay as my response to everything I was asked or had to think about in life.

This did not mean that I was happy about everything or that everything that occurred was okay with me. Okay meant acceptance, not acquiescence. It meant that when something happened, I merely said, "Okay, I accept that whatever just happened actually happened." It was a tacit acknowledgement of reality.

It seems so simple to acknowledge the obvious, but for me with Parkinson's, this was incredibly liberating and calming. Previously, my approach to life was that I needed to change the things I did not like that had already occurred—because that is what I did, or thought I could do—only to criticize myself afterwards for my inability to undo what already had occurred.

And, I felt I had every right to be angry and frustrated and exhibit stress and anxiety. Ultimately, though, I decided to give up those rights to help me get better from Parkinson's.

The negative emotions I faced with Parkinson's were a constant uphill battle. What I concluded was that I had become uncomfortable experiencing positive emotions—they came with a feeling of selfishness or guilt.

As I had gone through life, I had learned that I had the right to be angry if something happened that I did not like; "you have every right to be angry." This permeated other negative feelings and gave them the status of "you have the right to be frustrated, resentful, worrisome, fearful, stressful, anxious, unforgiving, critical, and self-critical." To have my Parkinson's recovery, I needed to give up these old rights.

The reason I call all of these negative emotions "rights" is because that is how they were treated in my life. The following example illustrates this.

Pre-Parkinson's behavior: I am driving on the highway and somebody cuts me off. I slam on the brakes barely avoiding an accident, and the person who cut me off speeds away. I become angry. I am angry that I got cut off, angry and frustrated that he sped away, angry and frustrated and resentful that nothing bad will happen to this person to punish him for having cut me off and almost causing a serious accident.

When I would tell my family and friends about it, with the anger spilling out of me, everybody would say, "You have every right to be angry. I would be angry, too!"

Now, using the same scenario post-Parkinson's: I would slam on the brakes avoiding the accident, catch my breath, and then I would give gratitude (lots of gratitude) for being safe and sound with no damage to the car or any of the occupants. And then I would let it go. However, if I were to mention the situation, I would imagine a response something to the effect of, "I am happy there was not an accident and nobody got hurt, but I do not know how you can be so calm about it. The other guy got away with it and you have every right to be angry; I know I would be angry if I was in your shoes."

In my life, I had been taught that these negative emotions were my rights, and most of the time, I was rewarded by inclusion when I exercised them. The way things are now, post-recovery, I am questioned as if there is something wrong with me when I choose to not exercise these "rights."

What I realized in my recovery is that nobody ever sat me down and said, "You have the right to be joyful, happy, fearless, compassionate, content, loving, accepting, forgiving, and grateful."

I decided to introduce myself to my set of new rights:

I HAD THE RIGHT TO BE JOYFUL, HAPPY, FEARLESS, COMPASSIONATE, CONTENT, LOVING, ACCEPTING,

FORGIVING, AND GRATEFUL!!!

The negative emotions were in my mind, and my mind ran rampant with negative ideas of what life was like with Parkinson's and with Parkinson's symptoms. My new rights came from my heart!

I had to make the transformations that would change my life. As the negative emotions surfaced, I transformed them into the positive emotions. The negative emotions were habitual, though. Simply put, they were so strongly built into me throughout my life that they just surfaced in response to the events of life.

However, this turned out to be a gift of Parkinson's symptoms. My Parkinson's symptoms got worse when I experienced any of the negative emotions. Those symptoms provided a built-in notification system that said, "My reaction to what was just said or done is an exacerbation of symptoms." When I received these kinds of notifications and developed this kind of awareness, it put me in the position of being able to exercise my positive emotions, my new rights.

Using my car example above, I now transform anger over the situation to gratitude over the outcome. The mind is very tricky. The mind wants to pull out its parade of horribles and say, "If the other car would have hit you, think about all of the terrible things that would have occurred." The mind pulls people out of the moment and it runs to all of the terrible outcomes that could have occurred.

The heart keeps one in the moment and says with gratitude, "Look at what really happened here. You avoided an accident, there is no car damage, and nobody in the car got hurt. Feel gratitude."

The bottom line was this: *keeping my old rights was a choice.*

Giving up my old rights and transforming them into my new rights also was a choice.

I had come to realize that when I chose my mind over my heart, I had been choosing anger, frustration, resentment, stress, anxiety, worry, and fear.

Likewise, I had come to realize that when I chose my heart over my mind, I had been choosing joy, happiness, fearlessness, compassion, contentment, love, acceptance, forgiveness, and gratitude.

Ultimately, to have my recovery, I needed to give up my old rights by transforming them into my new rights. Then, I was able to view the world and participate in life from my heart. This is not an easy transformation to make, but I found it to be absolutely necessary for having a healthy life. It certainly was worth the effort to make the changes.

Part of giving up my old rights and exercising my new rights was getting back to my new habit of saying "okay." Instead of living in turmoil, trying to be perfect all the time, trying to control everything that was going on, and then being angry and frustrated with myself because I was not perfect and controlled very little, I would just say "okay."

As stated earlier, "okay" really meant, "I accept that this just happened, so what am I going to do about it." And then I created a solution instead of creating anger and frustration and stress. Imagine that! Seems so simple. I can assure you that it was not simple. However, it was worth the effort.

This is how acceptance looked in real life: instead of spending hours and days trying to undo something that already had happened, I actually spent minutes doing something about it. Life became easier and less stressful this way.

As I became more accepting of life, I shook less and was rigid less. Also, I was becoming more accepting of myself: "Okay. I accept that I have Parkinson's. What am I going to do to solve this problem? I am going to do the Recipe!"

This meant learning to transform my anger. Anger is at the top of my list of the three causes that bring Parkinson's symptoms to the diagnosable surface. Part of Parkinson's recovery required letting go of anger, or as is discussed earlier, giving up the right to hold onto anger.

Anger is like drinking milk that is beyond its expiration date and has gone sour. Suppose a person went to the grocery store yesterday and bought a quart of milk. His mind was wandering and he did not look at the expiration date. He got home and threw away the receipt that went out with the garbage that was taken away early that morning. He opens the milk, pours a glass, and it is sour and disgusting and starts to make him sick. He looks at the expiration date and it was two weeks ago.

Here it comes. *Anger.* He is angry with the manufacturer for having expired milk on the shelf. He is angry with the stocking person at the store who left it on the shelf. He is angry with the cashier because she took his money when the milk was expired. Ultimately, he turns the anger on himself because he should have checked the date and he should not have thrown out the receipt, and there will be no justice after he has been wronged.

Whose fault is this? In the end, he decides this is his fault because he was not perfect, he could have prevented the situation, he was asleep at the switch, and now he has sour milk. At this point, he has two choices: 1. Continue to drink the milk; or 2. Let it go; throw it away.

If he continues to drink the milk, who is harmed? The manufacturer? No. The stocking person? No. The cashier? No. Him? *Yes.* Only he is harmed. But he chooses to continue drinking the milk and harming himself because it is his milk and he paid for it and he will never get his money back. This is why anger is like drinking milk that is beyond its expiration date and has gone sour. The person himself is the only one who is harmed if he does not let it go.

This is a description of me, how I was pre-Parkinson's. I had to look inside myself and visit where the anger came from. I needed to know if it was from current events or events from long ago. I had come to realize that holding onto my anger only hurt me! Acceptance of the events taking place in my life helped me let go of the anger and get control of my emotions. "Okay, this happened. If I do not let it go, it will make me ill and keep me ill. I want to get better, so I am giving up my right to be angry and throwing out the sour milk."

Getting control of my emotions became critical in my recovery. Pre-Parkinson's, when one of my children came to me and told me there was a virus in the children's computer, my reaction was anger. Anger was followed by interrogation of the bearer of the bad news, something to the effect of, "What did you download that you weren't supposed to download? What web site were you on that you weren't supposed to be on?"

I would be consumed with anger over the event, frustration over how my time was going to be interrupted to try to remove the virus, and resentment over the fact that somebody had been doing something they were not supposed to be doing and now we had a virus in the computer.

This reaction had a resounding ripple effect. I would not release the anger. The entire time I was removing the virus out of the computer, I was angry. And after it was removed, I was angry and dwelled on it. Whichever unfortunate child happened to be the one who told me about the virus was angry because I got upset with them and they viewed my behavior as unreasonable.

Also, I realized in my recovery that what was fueling my anger was fear over all the terrible things that could have occurred had I not been able to get the virus out of the computer. The more incredible thing I realized was that the fear continued to consume me after I had gotten the virus out of the computer. How sad is that? Part of my anger had been driven by fear of events from the past that did not take place and never would take place because the virus had been removed from the computer.

It was this type of emotional reaction to life that, along with other things, helped weaken my liver and allow Parkinson's Disease to overtake my body. One of the things I had to do to recover from Parkinson's was calm myself and not allow my negative emotions to rule my outlook of life or taint and control how I reacted to life's facts and events.

Almost a year after my Parkinson's recovery, one of my children came to me with the dreaded news, "Dad, there is a virus in the computer." She also said, "Because I know how you feel about this, I tried everything to fix it...I removed the program I had downloaded, I rebooted the computer, I downloaded tools to remove the virus, and it has just gotten worse. I am sorry." After she told me this, I noticed that my pre-Parkinson's emotional reaction of anger to this situation was non-existent. I was calm about it, and I looked at her and said, "No problem. I will take care of it."

This may seem hard to believe, but it is true. My daughter had the same reaction. She looked at me with the kind of bewilderment that said, "You're not my father. What did you do with him?" I fixed the computer and the only other thing said to her was that since she knew what it was that she had downloaded that had caused the virus, let's not do it again in the future and we will probably avoid the virus.

Parkinson's taught me that I needed to change my emotional reaction to the facts and events of life as a part of living a healthier life and as part of my recovery from the disease. I knew I needed to focus on the solution to the problems rather than focusing only on the fact that I had problems.

It circles me back to the issues of surrender and acceptance that life is messy. Sometimes in life a doctor tells a person that he or she has Parkinson's Disease. It is unrealistic to think that at that moment, the person will just say "okay" and go about his or her life as if the doctor had said it was a hangnail.

When the person gets the news he has the disease, it is only natural for emotions of anger, resentment, frustration, and fear to quickly rise to surface. I learned that the important thing for me was to let go of these negative emotions and to not let them control how I was going to deal with the diagnosis of Parkinson's, or I should say, how I was going to deal with the facts and events going on in my life.

As mentioned earlier, a tool I found extremely useful in working on acceptance was the simple, but powerful word "okay."

"Okay!" When I could look at my life and my Parkinson's and say, "okay," my Parkinson's really saw "okay" as a scary word. "Okay" became so powerful in my recovery that it made my Parkinson's afraid of me. It was liberating to have my Parkinson's afraid of me for a change.

There was a certain emotional detachment that came with "okay," but that type of clear-headed emotional detachment was what we needed to beat this disease. However, I have to admit that it was Sally who first used the "okay" strategy when we discovered that I had Parkinson's.

When I first realized I had Parkinson's and Sally and I discussed it and then cried together, she settled down and said, "Okay, we need to put a plan together and figure out what we are going to do about this." Looking back, I know this was the most loving thing she could have done because I had to put my "poor me" away and start to work on a solution. As I went through my recovery, I learned that "okay" meant acceptance. It was very important for me also to know that acceptance did not mean acquiescence.

For me, "okay" came to mean, "I accept the situation as it is, right here, right now. What is my solution? What am I going to do about it, right here, right now?"

I have tremors all the time…"okay."

My legs hurt…"okay."

My back hurts…"okay."

I am constipated…"okay."

I have to hold on to the railing when walking up the stairs…"okay."

I can't get my utensil to my mouth…"okay."

"Okay, okay, okay!"

Each "okay" meant this: "'Okay,' this is what is happening right here, right now, what am I going to do about it?" This is quite different from, "My legs hurt, and this means my Parkinson's is worsening, soon I won't be able to walk without a walker, and soon after that I will be in a wheelchair."

"Okay" was a call to action.

It identified an issue and worked toward a solution. The other response was emotions. It was fear, worry, and anger about the future. It caused paralysis of the spirit, which caused paralysis of the mind, which caused paralysis of the body.

This was the one situation where fear of the walker and wheelchair, and doing nothing to discourage or transform that fear, would have provided me the paralysis I would have needed to end up with the walker and wheelchair.

I elevated myself to be able to say, "I have Parkinson's and this is my Parkinson's body…'okay.'" Accepting my Parkinson's and my Parkinson's body, with all of my newly discovered physical limitations and pains was part of the process of recovery.

It required a lot of faith to take an "okay" attitude toward my Parkinson's. It was the type of faith that said, "I know I will recover and I am getting on my path and I am not getting off until I recover." Every morning after I finished doing the Recipe, I understood that everything else that was going on that day was actually my life.

I understood that for a time, Parkinson's was going to be part of my life. Also, I understood that Parkinson's was not my whole life and it would not always be a part of my life.

There was a meditation method I used to help me calm my mind at a higher level than my relentless awake-mode-self-talk-acceptance called "okay." It was called sitting zazen. Sitting zazen was a meditative form of breathing and counting. Since I knew nothing about meditation, I thought this would not be too difficult because breathing and counting were two things I already know how to do.

I was incorrect about how easy it would be. However, ultimately, I was able to breathe and count my way into a meditative state, and I feel it helped immensely with my recovery.

BREATHING AND COUNTING

Sitting zazen was the form of meditation I used with my eyes not completely closed so I would not fall asleep. I did it for ten minutes a day. I could not sit on the floor in a lotus or cross-legged position, so I did it sitting in a chair. Here is how I did sitting zazen:

1. I began with an exhale. Exhale and then inhale. That was 1.
2. I continued exhaling and inhaling while counting from 1 to 10.
3. When I got to 10, I started at 1 again.
4. I continued this exhale–inhale, counting 1–10 and starting again at 1. For the entire ten minutes I was sitting zazen.

By concentrating on breathing (in an opposite manner from how I generally viewed it with the exhale first), and by simultaneously counting those breaths (having to go back to 1 each time I hit 10), my mind was focused on these two things only.

As I mentioned, I could not sit that long on the floor. I improvised. I sat at the front of a hard, straight-backed chair, feet on the floor pointing straight, hunched forward with hands on knees. I set my timer for ten minutes, closed my eyes about 75% (eyelids cracked to assist me in not falling asleep), and I started counting my breaths on my exhale.

When I reached 25 or 26, it occurred to me that I must not have been paying attention because I was supposed to go back to 1 when I reached ten. I started at 1 again. After a few 1–10 sequences, I looked over at my timer to find that I had about seven and a half minutes remaining. I thought I was going to lose my mind (I had yet to realize that losing my over-thinking mind was the whole point of the sitting; I was a slow learner at the time). I looked at the clock a few more times over the next few minutes. My initial thought was, *what a waste of ten minutes; why in the world would anybody sit zazen for thirty or forty minutes?*

However, as was the way in my recovery, when I started something new, I stuck with it for a month so I could properly assess its usefulness. It took me quite a few days to make it through ten minutes without looking at the timer.

In my mind, I had really good reasons for looking at the timer: *I am certain I have been sitting here for a long time, but I am so focused on my counting, that I did not notice the timer when it buzzed,* and *I feel like I have sat here twice as long as yesterday, so the timer must be broken, I better check the time.* It is embarrassing to say, but this is just the beginning of a long list of reasons for looking at the time during the ten minutes. Instead of just doing—that is, breathing and counting—for most of my ten minutes I was involved in self-judging, self-criticizing, and over-thinking.

Then, one morning, it occurred to me that I needed to shoot down every excuse to look at the timer because part of what I was trying to accomplish was not over-thinking things and not worrying about the future. It hit me that worrying about the time prevented me from being in the moment. My mind was in a "what's coming next" mode instead of living in the moment, and I was preoccupied with the future (and sometimes the past).

Parkinson's had a way of creating a preoccupation with how I got Parkinson's and what the future would be like with Parkinson's until I reached my recovery. Doing, instead of thinking too much, was how to be in the moment. Sitting zazen, the functional equivalent of doing what looked like *no* thing (just sitting) turned out to be *some* thing special; it brought me into feeling the reality of the moment.

This was an important realization for me. I became better equipped for embracing the disease. It brought me to this level of realization of my Parkinson's experience: in the present moment, I had Parkinson's. At some time in the past, I did not have Parkinson's. At some time in the future, I would not have Parkinson's. However, if all I was doing was thinking about it, then it would cause me to stop living. Sitting zazen assisted me in calming my mind and starting to truly live life again.

In my discussion above, I explained how calming my mind, getting rid of negative emotions, accepting life, and sitting zazen all helped my recovery from Cause 1, Qi and Blood Deficiency.

Now, I will address Cause 3: "Kidney and Liver Wind; deficiency that is caused by overwork and insufficient rest which unbalances the body's natural rhythm." In simple terms, my kidneys and liver were worn down because I had been burning the candle at both ends and in the middle. This is the adrenaline-mode mind, which runs from fear (fight or flight), and wears down the kidneys and liver, making them susceptible to being invaded by wind, which causes shaking (tremors) and deficiencies in their functioning.

Here is how I saw the connections of the physical body imbalances and mind imbalances that result in Parkinson's symptoms breaking through the surface:

Adrenaline—Situations occurred in my life that had put me in the fight or flight mode (adrenaline mode). When my survival mode adrenaline kicked in, the rest of my body suffered. Eating correctly, drinking enough water, urges to go to the bathroom, and happy feelings took a back seat to the adrenaline. As a result, my dopamine flow suffered.

Adrenaline Mode—My pre-Parkinson's mind kept running well after the stressed filled years stopped being stress filled. Fear is what kept my mind running, and running, and running, and running, and running, and running, and running, and running.

This was where I had found myself in September of 2009. It was the "me" who I had become, whose tremors were so severe I no longer could ignore all of the physical changes and limitations that I had been ignoring for the previous years.

I had run in adrenaline mode for ten years, culminating in my tremors and my Parkinson's. I had practiced law from 1986 until 1999. In the early part of 1999, I accidentally stumbled upon what looked like corruption in the court system.

From that point forward, my life was in turmoil. My office was broken into, our home was broken into, a half dozen of my clients went from being happy clients to filing complaints that I was not keeping them fully apprised of their case statuses and returning their phone calls quickly enough.

I went from the public appearance of good lawyer to the public appearance of terrible lawyer. Back in those days, I was stubborn and I had a big ego. I was too stubborn to be afraid.

I decided that I was "going to fight City Hall," so to speak. I had an upcoming hearing with the Florida Bar regarding the six complaints, and I was preparing to testify about everything I had stumbled upon as my defense to what I felt were unfounded complaints. I had ignored the Florida Bar letter offering me a voluntary resignation with a right to re-apply to practice law in three years.

As I said, I was stubborn and I had a big ego. Also, I did not understand the seriousness of what I was about to do—of exposing court corruption. Then came the call that ended it all.

I received a telephone call from Sally's mobile phone from an individual who said if I wanted to see Sally and the children again, I would resign from practicing law. To be clear, the call did not come from the Florida Bar; rather, it came from someone who apparently was going to be negatively impacted by my exposure of the court corruption. In that moment, my stubbornness and ego went out the door. I told him absolutely yes, I would resign. I called the Florida Bar immediately and told the investigator she could cancel the hearing that week because I would be accepting her offer to resign.

Fear. I had never been so afraid in my life. The Florida Bar came to my office and the papers had the "right to reapply to practice law" increased to five years, and I willingly signed. They mentioned to me that when lawyers go from being good lawyers to being bad lawyers, it is usually something like marital problems, or alcohol or drug problems that bring on the change.

I told them it was none of those things, because it was not, and they went about their business. A couple of days later, my resignation was the lead story in the local news section in our newspaper…and I had my first experience with tremors…but I knew I was having a panic attack. Those tremors went away after a couple of hours.

Not only was my life as I knew it officially over, but everybody was reading about it. I had not had time to tell my family or friends, or my clients or colleagues. They got to read about it with their Saturday morning coffee.

As the weekend settled down, I knew my resignation was going to be the only thing people wanted to discuss with me, and I was afraid. Fear is powerful, and there was no way I was going to tell anybody the truthful story of what was occurring. I was too afraid.

However, I thought that the bright spot in this dark cloud in my life was that by resigning, I was removing myself from the legal system, so they would just leave me alone. I was wrong.

Leaving me alone was not on their agenda. After resigning, I was sued and I had criminal charges filed against me alleging crimes I had not committed. I was nowhere near being left alone or removed from the legal system. Apparently, they needed to destroy my credibility in case I ever attempted to go public with what I knew.

After I had criminal charges for crimes I had not committed filed against me in March of 2001, I was arrested at my home in front of Sally and our young children, and I was taken to jail. Talk about fear.

My blood pressure was so high, they told me they might have to put me in the infirmary instead of the general population at the jail. Fortunately, I bonded out of jail, and when the room emptied to take everybody into the general population, I was left alone to sit and wait a number of hours until I was released.

One and a half years earlier when I resigned from practicing law, I felt that my life as I knew it was over. But that was nothing. This made me feel like my entire world had been turned on its head.

Whatever fears I had in the past were nothing compared to this. I was defending criminal charges, defending civil lawsuits, trying to earn a living, sometimes working two or three jobs at a time to make ends meet, and having my heart race every time the doorbell rang, "Is it another lawsuit?" "Are they revoking my bond?" "Is one of the people who has called the house or come to the house and threatened my life actually going to carry it out?"

My fear had a mind of its own. I was becoming paranoid about everything. As time went on, it became clear to those involved that my criminal charges were nothing more than something to harass me. Over a year after the criminal case against me began, I filed a motion to have the case dismissed because the prosecution could not prove even the most basic case of guilt.

On July 9, 2002, the day of the hearing on the motion to dismiss and throw out my criminal charges, prior to the Judge ruling on the motion, the State of Florida issued a *nolle prosequi*, voluntarily dismissing all criminal charges against me.

My relief was short-lived because I soon learned that there were civil lawsuits pending against me of which I had no knowledge at all. Fortunately, the Clerk of the Court offices had modernized enough that I was able to do an Internet search and find the cases against me.

In this search, I learned that a judgment had been entered against me for over $200,000 in a case brought by a man serving three life sentences. I had been a court-appointed lawyer for his appeal in the early 1990's.

I had known about the case, which had been sitting dormant since the mid-90's. It had been the least of my worries when facing resigning from practicing law in 1999 and facing criminal charges in 2001. The $200,000 judgment effectively placed a lien on our home and was collecting interest at twelve percent per year. I filed a motion to set aside the judgment. We fought about this in the circuit court and appellate court for years.

On January 10, 2008, the judge ruled 100% in my favor, vacating the judgment (removing the judgment) against me, finding that it had been acquired through fraud. He then took the further step of dismissing the entire case against me, finding there had been fraud against the Court.

Was the nightmare over? No. The life prisoner appealed the decision, and on June 10, 2009, almost a year and a half after the original ruling, the appeals court affirmed the decision, which means they ruled in my favor, agreeing that it had been correct to vacate the judgment against me and to dismiss the case against me for fraud against the Court.

Nightmare over. Nearly ten years from the day I signed my resignation from the practicing law, my final case was over. However, did my mind stop running from the lion? Of course not. Three months later, I started shaking with tremors. This time it was not a panic attack. This time it was full-blown Parkinson's Disease.

In my Parkinson's recovery, I learned that my brain was hard-wired to fear. Fear had been pretty strong prior to my ten years of running from the lion. However, those ten years took an-already-overactive-fear-based-mind and put it into overdrive.

As soon as a situation occurred, my brain's reflex action was to jump on the fear train and put it in full throttle.

Fear of what? Everything! Fear of: "Maybe I won't be prepared for _____;" "Maybe I won't know the answer to _____;" "Maybe I am not good enough for _____;" "Maybe _____ (bad thing) will happen." As you have seen, there were plenty of unpleasant things that had not been on my radar until they manifested themselves in my life, including Parkinson's.

This is the short list of my fears. It is the list of things that could have happened that I felt compelled to have all of the possible scenarios examined. Why? So I would be prepared for everything that could possibly happen for the rest of my life. Why? So that nothing would go wrong or bad, and everything could happen according to my plan. Fear of what? Life!

I absolutely had become afraid of life.

If someone is afraid of roller coasters, he doesn't go on them. If someone is afraid of scary movies, he doesn't go to them. If someone is afraid of the dark, he can sleep with the lights on. I was afraid of life; my options were limited. I could come up with two options only: 1. Continue to live in fear, or 2. Face the fear and get beyond it.

I knew that continuing to live in fear meant I would not be recovering from Parkinson's, so number 1 got scratched from the list. That left number 2. Face the fear and get beyond it. I had no choice. Once again, Plan A, with no fallback Plan B option.

The interesting thing about having a Plan A choice only is that I chose it, and then I forced myself to deal with everything that came afterwards. How did I choose to "not be afraid?" That was no easy task. First, it took a lot of faith (more about that later). Second, it required me to face the fear that had become so much a part of me, or should I say, a part of who I thought I needed to be.

That was the crux of it: Fear to not be who I thought I needed to be because "that guy" was the one who had Parkinson's. The thing about Parkinson's, getting it and keeping it, was that when I jumped into adrenaline-mind mode, also called fight-or-flight mode, I struggled to not fight, and my tendency was to flee. Adrenaline-mind mode *always* meant fear *equaled* flight. Consistent with what had become my nature, I fled in fear.

Why did I flee? It was not my nature to be involved in conflict. I avoided conflict, and my Parkinson's knew it. And when I was faced with conflict, I was filled with fear of failure.

I was so deeply entrenched in fear of failure that I would flee to avoid conflict at all costs. Quite a few times while my criminal case was pending, Sally would ask what was going on with the case and I would say, "Oh, they set it for trial next month and there is a pre-trial conference in a couple of weeks."

And she would say something like, "Aren't you concerned about this?" And I would say, "I didn't commit the crimes, so they will come to their senses and it will not go to trial."

This is what I mean by fleeing; I was in denial of the seriousness of the charges against me. Actually, I was avoiding conflict, even with the people who were prosecuting me for crimes I did not commit. Sally was, and still is, a wise woman. She said to me that nothing good ever came from being afraid, and that I needed to be pro-active.

Ultimately, the case was not going away on its own and I had to fight. I had to say, "It is enough; you have been prosecuting me for over a year and there is not one bit of evidence against me that shows guilt."

By fighting, it forced the issue. In the courtroom as we all were standing in front of the Judge expecting that he would be dismissing all criminal charges against me, the prosecutor announced that the State would be voluntarily dismissing all criminal charges against me.

I had been forced to do something that was not my nature—fight on behalf of myself. When I practiced law, I fought for my clients. But when faced with criminal charges, it absolutely pained me to fight for myself even though I knew I had not committed the crimes. When fear of failure reared its ugly head, it made it even more difficult to fight for me. Thank God for Sally.

One of the things about avoiding conflict and running for my life, so to speak, was that they both were fleeing behavior, or avoidance of life behavior. And, while I was fleeing, my mind was racing faster than my legs.

My mind was engaged in this type of dialogue: How do I avoid this conflict (the fight)? What are all of the possible options? If I go with option 1, then what are all of the possible consequences? If I go with option 2, then what are all of the possible consequences? If I go with option 3, then what are all of the possible consequences? If I go with option 4, then what are all of the possible consequences?

The list of options was never-ending and the list of possible consequences was never-ending. My brain did not get a break, my body was worn to a frazzle, and my spirit had all but given up on me because all I wanted to do was flee and flee and flee.

My mind was telling me that if I stayed and fought, there would be two possible outcomes only: success and failure. Most certainly, I did not want to fail, so I would flee and look for another solution where I could justify my actions and not have the possibility of a dreaded failure.

That had become my nature. I avoided conflict and I made other people happy, even if on some occasions it meant that I was not happy. However, when others were happy, they liked me and life was easier, plus I avoided conflict. When Parkinson's was standing on my path to recovery, Parkinson's bet the farm that I would flee.

Why? Because it knew what had become my nature. It knew that my nature was part of what brought my symptoms to the surface in the first place. It knew that to recover, I would have to change what had become my nature; I would have to revert back to what was my true nature in my heart and soul.

To get back to being who I truly was, I would have to fight. I would have to fight my fear. Recovery from Parkinson's was do or die; I had to fight my Parkinson's.

When my Parkinson's saw in my conviction that I was digging in for the fight, it decided to force me to flee. It gave me some extra tremors, and it gave me some extra pain, and it gave me some extra stiffness, and it gave me some extra fear. It expected me to flee.

But I did not flee. Why? Because I was willing to change the nature of whom I had become and be my real self again...and fight! I was willing to look Parkinson's in the eye and say, "I am more than this body." I was willing to look Parkinson's in the eye and say, "I am more than this mind." I was willing to look Parkinson's in the eye and say, "I am this soul. This is me. I am strong in spirit and you cannot touch my soul!" I fought for me. This caught my Parkinson's completely off guard.

The thing about my real nature that was critically important in my fight against Parkinson's was that once I set my mind to something, I stayed at it relentlessly until I won. Failure was not an option. It was deep within my core to win this fight and fully recover.

Along the journey, I had to realize that I was worth fighting for. It had become my old-self nature to flee, but I knew I needed to change that part of my old-self nature to my real self and to fight.

Also, in the fight against Parkinson's, I had to realize that there was no such thing as failure. Success was the fight, the journey toward recovery, in and of itself! Success was every time I said to myself, "I am going to do the Recipe today."

Choosing a journey of recovery in my life, getting on the path, and staying on the path, in and of itself, was a SUCCESS! There was no failure, so I realized that I had nothing to fear, not even worsening symptoms.

If worse looking symptoms meant failure, then from my physical appearance, I had been failing almost every month I was working on my recovery. In May of 2010, my outward appearance and my physical suffering from symptoms became so pronounced that people were telling us that what I was doing was not working and that I should quit.

My tremors were raging, and even though nobody else could see them, I could feel them shaking me all day long. My rigidity reached a heightened level where I was so stiff that I felt like I was walking in mud with two metal poles for legs.

My pain was extremely severe, and on many occasions all I could do was curl up on the floor and cry. I would do my best to meditate and pray. Also, at the time I was suffering like that, I had no way of knowing that one month later, I would be fully recovered from Parkinson's. Even without that knowledge, I refused to give up faith in my recovery; I had begun to understand what was occurring.

The reason I suffered like that was because I was resistant to everything I have written here about the mind. The more I was resistant, the worse my symptoms got.

My mind would say, "But you have to worry about what the other people think about you. How can you let go of that?" My mind would say, "But you have to strive to be perfect. How can you let go of that?" And my mind would say, "But you have to be in control of everything. How can you let go of that?"

This was a very long list, but here was where this was going: the things I thought were real, the things I thought mattered, the things I thought were most important…they were not real, they did not matter, they were not the most important…they were a life-long-adrenaline-mode-mind-chatter-running-from-fear-of-not-being-perfect illusion.

How, and who, I thought I needed to be was nothing more than thoughts that were not real. I was so resistant to expelling those thoughts that it literally brought me to my knees in agony.

The interesting thing about agony was that it made me rethink what was going on in my mind. It made me realize that I needed to find my soul, my essence, the "me" that made me truly "me," and nurture that seed to help it grow again from deep inside in order to break away the toxicity of my body and my mind.

I viewed the fight against Parkinson's as chipping away, day by day, to clear out the toxicity that started deep inside me and had worked its way to the surface.

Ultimately, it came down to faith, attitude, and action to make progress. I will begin with action because most people understand action.

ACTION

In the Recipe, there are Medical Qigong exercises that required me to take action to fight my Parkinson's. These were not general Qigong exercises that would be taught at an introductory Qigong class. These were Medical Qigong exercises designed to heal the liver and kidneys and help them function better.

QIGONG IN GENERAL

The hearts pump the blood through one's body. The lymph system needs assistance to move it throughout the body to build up immunities and cleanse toxins. Enter Qigong. Qigong is known as a soft exercise in that it does not require a whole lot of physical exertion, but it still builds up internal energy because one is moving one's body slowly and stimulating the lymph system.

MEDICAL QIGONG FOR LIVER AND KIDNEYS IN THE RECIPE

The slow Qigong movements are focused on these specific organs. However, there are additional benefits. The liver is paired with the gallbladder as an organ system. The kidneys are paired with the bladder as an organ system. And, the lungs (it is not possible to do these Qigong exercises without breathing in a whole lot more oxygen than just sitting around) are paired with the large intestine as an organ system.

By doing these Qigong exercises, I was working on healing my liver, gallbladder, kidneys, bladder, lungs and large intestine. It is why my first noticeable results in doing the Recipe were an increase in energy, an improvement in bowel function, and my sense of smell returned. Although these were small signs of progress, they were signs of progress nonetheless.

HOW I ENVISIONED THE MEDICAL QIGONG WAS WORKING

I did not get Parkinson's the day I got diagnosed, and it was not going to go away the day after the diagnosis. The captain of the Titanic only saw the tip of the iceberg, if that, but an ice mountain had been growing for a long time beneath the surface. When Parkinson's finally broke through my surface, there was a mountain of toxic layers below that needed to be dealt with to beat the disease.

First, I envisioned the mountain of ice below the surface that sunk the Titanic. Then, I envisioned that I was placed deep into the center of this mountain of ice and that I had a tiny hammer and chisel. My goal was that each day I would chip away at the ice in a symmetrical manner. To onlookers at the surface, they could not even see that I was inside the mountain of ice chipping away. To onlookers at the surface, the iceberg looked just as solid as it did the very first time they saw it.

Every day I was chipping away more and more, and every day the onlookers at the surface would see no progress. On one particular day, if somebody who knew I was in there was to tell an onlooker, "Hey, there is a person in the middle of that iceberg with a small hammer and chisel chipping away," the onlooker would shake his head and tell the person, "If that is so, they are crazy and they are wasting their time. I have been looking at this iceberg every day and I see absolutely no change at all."

My feeling in my recovery went this way: if every day I was inside that iceberg chipping away and watching the hole inside get larger and larger, wasn't I making progress? And, this way: if every day I was inside that iceberg chipping away and watching the hole inside get larger and larger, did it really matter what the iceberg looked like on the surface in determining whether I was making progress? And this way: when I chipped away at this iceberg in a symmetrical manner and I finally broke through the outer edges, wouldn't the entire iceberg go away and wouldn't it happen quickly?

There it is in a nutshell (or iceberg), how the Recipe worked for me. After nine months of doing the Recipe and seeing very little improvement of my symptoms, I started seeing a lot of improvement. Two weeks after that

I had no symptoms. The causes of the Parkinson's were removed and the disease went away, also known as full recovery.

The Medical Qigong in the Recipe amounted to me taking action. The Qigong in the Recipe amounted to me chipping away at the iceberg from the inside out. To an onlooker, I looked like I was accomplishing nothing, that I was crazy and wasting my time. Yes, my symptoms were an annoyance and an inconvenience, but I was not focused on relieving my symptoms.

Instead, I was focused on ridding myself of Parkinson's, and then the symptoms would go away. Actually experiencing the symptoms was what gave me the insight to understand what needed to be accomplished to beat the disease. I saw the enemy, I was able to endure what it had to deliver, I learned what I needed to learn to defeat it, and I took action. Every day I did something to defeat the disease, I felt I was making progress.

That was the result of Medical Qigong for the Liver and Kidneys… even though I could not feel my organs healing from deep inside, they were. How did I know this? Faith, and gradual success. And in the end, symptom-free full recovery.

FAITH

At the beginning, I had to have faith in my own recovery and faith in the process I was using to lead me down the path to recovery.

ATTITUDE

In keeping a good attitude no matter how I felt physically, I was making progress because I had faith that I was on the correct path.

ACTION

Faith without action was meaningless for Parkinson's recovery. Action proved faith! Action said, "I so firmly believe that I will recover that I am willing to do Qigong exercises every day even if I cannot actually feel them healing me from deep within and even if I do not get immediate relief of my symptoms."

Some people told me that this kind of faith was crazy. I felt that this kind of faith was what brought me to full recovery. I concluded that the same people who called this kind of faith crazy actually had no faith at all in recovery, so I could not concern myself with how they felt. I needed to stay focused on how I felt about my recovery.

PROGRESS

Every day I woke up in the morning, I was making progress on the path of life. Every day that I was doing something in furtherance of fighting my Parkinson's, I was making progress on the path of my Parkinson's recovery. With strong faith, a great attitude, and proper action, I became aware that I was making progress every day I was doing the Recipe.

One day I woke up making progress in the path of life and knew that I had successfully completed the path of Parkinson's recovery. It was overwhelming.

When I healed myself from the inside, chipping away day by day, saying "okay" to whatever it is that Parkinson's was throwing at me, I was making progress each day and I took control of my Parkinson's.

When Parkinson's said, "How about more tremors or rigidity or pain" and I said "okay," it was the Parkinson's who was knocked off balance. My Parkinson's got confused. It did not know if I was saying, "okay, let me have some more misery" or "okay, that sounds exciting" or, the one that put fear into my Parkinson's and gave it tremors, "okay, I know I am recovering, so I accept that whatever it is that you do to me, it is nothing more than something I will have to endure on my path to recovery."

The more fear I gave my Parkinson's, the more it ran away from me. When Parkinson's tried to give me fear, I chose faith. My faith, in turn, put fear into my Parkinson's. That is how I controlled my Parkinson's instead of it controlling me.

The medical profession said that with Parkinson's, dopamine was depleted in the brain and the basal ganglia controlling movement were 60–80% dead. Having lived in a Parkinson's body, thought with a Parkinson's mind, and held my firm faith with a Parkinson's soul, I feel that they are incorrect.

I saw Parkinson's as an electrical problem that Western Medicine was trying to manage with chemicals. I felt that the dopamine was there, but that the flow was low because of the mind being in adrenaline mode. Essentially, the dopamine flow was blocked, thus leading to a lower flow of dopamine. However, it was not depleted.

Adrenaline had taken over, which ultimately lead to dopamine taking a back seat. Just like anything else, after years of operating in adrenaline mode as explained earlier, the dopamine just turned down the faucet's flow to a trickle. I felt that prayer helped open it up.

Prayer may not be the correct word, but here is my explanation of what I did to slow down my adrenaline and open up my dopamine. I would pray/meditate like this: "Hello, adrenaline. Thank you for all of the years you have run my body. Without you in charge, I would not have survived. However, all of life's stresses that required you do be in charge are gone, and you can take a break and you do not need to run my whole body anymore. Hello, dopamine. It has been a long time. Thank you for all of those years you stayed closed and allowed adrenaline to run my body. I appreciate that you understood it was for survival. Now that those stresses are gone, I need you to flow again. The thing is, I do not know how much adrenaline needs to shut down and how much dopamine needs to flow to achieve the correct mix. The two of you need to figure this out with God, and I am going to meditate on something else so I do not get in the way."

In looking carefully at the last part of this, I said:

"The thing is, **I do not know** how much adrenaline needs to shut down and how much dopamine needs to flow to achieve the correct mix. The two of you need to figure this out with God, and I am going to meditate on something else so I do not get in the way."

I emphasized four words, "I do not know," because I would imagine that this was the first time in my life that I ever had said those four words in that order: "I do not know."

In saying, "I do not know," I actually said, "I am not perfect. I do not have all of the answers. I do not control all of the situations in life. I cannot worry what other people are thinking about me as a result of me not being perfect and not having all of the answers and not controlling all of the situations in life. AND that is okay. My best is good enough."

I wanted to be recovered so much that I was willing to admit that I did not know how much adrenaline and dopamine had to adjust themselves for my recovery. I had provided my body the tools and materials for my recovery, and then, I surrendered control of the outcome: "The two of you need to figure this out with God, and I am going to meditate on something else so I do not get in the way."

Once I started achieving a more regular calming of my mind, I realized there was one very big missing piece of the recovery: The final unblocking of my dopamine. I realized that it had to do with how I felt about me...I needed to open my heart with love...for me.

OPENING THE HEART, OPENING THE DOPAMINE FLOW

This part of my recovery involved reconnecting with my soul and opening my heart for dopamine flow.

I began my recovery journey with faith in my full recovery. I considered that to be the beginning of healing my soul and reconnecting with the essence of my being. Essentially, in my recovery, I learned to reconnect with who I really was as opposed to who I had become and thought I needed to be in life.

I feel that I was born with a purity and innocence that I had adjusted, changed, and lost somewhere in life. It was the return to that beginning, my reconnection with that beginning, which repurified me and helped me reconnect with my soul, the true essence of who I was.

Parkinson's was toxic, and it was the Recipe's repurification of my body, repurification of my mind, and reconnection with the purity of my soul that purified me entirely...and then there was no Parkinson's...it only could reside in a toxic environment, and it had to leave. As a result, I became liberated!

My body was an accumulation of food and drink, etc., over the course of my life. My body had Parkinson's symptoms; I realized that I was not that body. My mind was an accumulation of thoughts and ideas and emotions and fears, etc., over the course of my life. My mind had Parkinson's negative emotions and fears; I realized that I was not that mind.

My soul, the essence of who I was, had remained pure. However, as a result of being so focused in life on what was going on with my body and with my mind, I had made adjustments to the pure and innocent essence of my being, and my soul got buried deep inside me, covered up by my body's and my mind's toxicities of life.

But *it* was there and always had been with me. *It* remained pure and untouched by Parkinson's. The Recipe's healing of the soul worked for me. *It* was something inside me—that something buried inside me that when I had faced insurmountable odds in life, I had reached down deep inside me and felt that something. There had been previous occasions in my life when I had defied all logic and accomplished whatever it was that nobody thought was possible.

In those times, I had trusted myself. I had faith that I would do whatever needed to get done. I had dug down deep inside myself and found whatever *it* was inside me to give me the ability to reach the end.

It was that spark inside me. That spark I had gone to when I needed a boost of energy or a smile on my face in hard times or that sense that there was a greater purpose in why I was here in this life at all.

Some people call that spark soul; some call *it* essence; some call *it* a part of God or the Higher Power or the Divine; some call *It* part of the Greater Consciousness; some call *it* an electrical charge. It does not matter what anybody else called *it*; *it* was there, and I needed to re-connect to *it* as I knew *it* would help me in my recovery. *It* was my basis of faith.

As I was opening my heart and finding *it* again, it had been critically important to continue to keep my mind calm. Two important components of keeping my mind calm—acceptance and getting out of the fear-based adrenaline-mode mind—had their foundation in faith.

FAITH AND ACCEPTANCE

To propel myself forward in my recovery and to calm my mind from self-judgment and self-criticism, I had to achieve a level of acceptance that required a strong amount of faith in the importance of my own existence: "I accept that everything that has happened in my life right up until now has had to happen exactly how it happened for me to be where I am right now." This was a powerful realization for me: *I accept that everything that has happened in my life right up until now has had to happen exactly how it happened for me to be where I am right now.*

I finally had realized that what made me special was not my achievements or degrees or performance. What made me special was that I existed. I existed as a human being. This really resonated with me: "I am special just in the fact that I exist."

Everything that had happened in my life right up until whatever moment it was at the time, was simply part of my existence. When I extracted judgment of myself from my mind, I could accept that everything in the past had a purpose whether or not I understood it or liked it. Whatever it was, it was in the past. Just accepting that it had to happen exactly how it happened meant that I never had to look back and judge myself again. This was a critical part of freeing my mind and liberating my life.

The past was exactly that: THE PAST! I let it go and I let go of self-judgment, self-criticism, and self-loathing over what should have, would have, could have been.

I cannot stress how important a lesson that was for me: *I accept that everything that has happened in my life right up until now has had to happen exactly how it happened for me to be where I am right now.*

To assist me with achieving that level of acceptance, I would think of someone or something that existed in my life for which I was grateful. If there were things in the past that I did not wish to accept, or that those things had to happen exactly how they happened, I would come back to that someone or something. There was no way to know the ultimate outcome if I were to theoretically change my course of action in the past in order to negate the thing I did not wish to accept. Had things gone differently at the time, the result might have set off a course of action that led to that someone or something for which I was grateful ceasing to exist in my life right then.

Accepting the past without judgment of myself. What a liberating concept. Then a thought occurred to me: if I woke up each day without a memory of the past, I would be prepared to accept the day as it rolled out in front of me. There would be no judgment of "now" compared to "the past" because the past would cease to exist in my mind.

There would be no "my symptoms seem worse today than yesterday" for the exact same reason. There would be no "I should have done it this way instead of that way." There would be no self-judgment, self-criticism, and self-loathing over what should have, would have, could have been because the past would not exist.

Acceptance that the past had to happen exactly how it happened closed the door to the past and put me a step closer to being in the moment. However, there was another obstacle: fear of the future of what my life would be like until such time as I had my final recovery from Parkinson's.

FAITH AND FEAR

Acceptance closed the door to the past. Letting go of fear would be necessary for closing the door to the imaginary future.

A quote from the movie *After Earth* stuck out to me and speaks well to this philosophy: "Fear is not real. The only place that fear can exist is in our thoughts of the future. It is a product of our imagination, causing us to fear things that do not at present and may not ever exist. That is near insanity. Do not misunderstand me, danger is very real, but fear is a choice. We are all telling ourselves a story and that day mine changed."

Earlier, I wrote about the adrenaline-mode mind. It is fear based, fear driven, fear, fear, fear, fear, fear…and F.E.A.R. (False Evidence Appearing Real). Or, as stated in the quote above, fear "is a product of our imagination, causing us to fear things that do not at present and may not ever exist."

How did I get rid of fear? Doing the Recipe.

Fear and negative thoughts were a constant battle with the disease. Although I had a very positive attitude that some day I would recover, fighting the disease mentally and spiritual was a daily war. I learned that God was in a much better position to handle my fears and negative thoughts and that I needed to give them away so I could stay focused on my recovery.

I meditated on this and adopted the following prayer for when I felt negative thoughts or fears coming into the forefront of my thoughts: "Dear God, I have this fear and I do not have time for it to bring me down. I need to stay focused on positive thoughts. You are in a much better position than me to deal with negative thoughts and fears, so I am giving you this negative thought and fear and thank you for taking care of it for me." The first day I did this, it must have been a hundred times I repeated this phrase. After four or five days, the negative thoughts and fears diminished, and then they went away.

Here was another way of looking at it. If I was in a small boat in the middle of the ocean and suddenly it started taking on water from a hole in the bottom, what would I do? Start bailing.

If I started bailing like my life depended on it, which in this scenario it would, then I would need to give it all of my attention, strength and energy. Why? Because I would not want to drown, and also, there was a shark called Parkinson's swimming around the boat.

Sinking and drowning would be a quick and an easy way to go, but getting grabbed in the teeth of the shark called Parkinson's would make life very unpleasant. Bailing faster than the water was coming into the boat would be my key to survival.

Of course, in this scenario, the water I was bailing was fear and F.E.A.R., negative thoughts, self-doubts and self-criticisms, and they kept coming and coming and coming. They were relentless. So I needed to keep bailing and bailing and bailing. I needed to be RELENTLESS!

In this scenario, the boat is a vessel, and the vessel was actually my heart. I needed to bail out of my heart vessel fear and F.E.A.R., negative thoughts, self-doubts and self-criticisms. Then, I could fix the leak at the bottom of my heart vessel and have compassion for the rotten wood on the floor and feel love and joy as I varnished the teak, feel compassion for the waterlogged seats, and feel happiness as I brought them back to a state of repair.

As a result of bailing the fear out of my heart, my heart became open to the notion of accepting my positive emotions again.

That was how I filled my heart with compassion, forgiveness, love, peace, joy, and happiness. That was how I reopened the valve on my dopamine faucet and let my dopamine flow. That was how I would reach my full recovery.

LIVING MY LIFE IN THE PRESENT MOMENT FROM MY HEART

Faith and joy were important components in opening my heart for cultivating positive emotions, which was the key to opening my dopamine faucet and finishing my recovery. Here was how I did it.

Throughout my life, in my wanting to be liked and loved and accepted by others, I had been achieving my "happiness" in the form of feedback from accomplishments. This self-perpetuated into the adrenaline driven behavior that helped me get Parkinson's—always thinking of the next scenario, or juggling act, to keep the "I can do anything to keep other people happy so they will give me positive feedback and keep me happy" balls in the air.

Quite frankly, I had to admit to myself how lost I was in this person I had become. I had to know why I did not like me.

It would be easy to say that I did not like me because of the Parkinson's, but that is not accurate. I did not like me before Parkinson's. Parkinson's only gave me a new excuse for disliking me more.

I needed to get to the root of the problem, so I decided to explore the things in life that had given me a feeling that I did not deserve—or was not worthy of—good things happening to me, including Parkinson's recovery. Essentially, I looked back at my life to see if there had been times when things were said or done that made me feel badly about myself.

I did not know much about the subconscious, but I sensed that if I had felt badly about myself and left those feelings unresolved, they could have grown over time into a subconscious feeling of being undeserving or unworthy of my final recovery.

In a quiet, meditative time, I explored my life from as far back as I could remember. I found some times when I was younger where things were said and the net result had been that I did not feel good about myself. I worked through these issues and gave them finality. I felt better about myself after having accomplished this and I will discuss this more in-depth later.

With this potential blockage out of the way, I was open to the realization that in life we all are connected at some level and the best way I could start

95

to open my heart and cultivate from the inside the positive emotions of happiness, joy, compassion, and gratitude was to share these with other people. I realized that this was much different than the "doing things for others so they would give me feedback so I could be happy" scenario that had helped me get Parkinson's. Absolutely, this was different.

The idea came from the realization that there was a substantial likelihood that every person with whom I would come into contact was suffering at some level—physically, mentally, and/or spiritually. I sensed that if I could assist people in feeling a little better about their own level of suffering, my suffering would become less because it would open my heart and my dopamine would flow better.

Also, it would bring me closer to God and closer to reconnecting with the *it* inside me, my essence, my soul. I did what had become an unnatural thing for me to do with my Parkinson's—I ventured out of my house to places with people and I talked to them. I introduced myself with a big smile and sincerely asked them how they were doing. People were responsive, and my heart opened from the absolute joy of helping other human beings feel a little better about their situations in life.

They knew they were not alone because this stranger, me, actually seemed genuinely concerned with how they were doing and was compassionate over their situation. It was amazing. I started easy—talking to the cashiers and baggers at the grocery store.

It made me feel so good to see the smiles light up on people's faces, that I started talking to anybody I could. Yes, some people looked at me with questioning eyes and walked the other way, but most people warmed up to the idea of having a chat.

It was my expanded realization that although we all are connected in this life, we spend so much time disconnecting ourselves from the other people. In reconnecting with other people and helping them feel a little better about their lives, I began to reconnect with my soul, the essence of who I was, and it felt great! My dopamine began to flow.

As a result of my faith, I was beginning to feel real joy in my heart. This assisted me in feeling compassion—for myself with Parkinson's, and for the rest of humanity as well.

I began with compassion for myself.

I was not my body. My body had Parkinson's physical symptoms.

I was not my mind. My mind had Parkinson's stress, anxiety, anger, frustration, worries, and fears.

I was my soul, my essence, my spot of grace, my "something" inside me that powered the rest of me and made me uniquely me. That part of me was untouched by Parkinson's. It was just covered up by the toxins of my body and my mind.

Let's say I went to the store and bought a shining silver teapot. I take the teapot home and put it on the sideboard to admire it. Then, I get busy with life and I do not spend any time with the teapot for the next six months. When I return to the sideboard, I am horrified to see that my teapot has become tarnished.

At first I think, "Oh no, what have I done. I have neglected my teapot and it is ruined." Fortunately, somebody points out to me that if I get silver polish, I can remove the tarnish. I get the silver polish, grab the teapot, and head to the kitchen sink.

I moisten the sponge, dip it in the silver polish, and I begin to rub the teapot. The first thing I notice is that it begins to look worse than when I started—there is black and gray pasty junk and it smells bad. In this moment of cleaning crisis, I think, *I have faith that the silver polish will work,* and I press forward.

Eventually, I have cleaned the entire teapot, washed it, dried it, and shined it. It looks like a brand new teapot. However, in that moment of admiring my "brand new teapot," it occurs to me that I am admiring the original, beautiful teapot that I brought home from the store six months ago. I realize that although the teapot had been covered in tarnish, the tarnish did not damage the essence of the teapot at all.

The original shining silver teapot was under there the entire time, unblemished by the tarnish. I would imagine that when somebody would come over to my house, they would say, "That is a beautiful new teapot you got to replace the old tarnished one." And I would just smile and say "thank you" because deep down I would know that they were staring at the original teapot, and it would shine.

Original me, my soul, my essence, my spot of grace, my "something" inside me that powered the rest of me and made me uniquely me...*it* was inside me. With the Parkinson's, *it* was covered up with a tarnish. The Recipe was my tarnish remover.

The Recipe helped bring my life back into balance by healing my soul, mind, and body. It helped me remove the toxins in my body so my organs were clean and functioning well. It helped me clean the toxins in my mind by calming my mind so my stress, anxiety, anger, frustration, worries, and fears would leave me and not return. Finally, it helped me to not be afraid to be the real me by opening my heart to myself and to the world fearlessly, and then my dopamine flowed and my soul shined again.

I needed to be compassionate to myself by being the real me, the new me as it seemed to others, but which actually was the original me. Throughout life, in my quest to be liked, and loved and approved of, I had made adjustments to the essence of who I was, the real me. Compassion toward myself allowed me to be my authentic self.

To others who had known the old me (the Howard who I had become through the adjustment I had made in life), I appeared to be a completely new person. However, I knew that what they were seeing was the original me, the real me, the authentic me, the me I no longer was afraid to show the world, and I shined.

I viewed the healing of my soul primarily as a 4-step process:
  1. **Learning to love myself**
  2. **Practicing Forgiveness**
  3. **Closing the door to the past**
  4. **Protecting my soul going forward**

1. LEARNING TO LOVE MYSELF

This was a very difficult topic for me when I had Parkinson's. However, I really wanted to get better from Parkinson's and I sensed that this was a necessary step in healing my soul, so I worked on it.

It was the "learning to love myself" that enabled me to see that it was not selfish to say, "I am worthy and deserving of my Parkinson's recovery." It was not selfish at all. It was NECESSARY!

I began by exploring the relationship I was having with myself like this. Let's suppose I was in a relationship with another person, and for most of the day, every day, the other person told me these things:

1. You are not worthy.
2. You are not deserving.
3. You are not handsome enough.
4. I do not like your tremors.
5. I do not like your stiffness.
6. I do not like your slowness.
7. Your speech is poor.
8. You are not good enough.
9. You are wasting your time doing this Parkinson's Recipe for Recovery.
10. It is selfish of you to put yourself first in your recovery.

Being completely honest with myself, I had to admit that this would be an unhealthy relationship. It would be such an unhealthy relationship that at some point I would have felt compelled to say, "Enough! I have to end this unhealthy relationship."

Here is the difficult part:

I realized that this was the relationship I was having with myself!

I absolutely struggled with this issue. How could I expect to move forward in my life and in my Parkinson's recovery if I thought so little of myself? This was such a difficult issue that for many months when I had Parkinson's, I would have a morning argument with myself about all the reasons why it was pointless to be doing the Recipe.

It was incredible how many excuses my adrenaline-driven-mind mode could spew out, rapid-fire, to try to derail my Parkinson's recovery: *The Recipe won't work. Who are you to think that you will develop the cure? Sally and the children are sleeping so who will know if you skip today? Do you really think you are worthy and deserving of being cured? Face it, your tremors and slowness and stiffness will be with you forever. Why are you wasting your time?*

Why are you being so selfish having Sally and the children help you do things you used to do yourself? This was a very long list filled with negativity and self-criticisms.

I needed to explore what were the attributes of a healthy relationship in an attempt to have a healthy relationship with myself. Let's suppose I was in a relationship with another person, and for most of the day, every day, the other person told me these things:

1. You are worthy.
2. You are deserving.
3. You are handsome.
4. Your tremors do not bother me.
5. Your stiffness does not bother me.
6. Your slowness does not bother me.
7. Your speech is fine.
8. You are good enough.
9. You are not wasting your time doing this Parkinson's Recipe for Recovery.
10. It is not selfish of you to put yourself first in your recovery. It is necessary.

Being completely honest with myself, I had to admit that this would have been a healthy relationship. It would have been such a healthy relationship that at some point I would have felt compelled to say, "I love you, too!"

Here was the difficult part:

How was I to make this relationship the one I was having with myself?

I knew I needed to end the unhealthy relationship with myself as it did not serve me well and it was preventing me from serving others well.

This unhealthy relationship with myself made service to myself and others come from the mind: *I have to do this because it is expected of me or it will help me avoid conflict or it will make others like me or love me or maybe I can feel good about myself because somebody will say 'good job' or 'thank you.'* This was my unhealthy fear-based service from my mind.

A healthy relationship with myself would make service to myself and others come from my heart: "I am doing this because I want to or because it enhances my joyful feeling inside or because it just feels right." This would be healthy joy-based service from my heart.

To start building a loving relationship with myself, I started telling myself these things:

1. I am worthy.
2. I am deserving.
3. I am handsome.
4. My tremors do not bother me.
5. My stiffness does not bother me.
6. My slowness does not bother me.
7. My speech is fine.
8. I am good enough.
9. I am not wasting my time doing this Parkinson's Recipe for Recovery.
10. It is not selfish of me to put myself first in my recovery. It is necessary. I am worth it!!!

Starting to have a healthy relationship with myself was not easy. I will explain the process I used to learn to love myself, and in the end, how I learned that it was not selfish to love myself, but that it was, in fact, necessary for my Parkinson's recovery and for my life.

With my Parkinson's, I did not look forward to going out in public. I was self-conscious, and the self-consciousness made my symptoms worse, particularly if I felt my slow-moving, hunched-forward, shuffling manner had caught somebody's attention (as if a 49-year-old man shuffling like a 90-year-old man with a back problem wasn't going to catch somebody's attention). Clearly, I was completely in my mind when I was in front of other people.

Eventually, I surmised that probably nobody was looking at me and thinking bad things about me. So, why did my symptoms rage in public? After some deep introspection, I had to admit to myself that I was the only one looking at me and thinking bad things about me. I did not like how I looked. I did not like how I moved. I felt I had let down Sally and our children. I did not like me.

However, that harder thing I had to admit to myself was that having Parkinson's was just another reason why I did not like me. I realized that I had not liked me for a very long time.

It occurred to me that I needed to find out why I did not like me because my feelings about myself made me feel unworthy as a human being, which also meant I felt unworthy of my Parkinson's recovery. At that point, I also realized that I had been trying to get better for Sally and our children. I was not even on the list of people for whom I was trying to get better.

After some meditative quiet time, I decided that I needed to explore times in my life when things were said or done that made me feel bad about myself. Maybe I had held onto those feelings and they had festered into a subconscious blockage in my life and my Parkinson's recovery. Here is what I did to explore this concept.

I sat in a relaxed manner, closed my eyes and went back as far as I could in life hoping that something would jump out, and something did. When I was young, I was a very sensitive child, which is a polite way of saying I cried a lot.

When I was about four or five years old, my father would scream at me to stop crying like a girl. From then on, when I felt the tears coming, I would bite the inside of my lip to suppress the tears.

I need to sidetrack for a moment here to explain that this situation from my childhood was something I thought I had resolved in my adult life as a stupid thing to say to a child. What I learned in my Parkinson's recovery was that it was only resolved at the intellectual level, but that it was not resolved at a deeper emotional/spiritual level.

Seeking emotional/spiritual healing, I visualized my four- or five-year-old self. I found him sitting there feeling really badly about himself. I sat down next to this younger version of me, put my arm around his shoulder and told him, "Dad was wrong. It is okay to cry. Crying is natural and you were not doing anything wrong when he screamed at you to stop crying like a girl."

Young Howard stared at me, and I told him it really was okay to cry. He started to cry, and then I started to cry. Forty-five years of self-criticizing, suppressed crying came to the surface and I sobbed and I sobbed and I sobbed. My tremors were out of control. A couple of times I thought I was going to pass out as a result of being unable to catch my breath. And then, the crying subsided.

As if I had not had enough surprises already, what came next nearly pushed me over the edge—ANGER!!! Young me was really angry with my dad, his dad. ANGER: the emotion that I had spent the previous seven months extricating from my being. That ANGER! And with that anger, I had a transformation.

I told young me that I was he in the future and I had not turned out so badly. However, I had this Parkinson's Disease, and I could not have anger in my life. I needed him to help me get better, and I needed him to join me in looking at the facts of 45 years earlier to help me get better.

I told him that when dad said this, it was the early 1960's in Miami, Florida, and I would imagine that he was trying to protect young me from being teased or beat up by the other children if I cried in front of them. It was not offered out of hatred for young me, but instead out of protection and love.

Yes, I still felt it was offered in a stupid manner, but dad had come into our relationship with 28 years of his own issues in life. I told young me that instead of anger, he needed to offer dad understanding, compassion, and forgiveness. Young me complied.

And with this compliance, I had another transformation. For the first time in my life, I viewed my father as another human being, not as a father figure. He became just another human being who was suffering from things just like everybody else, doing his best to be a good husband and father, coming into all of those relationships with his lifetime of baggage and issues. And I cried.

The crying was cleansing and I knew I needed to keep moving forward with this process as an emotional/spiritual shift was taking place inside me. This is the next major thing that came to mind and heart.

When I was young, I was a very good student. After two years of straight A's on my junior high school report cards, I came home with my first B. I had tried my hardest, done my best, and I had been okay with the B. In those days, our parents had to sign our report card.

With a bit of nervousness, I handed my report card to my father to sign. He signed it and returned it to me. As I turned to walk away, he got my attention and I turned back around to face him. He then said, "If you would have tried harder, you would have had all A's."

I remember the sick feeling that came over me. I remember the anger that raged inside me. I remember sitting down with Sally as we were having children and recounting this story followed by the words, "Grades will never be important in our home."

If you ask our children, each probably would tell you, "Mom and dad never put pressure on me about my grades. I put my own pressure on myself." And, of course, I would look at Sally and say, "I wonder where we got these perfectionist over-achievers from; certainly not from me." And we would laugh.

As you can see, I felt that this grades issue was long-before resolved. WRONG!!! Not even close. In my Parkinson's recovery, I realized some startling things when reviewing this situation at a deeper emotional/ spiritual level—the day my father told me, "If you would have tried harder, you would have had all A's" was the day I learned that my best was not good enough.

And it was the day I learned that my parents' love, affection, and approval was tied to performance. (Not my father's intention, but how the fourteen- year-old hurt-feelings me sub-consciously, unknowingly took it in).

Much in the same way that I resolved the other handful of issues I had located while reviewing my earlier life, I sat down with this younger version of myself to console him, to tell him that he had not done anything wrong, to let him know that it was a stupid thing to have been told, and inform him that we needed to let it go. Here is what I saw for the first time in my life, and I saw it through my younger-self's eyes and through his heart:

STRESS, ANXIETY, WORRY, FEAR, SELF-DOUBT!!! I saw myself through the next 10 years of school (high school, college, law school) studying long hours and never feeling like it was enough, and feeling stress every time I went to take a test or turn in a paper.

I was filled with self-doubt, and each test would be part of a grade that was going to determine the level of my parents' love, affection, and approval. It is a good thing that I had released crying already or I would have exploded as those memories were opening up. Instead, I cried, and it was a very healing cry.

Just like I explained with the four- or five-year-old me once I settled down, I had a heart-to-heart conversation with fourteen year-old me and asked him to listen to me as I explained how I (then-current with Parkinson's) saw the situation.

Dad worked hard his whole life. As I was growing up, most of the time he worked at jobs requiring him to work six days a week, including a couple of holiday seasons where he took on a second job stocking warehouse shelves in the evenings at a local toy store to earn extra money to buy presents for us.

I explained to my younger self that dad's statement, "If you would have tried harder, you would have had all A's" meant one thing and one thing only: "I want you to have things better than me." It was a statement about him, not about me.

With that understanding, my younger self had an enormous transformation and found overwhelming compassion and forgiveness for our dad. I realized in my recovery—and this was a very important point for me to understand—that it did not matter what was said or what was done or what was the other person's intention.

What mattered was how I took it in. It is the "how I took it in" that made their issue my issue. It is the "how I took it in" that got lodged in my sub-conscious. It was the "how I took it in" that made me feel bad about myself.

This is what lead to one of the biggest transformations of my recovery: I realized that whatever somebody was saying or doing was about them, not about me, and chances were that they were suffering from something physically, mentally, and/or spiritually. With that realization, I lost my mind and entered my heart.

That was a critical component of my transformation from illness to health.

Instead of looking at what people were saying and doing, and internalizing it with judgment from my mind, I started viewing what people were saying and doing from my heart and feeling compassion for their suffering.

I realized that I needed to view myself the same way. I was a suffering human being with Parkinson's who needed my compassion, not my judgment. I offered compassion to myself, and I learned at a deeper emotional/spiritual level that my best was good enough. Finally, I felt worthy and deserving of my recovery.

I had learned to love myself. I became able to put myself first in my recovery. I learned that this was not selfish, but quite to the contrary, it was necessary.

Also, I understood in my heart and soul that I was uniquely me. It was not my accomplishments that made me special. It was not straight A's that made me special. It was not hitting the home runs or scoring the most points or getting the lead in the play or the solo in band that made me special. It was not the great job that made me special, or the promotions or the raises, or the leadership positions I held that made me special. It was not the schools I attended or the degrees I obtained that made me special.

My thinking for almost all of my life had been that these were the things that made me special. However, that type of thinking was nothing more than the illusions I had created in my mind. I felt that I needed to be an over-achieving perfectionist in order to be special...in order to be accepted and liked and loved.

I had gotten the impression that acceptance, being liked, and being loved was based upon performance and achievement. This was because no matter how hard I tried and no matter what were my achievements, it never seemed to be good enough.

In my recovery, I understood that my achievements had been more than enough. However, I gleaned that the people from whom I was seeking approval, being liked, and being loved had been incapable of expressing these things to me as a result of their own life issues.

Ultimately, this brought me to a place of not approving of myself as well as not liking or loving myself. I felt that my best was not good enough. The people who had given me this impression had moved on in life. However, I was the one who had gotten stuck internalizing unhealthy feelings about myself.

Then, I broke free and became liberated. I understood that I was special simply because I existed.

My lifetime of self-criticizing stressful turmoil was because somebody said or did something (or many things) in my life that I held inside myself with silent, sub-conscious agony. That silent sub-conscious agony set up a fortress of self-protection.

That fortress of self-protection said, "If I am invulnerable, control everything, over-achieve, strive for perfection, never feel that my best is good enough, do everything for everybody as they expect I should be doing, and never ever make a mistake, I have a chance to be happy."

Since this notion absolutely was impossible to achieve, I became an expert beyond comprehension in one thing and one thing only: self-criticism. All of this because of the illusions created in my mind. I learned to let go of those illusions in favor of what was real, what I felt in my heart and soul.

The spiritual part of the Recipe helped me grow the happiness and joyfulness I was beginning to feel in my heart into compassion for myself, followed by forgiveness, acceptance, and liking and loving myself. When I achieved this, I became aware that viewing the world from my heart actually was what was real.

It is where I found God, the Universe, the Higher Consciousness, and the Energy that surrounded me and connected me to all of what was. It is where I found love, peace, and liberation from what had been the illusions of my mind.

It is where I could look at myself and realize that loving myself was not selfish, but instead, it was necessary, absolutely necessary to being a complete human being. And I let go, I surrendered, I voluntarily gave up the shackles of the illusions that had kept me a prisoner in my own body, and in my own mind.

I realized that what was in my heart was actually me, and that he was BEAUTIFUL!!! What made me special had been with me all along. However, my strong mind had convinced me otherwise.

When I lost that mind, I found the real me in my heart.

2. PRACTICING FORGIVENESS

In practicing forgiveness, I came to see that forgiveness was a gift I was giving myself as an effective tool for releasing myself from the bondage of those I had not forgiven; call them my tormentors. This included releasing myself from myself. In many ways, I had become my worst tormentor.

Whatever had been said or done in life that was so terrible that I harbored the ill will that said, "I never will forgive that person," was destroying me and destroying my health. Whoever had been my tormentor had moved on. The torment only lived anymore because I continued to carry the burden.

It reminded me of a quote I had heard that has been attributed to many different people throughout history, but it really hit the point here: "Resentment is like drinking the poison and then hoping the other person will die."

I needed to stop drinking the poison, and forgiveness was the gift I could give to myself. What a heavy burden I had been carrying all those years, being angry and feeling bad about myself when the person who had dropped on me those burdens had moved on.

I was the only one still living with the burdens that had been given to me. Forgiveness—and this was done in silence from my heart—said, "I have carried this burden long enough. I forgive you and I now remove this burden from my life."

Sometimes I did this forgiveness practice in the morning with my meditations, and sometimes throughout the day, I would sit down to have some quiet time and do the forgiveness practice.

As an example, using one of the things I mentioned earlier about my father, "If you would have tried harder, you would have had all A's." I looked at the situation, saw my father as a suffering being, and silently told him, "Dad, I forgive you." Although this may not seem like a meaningful thing to do as related to him, it was a liberating thing to do as related to me.

Those words were the functional equivalent of saying, "Dad, you laid this grade burden on me thirty-five years ago, and I have carried it long enough. It is not my burden, so I am taking it off of me. You are forgiven."

I was liberated; burden after burden after burden. I gave forgiveness and unloaded the burdens. I felt lighter, cleaner, the shackles began to fall off, and I had set myself free, so I thought.

Forgiveness began to flow from me naturally, except for the most difficult forgiveness of all, which was forgiving myself for whatever it was that I felt I had said, done, hadn't said, or hadn't done that had forever placed me in my own personal unworthy and undeserving category of life.

FORGIVING MYSELF!!! I KNEW THAT AS IMPOSSIBLE AS IT SEEMED, IT WAS NECESSARY IN MY LIFE AND IN MY PARKINSON'S RECOVERY!!!

I was my own worse critic, and many of the criticisms were the negative tapes I had been playing in my subconscious. These were primarily negative tapes created by somebody other than me. The negative tapes kept playing because they had been there for so long that I mostly did not even recognize they were there.

They were telling me that I was not worthy enough, that my house was not clean enough, that I was not smart enough, that my job was not good enough, and _____ (filling in the blank of this long list would require another book).

My mind had collected, sorted, and categorized for easy retrieval, every mistake I had made in my life, and the more I tried to open my heart with compassion and forgiveness for me, the more my mind would bombard me with mistakes from my life about which others had been quick to criticize me.

Somebody dropped these negative bombs on my head and I had been playing them in my mind time and again, ultimately accepting them as true and then playing them against myself.

In my recovery, it was necessary for me to lose my self-criticizing mind and to open my compassionate heart. I had to forgive myself and not utter another critical word about myself or think another critical thought about myself. All of the criticisms were judgments.

I needed to stop judging myself! It wasn't that I was thinking that I was not worthy, but I was thinking that I was not worthy **enough**. It isn't that I was thinking that my house was not clean, but I was thinking that it was not clean **enough**. It isn't that I was thinking that I was not smart, but I was thinking that I was not smart **enough**. It isn't that I was thinking I did not have a good job, but I was thinking that my good job was not good **enough**.

Finally, I had to say to myself: **ENOUGH!!!** I needed to stop judging myself based upon on my, and somebody else's, measurement of "beyond perfection" and then thinking that whatever I was doing in life was not good enough. I needed to forgive myself, and I needed to know a very important fact: **MY BEST WAS GOOD ENOUGH!!!**

And then, I had to give myself a hug. I really needed a hug from me.

By practicing forgiveness, I unloaded my burdens, released my shackles, set myself free, and could really live. I wasn't just alive, but I started living the wonderful life I was meant to live. Forgiveness helped me wipe my lenses clean so I could see clearly the beautiful life I had ahead of me.

Forgiving myself was such an important part of finishing my recovery that I feel the need to cover it a bit more.

I realized that with my lack of forgiveness for myself, I was tormenting myself with self-judgment and self-criticism. Essentially, I was the victim of my own torment. And, on top of that I was judging myself for being non-forgiving of myself and tormenting myself more.

In this scenario, I realized that I was the judge, and the tormentor, and the victim. I was involved in a vicious cycle of tormenting myself with self-criticism and then punishing myself with worse feelings about myself. It was like running around a hamster wheel and never being able to get off.

Taking this to the logical end, I was the jailer who put me in the jail cell as my punishment from me, the judge, for tormenting me, the victim.

I realized, though, that if I was the jailer, then I was the one who held the key to my own freedom. That key to my freedom was called forgiveness of myself.

Forgiveness of myself in a nutshell looked like this:
1. Agree to stop judging and criticizing myself.
2. Agree with myself to not utter a negative word about myself.

3. Agree with myself to not think a negative thought about myself.

4. Do not break these agreements, ever!

Many mornings when I was doing the physical part of the Recipe, it was very difficult. Also, my balance was extremely poor when I shifted my weight to the back. In Medical Qigong for the Liver, there is a part when the instructions said to bend backwards.

I could not bend backwards. I was doing the Qigong exercise to the best of my ability, and bending backwards was not part of my life with Parkinson's, as I would have fallen down. My Parkinson's mind would tell me that if I could not do the Qigong exercise as it was written, then I could not have a recovery.

I had to tell myself that my best was good enough and that not bending backwards on one Qigong exercise was not going to stand in the way of my full recovery. It felt so good to not feel the need to be perfect. It was the beginning of a long process of derailing the negative thinking of my Parkinson's mind.

Accepting that my best was good enough included that my life was a learning experience. I was learning through experience, which meant that I always had the opportunity to learn something new.

Sometimes, I would be learning that things did not turn out how I wanted them to turn out. However, instead of self-criticism for a result I did not like, I learned to say, "Okay, that did not turn out how I wanted. I will do it differently next time." Then, I would move on to the next experience. Learning and moving on with no self-criticism was a formula for a healthy life.

3. CLOSING THE DOOR TO THE PAST

Once I had worked out the earlier life issues and learned to love myself, and then I had forgiven everybody, including myself, there was one more critical step to moving forward in a healthy manner—closing the door to the past.

I mentioned this earlier and want to reiterate it now. This is the level of acceptance that closed the door to the past: *I accept that everything that has happened in my life right up until now has had to happen exactly how it happened for me to be where I am right now.*

Okay! With the door closed to the past, and me being filled with love and forgiveness for others and myself, where was I to go from there?

4. PROTECTING MY SOUL GOING FORWARD

After I closed the door to the past and realized that my soul was just as pure as the day I was born—my shining teapot—I knew that I did not want to allow the toxins to cover up my soul again. Here is what I did:

I worked extra hard to keep control of my mind so I could stay in my heart. I knew that this was necessary to help me to not worry or be fearful, to not have stress or anxiety, to not have things anger or frustrate me.

I wanted to proceed forward in my life through my heart and soul, and I understood that these negative emotions had been the toxins that had placed tarnish over my soul. First I healed my soul this way, and my mind and body had no choice but to follow.

Freeing my mind: My mind would say, "worry." I would say to myself, "Worrying is a toxic thought about the future that may not ever take place and it tarnishes my beautiful soul and hurts my recovery in the present moment. I need to decide to not worry. If the thing I was going to worry about ever actually occurs, I will deal with it in the moment when it occurs. I choose to not worry."

Freeing my mind: My mind would say, "That person insulted you, you need to be angry and 'let him have it.'" I would say to myself, "This anger is a habitual reaction to life's events and it fills me with toxins that tarnish my beautiful soul and hurt my recovery. I will view the other person from my heart and realize that somebody who would utter such insults must be suffering, and suffering beings need my compassion, not my anger. My anger hurts both of us, and my compassion is healthy for both of us. I choose compassion."

I came to understand that my negative emotions surfaced as part of life, but that I could choose to transform them into something positive. It took a constant conversation with myself to undo old habits and old ways of thinking and responding to life. However, this is what protected my soul from getting covered by all of the toxins and tarnish of life.

Over time, this gave me control of my mind. Once I reached the point where my mind was following my heart and soul, my mind did not interfere with my body as much.

What I mean by this is that my mind was so much under control that it stopped telling my body, "you are not getting better, Parkinson's is not curable, more tremors is a sign you are getting worse and not a sign you are getting better from increased energy, etc." The negativity of my mind vanished.

As a result of my mind not being so negative to my body, my body said, "Thank you, thank you, thank you, for removing all of that negative chatter from my recovery, I can finish recovering now."

Also, I learned to be me, the real me, the me-that-I-had-been-so-afraid-was-not-good-enough-and-that-nobody-would-like-or-love-or-approve-of me. I HAD BECOME HIM, AGAIN—THE REAL ME!!! In fearlessly being the real me, I radiated my essence and was not afraid to show my luminosity! I realized that it was the compassionate thing to do for myself, and it was the compassionate thing to do for others.

AND THEN I FOUND GRATITUDE, WHICH HELPED ME FINISH MY FULL RECOVERY

Parkinson's is a symptom of life out of balance, physically, mentally, and spiritually. I decided that it would be progressively degenerative disease for which there was no cure for me ONLY if I accepted it that way and did nothing about it.

If you have read this far and still are here with me, then you can see that I decided to do plenty about it! I knew I needed to bring my life back into balance and rid myself of the symptom called Parkinson's. Gratitude helped me open the final door to my liberation.

GRATITUDE!

My story of a life out of balance. As explained earlier, in the years leading up to the fall of 2009 when the tremors appeared with all the other things that had been going wrong with me and the neurologist pronounced "you have Parkinson's," I had been running from the lion for a decade. My adrenaline-mode fear-based mind was always running. This brought me completely out of balance in my life.

While working on my recovery, I realized just how out of balance I truly was. When things occurred that I did not like, my habitual stress, anger, and frustration surfaced. I did not express it on the outside. I held it in. I did not know that I was harming my liver by doing this, but I was harming my liver just the same.

I realized in my recovery that I had been refusing to accept reality, and with the surfacing of stress, fear, anger, and frustration when something occurred that I did not like, I was constantly "trying to undo what had just occurred."

I was not dealing with life as it was rolling out in front of my eyes because everything was not occurring the way I thought it should be occurring. So, I was trying to undo what had occurred instead of dealing with life, accepting the situation, and creating a solution.

Ultimately, this would cause me to turn the anger directly at me: "you should have known this was occurring, you could have put things in place to have prevented this from occurring, I can't believe how stupid you were for not being prepared...." Simply put, I lacked acceptance of the things I did not like in life and ultimately blamed myself for them. Mentally and emotionally, this brought me out of balance.

On the issue of gratitude, I had no gratitude. This is not because I was not happy about good things when they occurred. It was because I did not expect them to last. I realized in my recovery that I felt so unworthy and so undeserving of the good things lasting that I could not bring myself to a point of gratitude; it would only hurt that much more when the good things went away.

Why give gratitude for something when it won't last and thus cause myself more pain later when it is gone? In short, I lacked gratitude for the things I liked in life. Spiritually, this brought me out of balance.

To bring balance back to my life, which would lead me to my Parkinson's recovery, I had to adjust these imbalances. To physically bring my life back into balance, I needed to heal my internal organs. To mentally and emotionally bring my life back into balance, I needed to learn acceptance.

To spiritually bring my life back into balance, I needed to practice gratitude. This seemed like an easy task. I would think about things for which I was grateful and give thanks.

However, my problem was bigger than that. How was I to give gratitude when I did not feel that I was worthy and deserving of the good things that had occurred in my life? I had the most wonderful wife and we had been blessed with three magnificent children. But I had Parkinson's. How could I have done this to them? This was so unfair to them. Having done this to them, how could I be worthy and deserving of anything?

How much more out of balance could I have been than that? I was doing the Recipe every day for my family because my Parkinson's was so unfair to them. Sadly, I was not even on the list of people for whom I was trying to get better. I did not like myself enough, certainly did not love myself, and absolutely felt it would be selfish to be trying to get better for me. I was so out of balance and I was completely incorrect on this point.

This was such a critically important point in my recovery that I need to discuss it again.

I needed to see myself as worthy and deserving of good things in life, including my recovery. I needed to like myself. I needed to love myself. I needed to want to get better for me. I needed to want to get better for me FIRST! Yes, for Sally and the children, too, but for me first.

AND I NEEDED TO KNOW THAT PUTTING MYSELF FIRST IN MY PARKINSON'S RECOVERY WAS NOT SELFISH. IT WAS *NECESSARY!* AND, NOT ONLY WAS IT NECESSARY, IT WAS GIVING!!! It was giving because I would be serving others and myself graciously from the joy in my heart rather than from some obligation in my mind.

Once I realized this, I started giving gratitude for my life. I realized what a gift it was to be alive. "Thank you God for another day of being alive, even in a Parkinson's body. There is so much I can do with my soul inside a human body. I am grateful."

And with that beginning to each day, I began working on spiritually bringing my life back into balance.

Each time I gave gratitude, it was an internal announcement that I was worthy and deserving of good things in life and that the good things in life could and would last. Why? Because I was worthy and deserving and abundantly grateful for them. I know this sounds like circular reasoning. It is circular reasoning. But it worked!

The more grateful I became for my life and everything in it, the more accepting I became of everything in my life. "Okay" was my new way of living. For the first time in my life, I was completely accepting of my life as it was rolling out in front of me.

In my recovery, to help me keep a positive attitude, and because I knew it was true, I looked at everything that was happening with me physically as "necessary for my recovery." I started taking that attitude into my daily life.

By accepting that whatever was happening in my life was necessary in my life's journey, I was able to reduce stress and anxiety, reduce anger and frustration, reduce worry and fear. Instead of being afraid of life, I explored it, one small shuffle at a time, just like the tortoise from the children's story, "The Tortoise and the Hare."

There are things I could learn from the tortoise every day. In proceeding forward like the tortoise, slow and steady, I tended to see many beautiful things in life that I used to just walk by without noticing. This brought so much joy into my life that it opened my heart and my dopamine flow as I was working on my recovery.

It occurred to me that when I was moving like the tortoise, slowly and steadily, I also had more time to notice all of the subtle unpleasant changes that were happening to my body. However, my faith was strong from doing work in the Recipe so I did not worry about the unpleasant changes that were occurring, and occurring in the best way for me.

Since my Parkinson's body had limited energy, I had to trust it to know where I needed the healing the most. Some days that meant I walked a little slower, some days it meant I had more tremors, and some days it means I had a big headache.

Here is the new look at acceptance I decided to undertake:

"Okay. Apparently, I am supposed to be walking slower, because if I wasn't supposed to be walking slower, I would not be walking slower."

"Okay. Apparently, I am supposed to be tremoring more, because if I wasn't supposed to be tremoring more, I would not be tremoring more."

"Okay. Apparently, I am supposed to have a big headache, because if I wasn't supposed to have a big headache, I would not have one."

The power of "Okay. Apparently..." is representative of true acceptance of what the Universe was offering me. It defeated emotional stress, anger, frustration, resentment, and fear.

Instead of looking at something and getting upset, I would just say, "Okay. Apparently, that was supposed to happen," or, "Okay. Apparently, I wasn't supposed to be doing that." The more I could look at unpleasant Parkinson's circumstances and say, "Okay. Apparently..." the more calm I became and less angry and fearful I became as I continued my recovery.

The one thing I knew I needed to keep constant in my recovery was doing the physical, mental, and spiritual parts of the Parkinson's Recipe for Recovery every single day.

That way, my body could say, "Okay, I know you are doing these things, and I know you are generating this energy. Thank you, now I can start fixing this mess." Faith, plus action, was key to this philosophy.

And with the Parkinson's Recipe for Recovery, faith plus action looked like this:

I have faith in my recovery. Plus, I am taking action to heal my organs by doing the Qigong exercises. I am recovery!

I have faith in my recovery. Plus, I am taking action to generate more brain activity and energy by doing the Brain Vibration Chanting. I am recovery!

I have faith in my recovery. Plus, I am taking action to make my body healthier by eating better. I am recovery!

I have faith in my recovery. Plus, I am taking action to balance my internal energy by doing Jin Shin Jyutsu. I am recovery!

I have faith in my recovery. Plus, I am taking action to calm my mind by meditating. I am recovery!

I have faith in my recovery. Plus, I am taking action to connect my Inner Divine to my Higher Power by praying; opening my heart; feeling love, joy, laughter and gratitude; and keeping the faith that I am safe and secure. I am recovery!

Getting back to moving like the tortoise, I realized there's a lot to the tortoise and hare story. The hare views "recovery" as winning the race, only...he's thinking about the end goal of totally symptom-free recovery. He fails to understand that, in and of itself, recovery is participating in the race. So when the hare gets off the path toward what he sees as recovery, the destination only, he never finds his way back to the path and he never wins the race.

The tortoise is recovery. The tortoise views recovery as each small advance toward the symptom-free recovery at the finish line. However, the tortoise, by its very nature, has to move slowly and steadily, and the tortoise cannot worry too much about the bumps in the road.

Instead the tortoise knows that every step toward the finish line is recovery, in and of itself, and the tortoise sees love, joy, laughter, gratitude, and fulfillment on the entire journey.

Oh, yes, and then the tortoise wins the race. There is much I learned from the tortoise. Gratitude for my life, gratitude for the journey, gratitude for moving so slowly that I saw flowers and birds and other grand things in nature that I never noticed before.

The more I accepted what was happening in my life was necessary in my life's journey, the more I came back into balance mentally and emotionally.

The more I learned to give gratitude for being alive, including for everything that was happening in my life as a result of being alive, the more I came back into balance spiritually.

Then, one day when I wasn't paying attention, for the first time in eight months, I walked down the stairs and back up without holding on to the railing. On another day, I was pushing a shopping cart and it felt like it suddenly got turbo-charged and we flew down the grocery store aisle. I had not walked like that in eight months.

These things were one-time events, but they were real and they signified the blessings of a full recovery on the way.

I kept up with the full Recipe, and on June 9, 2010, I had an enormous change for the good in my symptoms; I was excited. A couple of days later, I was staring at what I had written on my blog about my recent partial symptoms relief, and I noticed that I had written this: "I am not out of the woods with fighting Parkinson's. It will be a life-long battle, but I am making progress. On a sliding scale, I am on the plus side, beyond the 50% mark, between Parkinson's and not-Parkinson's."

Then it hit me. In staring at these words, I asked myself, "Where is the guy who knows he will be fully recovering from Parkinson's? How is he now the guy describing his Parkinson's as a life-long battle?" And then it came to me.

So many people had been so negative and so disbelieving of my fighting Parkinson's without medications and saying I was not going to have a full recovery, that I had fallen back into my old "safe-place" habit when faced with potential disapproval and conflict. I had become willing to keep Parkinson's to my detriment just to make the other people happy because if they were already negative toward me just with what I was doing in my treatment, how negative would they act toward me when I fully recovered.

With that awareness, I realized that I needed to be the real me and, by doing so, it would make me vulnerable. However, I also realized that being vulnerable was necessary to finish my recovery. I knew I would need to be vulnerable in all I did in life, fearlessly facing life as my real self.

The fear of being the real me is what had been holding me up. The more I resisted being absolutely vulnerable—being genuinely me—the more physically miserable I had become in the last month leading up to my recovery. And through that physical misery, I let go.

I surrendered fearful me. I awakened to the truth that the person who I had become was not the real me, the essence of me from birth. He was the "who I had become" based upon what I thought others expected from me. I had allowed people outside of me to influence the script of my life.

To be authentically me, I decided that my script of life going forward would have to be whatever rolled out in front of me, trusting and accepting that if it was rolling out in front of me then it was necessary in my life. I needed to accept life as it was and deal with it in the moment, moment after moment.

On June 11, 2010, at the end of my usual meditations and prayers before going to sleep, I added the following:

> *Dear God, I surrender my ego to you. I surrender my attachment to my Parkinson's Disease to you. I am not afraid anymore. I no longer fear Parkinson's. I no longer fear the scorn I may face by being cured from a disease the experts say there is no cure. I no longer fear the people who may say I was misdiagnosed or that I faked having the disease. I am surrendering my ego to you, that part of me that felt I needed to remain attached to Parkinson's because the experts say once you have Parkinson's you always have Parkinson's. I am forgetting about my old self (Parkinson's) and stepping into my new self (No Parkinson's).*

What happened next, I have never written about, although I have discussed it with some people over the years. I said, "Okay, God, I surrender all of me, my over-thinking adrenaline-mind me, to you. Take me, and I fully accept in advance however this turns out." The next thing I knew, I was walking with a bright white light. I stopped for a moment and glanced back over my shoulder.

What I saw was me, the body of me, lying there on the bed. In that moment I realized that I might not be in that body in the morning. However, instead of being afraid, a feeling came over me that I did not recognize at first. Then I realized that the feeling was absence of fear, and it was so peaceful.

I turned back to the white light and said, "I told you that I fully accepted in advance however this turns out, so if I am not in that body in the morning, Sally and the children will just have to figure it out." And I kept walking.

I awoke the following morning, June 12, 2010, with my remaining symptoms gone. I jumped out of the bed and was immediately on my hands and knees crying praise and gratitude.

In that moment, I knew my purpose. I promised God to help people with Parkinson's for the rest of my life. And, that is what I have been doing since June 12, 2010.

I had fixed the imbalances in my life, physically, mentally, and spiritually, and I had found me again. Physically, I had healed my organs to help them function better and to form a strong foundation on which to base my recovery.

Mentally, I had learned to calm my mind. Acceptance of life as it rolled out in front of me was the equivalent of taking my zazen practice into my everyday life.

Spiritually, fear of being the real me had stood in my way. It was this fear that made me afraid to be vulnerable and say how I really felt or act in a manner authentic to my essence. It was this fear that drove my Adrenaline mode mind. It was this fear that made me afraid of conflict and compelled me to make the other people happy even if it was to my own detriment.

Spiritually, I needed to detach from the fear of life. I surrendered fear. I opened my heart and learned to love myself, feeling worthy and deserving of a joyful, grateful life, including a Parkinson's recovery. I had found me, the essence of who I had been since the beginning, but who I had become too afraid to show to anybody except Sally.

The Recipe had been my daily companion as well as the roadmap for my recovery. It taught me to live a fearless, healthy life. I did not understand it until after my recovery, but taking the time each day to work on my recovery had been the beginning of my journey to feeling worthy as a human being.

Finally, I became aware that my full recovery from Parkinson's was not a destination. Although magnificent for me in ways too difficult to describe, my full recovery had been an exemplary event in my life's journey. On the day of my full recovery, I stopped doing the physical part of the Recipe; the mental and spiritual parts of the Recipe had become a part of how I lived my life and I continue to practice them daily.

I am joyful. I am grateful. I am blessed. And I am only seven years into the next part of my life's journey.

Part Three

What has been happening subsequent
to my recovery

June 12, 2010, was an incredible day. Full recovery from Parkinson's. It still feels good just thinking about it.

Also, June 12, 2010, was a bit of surreal day. Sally and I knew my recovery was real, but we held off telling anybody until we had a little time that day to sit with it. Sally's mother came over for a visit that day and we decided to not say anything because we were still grasping the full recovery ourselves.

After the visit, Sally walked outside with her mother when her mother was leaving. When Sally came back inside, she said, "Mother told me that you look particularly well today. I thought, 'Mother, you have no idea!'"

My full recovery was the final transformation of bringing me back into balance physically, mentally, and spiritually, bringing me from Parkinson's to no-Parkinson's.

As explained earlier, I had a final surrender that last night and awoke the following morning symptom free. I wrote on my blog two days later:

On Saturday morning, I was symptom free. On Sunday, I cleaned the garage. It was the first time I ever have viewed cleaning the garage as a blessing.

To finish my recovery, I needed to view my life, in and of itself, as the grand blessing that it was. I was giving gratitude each day just for being alive, and I still start every day that way now.

After Sally and I started breaking the news of my recovery to people, the responses came with mixed reviews. There were those who were genuinely, abundantly happy for us; there were those who were struggling with accepting my recovery; and there were those who simply did not believe I had a full recovery because the medical profession said it is not possible to recover from Parkinson's.

What I had learned in my recovery was that it simply did not matter what the other people were thinking. What mattered was my truth, the reality of what actually had occurred in my life. I had lived through the Parkinson's and prevailed; that was pure fact. That was my authentic truth and nobody's opinion could change that fact.

Post-recovery, I decided that helping people with Parkinson's would begin by sharing my recovery story with anybody and everybody who had anything to do with Parkinson's and Parkinson's research.

For six months, I made phone calls, sent letters, and sent emails, reaching out to many organizations such as The Michael J. Fox Foundation, The American Parkinson's Disease Association, and The National Parkinson's Foundation, as well as hospitals and health care centers involved in Parkinson's research.

My offers to share information, assist in studies, do whatever I could to get the word out that one could recover from Parkinson's fell on deaf ears, mostly. I did get the occasional unpleasant response stating that if I was saying I was better then I never had the disease or telling me I was being irresponsible to say I was recovered.

However, during those six months, people from around the world who had been following my blog began contacting me and asking if I could teach them my Parkinson's Recipe for Recovery. So I began doing some one-on-one work with them.

Also, during those six months, my already-scheduled neurologist visit occurred. On August 5, 2010, eight weeks after my full recovery, I walked into my neurologist's office fully recovered from Parkinson's.

Here are excerpts from that visit from my medical records:

> *This is a return visit for Mr. Shifke. He did not want to take any medications and has relied on alternative medicine including meditation, Chinese practice Chi-Gong, and a vegetarian diet. He feels that his symptoms have completely resolved.*

> *ASSESSMENT/PLAN: My assessment was that his symptoms have resolved. I suspect that his clinical features fluctuate and when he is in a good state of mind he has no symptoms, as in today I could detect no signs and symptoms. In any case, I have encouraged him to continue his current regimen of activity since they seem to be effective and making him have a sense of well-being. We will see him again in about a year.*

So, there I was completely symptom free, something not seen before by my neurologist, and he did not take away his diagnosis. In fact, he confirmed his diagnosis by stating that he suspected that my clinical features fluctuated, which means he still felt I had the disease, but that I was able to control the symptoms with my regimen and a good state of mind.

I accepted his feelings. It must have come as such a shock to see me symptom-free that his decades of Parkinson's research had to find an explanation for me being symptom free. The most important part for me is that he did not say I was misdiagnosed or faked having the disease. My diagnosis was confirmed even when I was exhibiting no symptoms on my exam.

As I was reaching the end of the 2010 year and was learning that it did not seem that any Parkinson's organization was interested in working with me and my recovery protocol, I was at a crossroads of what I should do next. I knew I had found my purpose of helping people with Parkinson's Disease, but I did not know how to accomplish this.

Sally and I had a few discussions about this because it was a really important topic in both of our lives. We were running low on money, so it looked like I was going to have to redo my resume and start looking for a regular job, and ultimately give up assisting people with my Parkinson's Recipe for Recovery one-on-one.

I decided that one way I could continue to fulfill my purpose of helping people with Parkinson's for the rest of my life would be to post on my blog my entire Parkinson's Recipe for Recovery, thus offering to the world at no cost everything I did, step by step, in my recovery.

In my final blog post of 2010, I concluded with this:

> I am going to spend some time with my wife and children over the next couple of weeks during the holidays, and I am going to gather everything I have to share with you. The things that are too difficult to explain, I will give you the book title and author as well as the pages I found meaningful in my recovery. In January, I will post my entire recipe for recovery.

During this time, I had become friendly with a woman in Boston who I was assisting in explaining the Recipe, as she had a client with Parkinson's. I shared with her was my intention was, as I saw no other way and I did not think my family was supposed to starve as a result of me fulfilling my purpose in life.

As the year wound down, she said she recommended I speak with a man in Japan for guidance. I asked how that would be accomplished and she said via Skype. At the time, I did not know what Skype was. However, I agreed.

She introduced us by email, and I scheduled a Skype call with the gentleman in Japan. After a lengthy conversation he concluded with this: Parkinson's recovery was a wonderful thing. As a showing of gratitude, I had offered my entire Parkinson's Recipe for Recovery to the world free of charge by posting it on my blog. However, there would be some people who might need one-on-one teaching to get started, and some people who might want one-on-one continued teaching of the Recipe throughout their fight against Parkinson's, so would I consider doing Parkinson's coaching full time?

He said that I had spent the majority of my time trying to convince the Western Medicine world that my Recipe worked and that my recovery was real, and they were not listening. Maybe the majority of my time would be spent in a more useful manner if I were coaching people who actually wanted to get better. And since everything else I was doing was free, there would be nothing wrong with charging a cost for my one-on-one coaching time.

I told him I would think about it and asked if we could talk again once I had discussed things with Sally and made some decisions about what I might or might not be doing.

Sally and I decided that this felt like the right path. A couple of weeks later, I had my second Skype with the gentleman in Japan. He explained to me that I would need to set up a professional full website, move my already existing blog to my new site, and decide what "Parkinson's Coaching" would be.

He then told me that he used a web designer in the Philippines and would provide me an email introduction. So I received the introduction to the web designer. I provided him with the layout of the website, all of the pages and page material, and my previous blog program that I had been using for about a year.

He took all of the information and set up the design of my then-new website, www.fightingparkinsonsdrugfree.com. Near the end of March of 2011, I launched the website, which included announcing Parkinson's Coaching. I have been running the website and doing Parkinson's Coaching full time since then.

So many wonderful things have occurred since launching my website in 2011, and I will do my best here to discuss the more monumental occurrences in the Parkinson's Recipe for Recovery world and in my life.

On January 5, 2011, I posted the entire Parkinson's Recipe for Recovery on my blog. A few weeks later, Marie, a woman who had Parkinson's, contacted me. This was during the time I was deciding whether I would be doing full-time coaching or not, and I decided to coach her in the Recipe.

Marie was very similar to how I had been in that she had been recently diagnosed and was not taking medications. I worked with her on my Parkinson's Recipe for Recovery. Over the course of time doing the Recipe, she had periods of symptom improvement.

That was something new to me. I had been pretty miserable in my symptoms all the way to the end of my full recovery, and I commented to her one time that even though I had been recovered from Parkinson's for nearly a year, I was still a bit envious of her diminishing symptoms.

In August of 2011, about 7 months into coaching Marie, I received a rather simple email with the subject line, "thanks." The content said,

> dear howard, my mom has parkinson stage 4. after reading your personal experience i am trying to help her out and i feel i am succeeding. thank you so much.
> bhavna
> india

I wrote back to Bhavna thanking her for her email and thanking her for helping her mom. Ultimately, Bhavna asked me about coaching her mom in her mom's recovery. This was going to be a challenge for a number of reasons.

Her mom, Pratima, was Stage 4 Advanced Parkinson's, wheelchair bound and bed bound, and she had not spoken in two years. Also, she was taking four Parkinson's medications and had been diagnosed about six years earlier. Oh, yes, and she spoke Hindi only, something not in my abilities.

I explained to Bhavna, who was fluent in English, that I would agree to coach her mom, but that I would need Bhavna's assistance for translation and for movement of her mom through the physical part of the Recipe.

She agreed, and I began teaching Bhavna, and Pratima, the Parkinson's Recipe for Recovery. Over time, Pratima became my extended-family Indian mother.

In November of 2011, on my blog, I issued what I called my "November to Remember, No Excuses November Challenge" for people to make a commitment to themselves to do a reduced version of the Recipe for thirty days.

Nine days into the November Challenge, this comment was posted on the blog:

I accepted an internal 30-day challenge from myself when I discovered fightingparkinsonsdrugfree almost a year ago. And that was just the beginning. I made a promise to myself that I would do whatever was necessary and change my life in whatever ways would support recovery, if it was really possible to have my condition improve rather than degenerate. As Howard so often says, "What did I have to lose?" I trusted Howard as my guide, and the bearer of good news that penetrated the bleakness of my fear and despair. I put my faith in my power to heal myself. The Recipe for Recovery was my lifeline. AND it is why I can happily and gratefully report to you today that the reason I am not accepting this challenge now is that I am symptom free! YES! Symptom Free!!!

Cheering you all on as you courageously overcome the disease. I am a happy example of the success of the Recipe for Recovery.

With love to you all~ Marie

Those who had been following my blog for a while were familiar with Marie as she had been writing comments on the blog for most of her recovery period. Marie has continued to write blog comments and encourage others for over five years since her full recovery. Thank you Marie, my dear friend.

Earlier that year, in the summer of 2011, my friend, Frederick Slone,

M.D., approached me regarding the potential of doing a study of the Recipe. Fred had known me for eighteen years prior to me getting Parkinson's, he saw me with the disease, and he had seen me for the year subsequent to my recovery.

Fred was a wonderful person, a brilliant doctor, and an excellent scientist. However, he is not a neurologist. Fred is a gastroenterologist, but he felt he could assist me in organizing the information of my recovery doing the Recipe to see if we could get a neurologist's support and do a study of the Recipe.

For six months I worked with Fred explaining everything I did and why I felt it worked. He utilized this information to examine if there was a reasonable Western Medicine explanation for what had occurred in my recovery. Ultimately, we had a good meeting of the minds and he felt comfortable that we had a very good chance of having a study approved, but we needed a neurologist.

I explained to Fred that it had been over a year since my neurologist had found me to be symptom free, so maybe it would be a good idea to schedule a follow up visit, get another solid confirmation of my recovery, and, out of respect to Dr. Sanchez-Ramos, tell him what we were up to and see if he was interested.

On December 22, 2011, I returned to my neurologist for a follow up visit. Here are excerpts from my medical records:

> *This is a return visit for Howard Shifke, who I had diagnosed with Parkinson's disease, stage 1. However, I saw him last August and found his symptoms had resolved using no medications.*
>
> *On his exam today, he is completely normal. Cranial nerves II through XII are normal. He has excellent facial expression. Normal voice volume. Face is symmetrical. Motor exam reveals supple tone throughout, even with reinforcement I can detect no rigidity. There is no rest tremor postural tremor. Deep tendon reflexes are normal and symmetrical. Sensory exam is intact to all modalities.*

Gait and balance are normal. He walks with a normal stride and arm swing.

This gentleman for two examinations in a row does not have signs and symptoms of Parkinson's disease. I cannot explain the mechanism for his improvement.

After my exam, I explained to my neurologist what Fred and I had been doing and that we were looking to move forward with a study of the Parkinson's Recipe for Recovery. I was very excited when he said he was interested in being the neurologist to oversee the study. I connected Fred and Dr. Sanchez-Ramos to work out the details of what was needed to apply for the study and get back with me. It was a wonderful way to finish the year 2011.

Fred got back with me after New Year's 2012, and on January 18, 2012, I posted on my blog, "Fighting Parkinson's, and it's time to heal the world." In that post, I announced what had been going on and asked anybody who had been doing the Recipe and was willing to provide supporting data for the application for the study to supply some basic information as well as his or her medical records.

Many people responded favorably to providing medical records and answering questions, and we began to gather the pertinent information to support our study of the Recipe. A number of months into doing this, Pratima had her full recovery. It was incredible.

On May 22, 2012, I posted "Fighting Parkinson's, and Pratima is symptom free from Stage 4 Parkinson's." The subheading to the post was "PRATIMA IS OFF OF ALL OF HER MEDICATIONS AND IS SYMPTOM FREE FROM STAGE 4 PARKINSON'S HAVING FOLLOWED THE RECIPE FOR RECOVERY FOR NINE MONTHS!!!"

The excitement over Pratima's full recovery is hard to explain. Here was a woman going from Stage 4 Advanced Parkinson's taking many Parkinson's medications who did not speak English but who learned the Recipe from me with the assistance of her daughter's translation skills, and while she was healing by doing the Recipe, she slowly reduced her medications down to complete elimination of her medications, and then she had a full recovery.

Pratima visited her neurologist on June 9, 2012, and he found her to be off of her medications, walking without support, and symptom free from Parkinson's symptoms. This was very exciting as we were moving forward to request a study of the Recipe. By mid-2012, there were three people with full recoveries doing the Recipe.

Over the next few months, I finished collecting 16 medical records from people in 6 different countries and supplied all of the information to Fred. He compiled the information, organizing it chronologically as well as by symptoms and patient improvement doing the Recipe as explained by the individuals who had sent me the information.

However, in September of 2012, we learned from Dr. Sanchez-Ramos that he had become very busy with other endeavors and the notion of doing a study would be put on the back burner at best, probably never to go forward with him.

After the initial blow of this news settled in, I had to utilize what I had learned in my recovery. "Okay. Apparently, he was not the right one to oversee this study and champion the cause." "Okay. What am I going to do about this? *What is my solution?*" It occurred to me that finding another neurologist when my neurologist was no longer interested in participating would be a futile endeavor.

My solution was to take the Parkinson's Recipe for Recovery on the road by doing an all-day workshop once per month in a different city in the United States and Canada over the following year. I felt that if Western Medicine did not want to study the Recipe then I would bring it to people's communities.

My thought was that if I did one-day workshops, not only would people get to meet like-minded people in their community who wanted to get better from Parkinson's, but also, more people would get one-on-one teaching of the Recipe directly from me.

Ultimately, I felt that once a large number of people had full recoveries doing the Recipe, maybe Western Medicine would take notice. Maybe not...but maybe.

My first workshop was in Seattle, Washington. At that time, I was coaching some people from in and around the Seattle area, and it made sense to go somewhere where people were open-minded and where I could meet in person some of the people who I was coaching but had only met on Skype.

The workshop went wonderfully well. There were 28 of us and we spent seven hours together. We discussed my Parkinson's philosophy in the morning and visited with each other over lunch. I spent the final three hours teaching the physical part of the Recipe, plus we meditated together and had a discussion of the spiritual work I did in learning to love myself and feel worthy and deserving of a recovery.

The people attending the workshop were very focused on learning about my recovery and the overall possibility of recovery from Parkinson's. Most were from Washington State, but five had made the trip down from Canada. It was wonderful to be able to share my story and Parkinson's experience with them.

Seattle was a beautiful city. It was my first trip to the northwest, and even though it was cold and raining, I enjoyed seeing the mountains. Also, the people were open-minded about my recovery, something I had not experienced in Tampa. I felt peaceful and at home.

My daughter, Genevieve, was in college in California at the time, and she came up for the workshop. I got to spend part of the weekend with her. This made having the Seattle workshop extra special for me.

The workshop was an exhausting and exhilarating day all wrapped into one. I was so inspired to be with people with Parkinson's who were open-minded in exploring the possibility of actually recovering from Parkinson's. On December 4, 2012, I wrote about the workshop on my blog and included a picture of some of the attendees.

Another great year was coming to an end. By the end of 2012, I had spent the previous twenty months doing Parkinson's coaching full time and was beginning to take the Recipe on the road with workshops.

In those twenty months, I had met, Skyped, FaceTimed, and spoken on the telephone to people with Parkinson's from around the world. I had learned very much from those interactions. This international group turned out to be the nicest, most kind and compassionate people I ever had the pleasure of meeting.

However, I also could see that they were just like I had been. They were nice, kind, and compassionate to everybody but themselves. I was receiving daily reminders of how difficult it was for these people with Parkinson's to see how truly beautiful they were on the inside.

In my final blog post of 2012, I included these affirmations of encouragement:

1. I have the power to heal myself. I am so much more than Parkinson's symptoms. I am alive, and I am recovery! Parkinson's is a symptom of my life out of balance, and I can repair the imbalances and recover. I refuse to allow appearances in my physical symptoms to make me fearful. Fear is a choice. Faith is a choice. I choose Faith. I am recovery. I am worth it!

2. I have the power to heal myself. Parkinson's is a symptom of my life out of balance. I am bringing my physical body back into balance, I am bringing my mind back into balance, and I am bringing my spirit back into balance. I choose Faith. I am recovery. I am worth it!

3. I have the power to heal myself. Parkinson's is a symptom of my life out of balance. I say "Okay" as my way of acknowledging acceptance that my Parkinson's is temporary and that my recovery is real. I say "Okay" as my way of acknowledging acceptance that my fear is actually False Evidence Appearing Real. I say "Okay" as my way of acknowledging acceptance that my faith is real. Okay. Okay. Okay. I choose Faith. I am recovery. I am worth it!

4. I have the power to heal myself. Parkinson's is a symptom of my life out of balance. As I wind down 2012, I say good-bye to anger and frustration and resentment and stress and anxiety and worry and fear and FEAR (False Evidence Appearing Real). As I begin to see 2013 on

the horizon, I feel a surge blossoming inside me filled with happiness and joy and gratitude and compassion and love...and FULL RECOVERY! I choose Faith. I am recovery. I am worth it!

5. I have the power to heal myself. Parkinson's is a symptom of my life out of balance. The tortoise is recovery. I am the tortoise. I view recovery as each small advance toward the symptom-free full recovery at the finish line. Just like the tortoise, I move slowly and steadily, and I realize that I cannot worry too much about the bumps in the road. Instead, I know that every step I take toward the finish line is recovery, in and of itself, and I settle in and enjoy the journey. In each step, I see love and joy and laughter and gratitude and fulfillment and compassion and contentment. Oh, yes, and then the tortoise wins the race. Oh, yes, and then I win the race and achieve my full recovery. Fear is so 2012. Faith is absolutely 2013! I choose Faith. I am recovery. I am worth it!

I began the new year 2013 with a Survival Guide/FAQ feature on my website. I had been receiving many inquiries through the holidays asking me questions about how I performed certain Medical Qigong exercises or how I calmed my mind or opened my heart. I decided that I would go back through my recovery, back through many earlier blog posts that explained my methodology as well as my philosophy of Parkinson's Disease, and put all of it on one screen on my site.

I initially posted it as a blog post, and then I added it as a permanent page on my website. I felt is was a good teaching tool to assist people in understanding more in-depth what I did, how I did it, and why I felt it worked for me.

In late January, I had my second Recipe on the road workshop; this one was in Atlanta, Georgia. I was coaching a couple of people in Georgia, so Atlanta seemed like a good spot for a workshop. On January 28, 2013, I wrote about this workshop on my blog:

> It was a very different workshop than the one in Seattle the previous month. There were sixteen people in attendance, and this group was very focused on the healing the soul part of my recovery. I shared with them the bad feelings I had about myself and what it took to learn to love myself and feel worthy and deserving.
>
> We laughed and we cried as we went through the day together. In our lunch conversation, there was one thing very clear: the reason people came to attend a workshop in Atlanta even though some were from Texas, South Carolina, and Florida was because none of them could find an "I want to recover" Parkinson's support group, and this was an opportunity to meet others who wanted to recover from Parkinson's, even if it meant a big trip to attend a workshop. There was a real comradery in this group.

The next workshop on the road was Tampa, Florida, where I lived at the time. In February of 2013, it had been over two and a half years since my full recovery, but acceptance of recovery in Tampa was virtually non-existent. The Tampa workshop attendance was a reflection of this point. On February 18, 2013, I wrote a blog post about this workshop.

> Sixteen people were in attendance, and there was only one person other than my wife Sally and myself who had a Tampa address. The other attendees were from other parts of Florida, Massachusetts, Ohio, and Pennsylvania. As a result of it being such a diverse group, it took a while for people to warm up, but then we had a very good workshop together.

One thing about that day really sticks out in my mind, and I wrote about it in the February 18, 2013 blog post:

And, my wife Sally was there. That made it extra special for me, and I feel her presence had meaning for the others who attended. When we were eating lunch, the woman sitting next to Sally asked her a question about the experience of me with Parkinson's. As Sally was trying to explain what it was like the day we told our children, her voice cracked and she started crying. Even two and a half years after my recovery, the memories weigh heavy and the emotions are strong.

The next stop for taking the Recipe on the road was Victoria, British Columbia, Canada. I scheduled that workshop so that Sally and our daughter Victoria could come with me and we could make a family vacation out of it as well. The timing coincided with Victoria's sixteenth birthday and her spring break from school.

None of us owned passports, so we began the year filling out the applications and moving that process forward. Our passports arrived well in advance of the scheduled trip. Okay, check that off of the list.

Fortunately, the commitment to do the workshop in Victoria was solidified well in advance of the "how are we going to get there" part of the adventure. To fly to that part of Canada from Tampa, Florida, in early 2013 required three or four connecting flights; all day travel that came at a very large expense.

Then we remembered that I had flown a few months earlier to Seattle at a reasonable cost and two flights only. Since we were going to need a rental car anyhow, we flew to Seattle, drove up to Canada, and took the ferry to Victoria. After eighteen hours of travel, we arrived at the hotel and passed out.

Victoria, Canada, was absolutely breathtaking. I was ready to move there on the second day, and it actually was this trip to Victoria that started Sally and me discussing the possibility of moving to the northwest at some future date.

On March 11, 2013, I wrote my blog post about the Victoria workshop. It was every bit as wonderful as the city itself.

As you know, on Saturday, March 9, 2013, I had my fourth workshop in taking my Parkinson's Recipe for Recovery on the road. This venue was Victoria, BC, Canada, and the day was absolutely astounding! Imagine: 45 of us, some with Parkinson's, some of their spouses and partners and friends, my wife and one of our daughters, a few health practitioners, some from the Island and some who took the ferry, all in one place with one purpose...Parkinson's recovery.

And I got to have Sally and our daughter Victoria, there, which made it even more special. For the people in attendance, I feel that meeting Sally and Victoria helped make my recovery real and more meaningful.

The workshop attendees were not afraid to be vulnerable in sharing their personal stories of Parkinson's, and this group encouraged each other to not fear the disease. By the end of the day, there was a strong feeling of empowerment in the group.

I remember thinking how wonderful it was to be with a group of people who had Parkinson's and to hear them encouraging each other to not fear the disease. Instead, they were encouraging each other to be proactive in doing something about the disease. I was grateful for all of them.

As we were cleaning up the room at the end of the day, a man came over to say thank you and good-bye. I noticed that he was struggling greatly with his walking.

As he was reaching the door, Sally went over to him and gave him some reassurance. She said, "Don't worry. Howard walked exactly like you, and look at him now." The man's face lit up with excitement.

When Sally returned to the table where we were cleaning up, I thanked her for encouraging the gentleman. Her response was, "I told him the truth. That is exactly how you walked." I was shocked and looked over at our daughter Victoria. She confirmed, "Yes, dad, mom is right, that is exactly how you walked. "

I was overwhelmed with emotions and cried. I had no idea. I realized it probably was a good thing I never saw myself walk as others saw me. I was overcome with gratitude for the blessing of my full recovery. I was not taking it for granted, not any day, and certainly not that day.

We made it back to the States, and the next thing I knew, I was preparing for a trip to Upstate New York for my next workshop. The workshop had eighteen people in attendance, including one who was friends with one of the Atlanta workshop attendees. It looked like word of the workshops was getting around.

On April 22, 2013, I wrote a blog post about this workshop. One thing sticks out in my mind about this workshop. As I was discussing my recovery and getting into the mental, emotional, and spiritual aspects of my recovery, one man started crying and left the room.

When he returned, he shared with the group that he thought he was going to a workshop to learn some exercises for his Parkinson's, but when he heard my story of my soul, mind, and body recovery, he saw a lot of himself in my words and it overtook him. The group circled around him like a family, and he felt safe and secure among friends, the friends he had made that day.

My next workshop was scheduled for June 1, 2013 in Tucson, Arizona. It was so different from the other workshops that the best way I can explain that workshop is to provide excerpts from my June 3, 2013, blog post entitled "Fighting Parkinson's, and the Tucson workshop was educational."

As you know, on Saturday, June 1, 2013, I was scheduled to have my sixth workshop in taking my Parkinson's Recipe for Recovery on the road. This fifth venue of 2013 was Tucson, Arizona and the day was educational! Imagine: 2 of us. That's right, 2 of us, a woman I am coaching and me. It was educational.

First, I digress, then back to educational. On October 3, 2012, I announced taking the Parkinson's Recipe for Recovery on the road with workshops. I felt the need to come to your communities and meet with you personally for a day of recovery where you could meet each other as well. Financially for me, it was going to be a matter of enough people coming to cover my expenses or I would be unable to do the workshops.

I would imagine that this fits under the category of vulnerability. I am not financially independent. My wife works and has health benefits for the family, and my income is from coaching and Parkinson's Recipe for Recovery manual sales. I knew if I could cover my costs of doing the workshops, then all would be okay financially. That occurred with the first four workshops, but not with numbers 5 or 6.

Back to educational. The woman I was coaching in Tucson had been out of the country for a number of months and returned about two months ago. I advertised the workshop in the same manner I have advertised the other workshops and she belonged to a large Parkinson's support group in Tucson. She provided my press release and workshop flyer to the head of the support group to send out to the members, and that's when the first part of the education took place. After hearing nothing back and trying to contact the person, she finally heard back -- my recovery was "too controversial" and the person was concerned about providing my workshop information to the group.

Here was my response in an email:

"Thank you for letting me know that your local contact to a larger Parkinson's group is so skeptical that she does not want to share with the group that I am doing a workshop on June 1st. I would ask that you please hit the forward button and send this to her, and leave this note to you in it so she will understand why you are forwarding it. Do not copy me on the forwarded email as you should keep her email address private between the two of you.

Thank you.
Howard

Good Day,

My name is Howard Shifke, and I understand your skepticism about my Parkinson's recovery. Many people are skeptical because the doctors say we cannot recover. My neurologist is Juan Sanchez-Ramos, http://health.usf.edu/ medicine/neurology/faculty/sanchez_ramos.htm, and he was my mother's Parkinson's neurologist for 24 years before she died with Parkinson's, Alzheimer's, and Dementia in 2007.

He diagnosed me, and he found me to be symptom free when I went back for my later follow up visits. I bring my medical records to all of my workshops for people to review. In summary, they reflect:

November 5, 2009 — diagnosis of Parkinson's. "The patient has the signs and symptoms of Parkinson's."

February 4, 2010 — diagnosis confirmed. "The patient has at least stage I Parkinson's disease."

August 5, 2010 — symptom free, but diagnosis confirmed again. "My assessment was that his symptoms have resolved. I suspect that his clinical features fluctuate and when he is in a good state of mind he has no symptoms, as in today I could detect no signs or symptoms."

December 22, 2011 — full recovery, no more Parkinson's Disease. Here is what my exam results were prior to my neurologist determining I did not have Parkinson's Disease anymore: "On his exam today he is completely normal. Cranial nerves II through XII are normal. He has excellent facial expression. Normal voice volume. Face is symmetrical. Motor exam reveals supple tone throughout, even with reinforcement I can detect no rigidity. There is no rest tremor or postural tremor. Deep tendon reflexes are normal and symmetrical. Sensory exam is intact to all modalities. Gait and balance are normal. He walks with a normal stride and arm swing."

I am not asking you to endorse my workshop. You do not know me, and you do not believe my recovery has taken place. However, two other people have fully recovered using my methodology of recovery, and many more around the world are reversing their Parkinson's.

What I am asking you to do is just share the information and allow those with Parkinson's to decide for themselves what they wish to do. I do not care if you put a big disclaimer out to the group that expresses your skepticism and that clearly points out that you do not endorse my workshop. That is fine. At least you will be providing people the opportunity to decide for themselves. This is my sixth workshop. Here is how the other 5 went:

http://www.fightingparkinsonsdrugfree.com/2012/12/04/ fighting-parkinsons-and-the-seattle-workshop-was- incredible/.

http://www.fightingparkinsonsdrugfree.com/2013/01/28/ fighting-parkinsons-and-the-atlanta-workshop-was- amazing/.

http://www.fightingparkinsonsdrugfree.com/2013/02/18/ fighting-parkinson%E2%80%99s-and-the-tampa- workshop-was-stupendous/.

http://www.fightingparkinsonsdrugfree.com/2013/03/11/ fighting-parkinsons-and-the-victoria-workshop-was- astounding/.

http://www.fightingparkinsonsdrugfree.com/2013/04/22/ fighting-parkinsons-and-the-upstate-new-york- workshop-was-healing/.

I am hopeful that after you click those links and look at the over-100 faces of people with Parkinson's and their loved ones, you will see that they are filled with hope and faith, and that they feel empowered to do something positive in their lives and their Parkinson's. I watched my mother decline from a beautiful, loving, caring person, to a mindless, crippled person in a wheelchair. Nobody should have to go that way. I am passionate about getting the message out that it doesn't have to be that way.

All I am asking you to do is share the information with anybody who has Parkinson's so that at least they will have the opportunity to decide for themselves. Here is the link with more details about my workshop,

http://www.fightingparkinsonsdrugfree.com/ parkinson%E2%80%99s-recipe-for-recovery-%E2%84%A2-workshops/.

Thank you.

Respectfully,
Howard"

The person declined. That was educational.

About two weeks prior to the workshop, when I still could get a reasonably-priced airline ticket, I discussed with Sally that I felt the need to go to Tucson. I booked my flight, already had paid for my workshop venue, and planned my trip. At best, some people would attend. Also, I knew if nobody attended (or even a few), I would have to put some rules on future workshops. On Saturday morning, I went to the venue, and nobody was there…educational.

A bit on "Okay" and acceptance. Prior to leaving for Tucson, I had to say "Okay" and accept that nobody might attend the workshop. It does not say anything about my recovery or the validity of my workshops. It does say a lot about getting people to workshops and it does say a lot about fear.

One person, the gatekeeper to a large group of people, was so filled with fear of what the others' might think for sending out a flyer about a Parkinson's workshop about recovery, that the one person's fear stopped all of the other people from getting an opportunity to exercise their own free will in whether to attend or not. One person's fear blocking everybody's knowledge. Educational.

My trip ended with "Okay" and acceptance when I arrived in Tampa last night but my luggage did not. My luggage was delivered to my home about 30 minutes ago. Okay!

Educational. What I have learned. My future workshops are a mix of vulnerability and "Okay" acceptance. From this point forward, unless I have a reasonable amount of people pre-registered for my workshops within 2 weeks prior to the workshop that will be upcoming, I will cancel that upcoming workshop and refund the registration cost of those who already had pre-registered. I will do this workshop-by-workshop. This is not to be mean or as a punishment. It is simple economics, mine. I cannot afford to do all of this traveling and pay all of these upfront costs if people will not be attending the workshops.

So, I put it out there to you. If you planning on attending a workshop or cannot attend but think the workshops are a good idea, then I need your assistance in helping me get out the word and letting people know I cannot wait until the last minute for them to register.

I open my heart to all of you, and I am "Okay," and fully accept however this turns out. I am optimistic that the future workshops will fall into place the way the first five did, and I fully accept that maybe number six turned out this way because I needed to express my vulnerability to all of you.

Thank you for listening. Looking forward to meeting

many of you at my next workshop on June 29, 2013 in Santa Fe, New Mexico.

Here I was, coming up on three years since my full recovery, still practicing the lessons I had learned in my recovery. This was, and continues to be, a very important thing in my life.

In my recovery, I had learned to be vulnerable. Also, I had learned that there was nothing wrong with me, that is, the essence of who I was. Moreover, I had learned acceptance, "Okay. I accept that if this is in my life then it belongs in my life. What am I going to do about it?" In its simplest form, life is a series of lessons followed by acceptance and solutions.

And then came June 29, 2013. This was a very exciting day for me because I was going to meet Marie in person for the first time. Marie, the same Marie who I had coached in the Recipe two years earlier and who had her full recovery in November of 2011. That Marie!

Twelve of us attended the Santa Fe workshop. On July 2, 2013, I wrote about the details of the workshop in a blog post.

> It was a special day. Two of the twelve people at that workshop had fully recovered from Parkinson's doing the Recipe. There was a very calm feeling in the room and a sense that many friendships were made that day where people could offer each other support going forward.

The following day, I drove to Marie's home and we had a lovely time. It was fantastic to share the space with Marie and her partner, a gentleman every bit as nice as Marie. It is difficult to describe what it was like to be with another person who traveled down the same path of Parkinson's recovery as me and was sitting next to me at her kitchen table having lunch.

Suffice it to say, my entire trip to Santa Fe was delightful.

My next workshop was scheduled in Boston on July 27, 2013. I few weeks earlier, I added this note at the bottom of a blog post:

NOTE: WORKSHOPS UPDATE. The Boston workshop

formerly scheduled to take place on July 27, 2013 is being postponed. Many of the places I contacted only can rent space to a non-profit company, some are doing renovations, and some are not available; late September looks like a better time to have the Boston Workshop. The Los Angeles workshop will take place on August 24, 2013. Marianne, a woman who I am coaching, has graciously offered the Community Room at her apartment complex as the venue for my Los Angeles workshop.

Four days prior to the workshop, I wrote a blog post entitled, "Fighting Parkinson's, and Betty M. is symptom free." I was elated to be writing about another full recovery doing the Parkinson's Recipe for Recovery. I was excited for Betty, and I was exuberant to be able to share the news with the workshop attendees in Los Angeles.

Betty previously had lived in Minnesota and had been seen for years at the Mayo Clinic. The following year, in July of 2014, eleven months after her full recovery, she made the trip back to the Mayo Clinic, and gave me permission to post the following results of her neurologist visit on my blog:

> At the Mayo Clinic, Betty was seen by two neurologists who first documented her history, beginning with, "This patient has had imbalance since 2006 when she began lurching to the left." The neurologists put her through all of their tests and then documented the following conclusion:
>
> "Neuro: I agree entirely with Dr. Scharf. There is no evidence of parkinsonism."

Betty M., the fourth person who had a full recovery following the Recipe received confirmation from two neurologists at the Mayo Clinic. This was outstanding news.

A couple of days after the post about Betty's full recovery, and I was off to Los Angeles for the workshop. Genevieve, my daughter who had attended the Seattle workshop, had stayed in Los Angeles to work all summer and was about to begin her next year of college. Part of the Los Angeles trip was to see her and help her move into her new apartment to start the school year.

On September 3, 2013, I wrote a blog post about the Los Angeles workshop.

There were fifteen of us, and the room was abuzz. I was delighted to observe the connections people were making with each other sharing the stories of their Parkinson's experience. It is the one workshop where I forgot to take a picture of the participants to share on my blog.

Here is what I had to say about it on the blog:

> I was so much in the moment of the workshop that when I awoke on Sunday morning, it occurred to me that no picture of the group had been taken to share with you. I accept responsibility for the lack of a picture, and I am sorry I do not have one to present to you. I am not perfect, and surrendering the "need to be perfect" was instrumental in my Parkinson's recovery.

Once again, the lessons of my recovery resurfaced in my everyday life. Recovery from Parkinson's was a reflection of a soul, mind, and body healing that brought my complete life back into balance. Keeping my life in balance was practicing the lessons that I learned and applying them to my life each day. This has kept me calm, and it has put a perpetual smile on my face.

As I neared September and was starting to look for venues for the Boston workshop, I finally gave in and stopped doing workshops. I had lost money on the New York workshop and had lost a lot of money on the Tucson workshop. Also, I had lost money on the Santa Fe and Los Angeles workshops.

I did not cancel the Santa Fe workshop because I wanted to meet Marie in person and I felt it would be very inspiring for people to have a workshop with two of us who had our full recoveries. I did not cancel the Los Angeles workshop because I had to go to Los Angeles anyhow to help

Genevieve move into her new apartment.

However, three weeks in advance of the Boston workshop and very close to the time when I would have to buy a plane ticket, book a hotel, rent a car, and pay for a venue, I had one registered attendee. I refunded her payment and stopped doing workshops.

The workshops had served many useful purposes. They were a great way to get people with Parkinson's out of their homes to meet others with Parkinson's who had an interest in hearing a story of recovery. Hearing about the workshops and seeing the pictures of the workshops inspired people around the world in their recoveries.

Personally, I loved meeting all of the attendees and having the opportunity to share my recovery experience with them. And finally, I brought my medical records with me to every workshop and had them available all day for anybody to review. This was important to me.

With the workshops and other talks I had been invited to do, my medical records have been put out on the tables for hundreds of people to see and review. In this day and age of the Internet, which makes people question what is real and what is not, attendees could meet me, hear my story, look at my medical records, and feel comfortable that I am a real person reporting exactly what I did to get better and what is contained in my medical records.

In October of 2013, I had just finished nearly a year of traveling and meeting many people. One question that appeared at every talk and every workshop was, "Do you still do the Recipe?" My answer was, "No, I stopped doing it the day of my full recovery, and except to refresh myself before a workshop, I have not done it since then. It is why I consider myself cured."

So, in a blog post dated October 2, 2013, I announced my feelings, "Fighting Parkinson's, and Parkinson's is curable!"

I began my post like this:

> Parkinson's is curable! There, I said it. Your turn...take a deep breath...now, all together, let's say it: Parkinson's is curable. Doesn't that feel great? Yes, I agree. It feels great!
> As a result of the medical profession saying there is no

Parkinson's cure, I have talked in terms of being symptom free or fully recovered. I felt that acceptance of what I had to say would be hampered if I used the words Parkinson's cure. However, after 3 years and 4 months of not doing the Parkinson's Recipe for Recovery, and still being symptom free and fully recovered, I know it is time to say Parkinson's is curable.

The way I saw it was that I was diagnosed with Parkinson's, I did the Recipe as my treatment, all of the signs and symptoms of Parkinson's resolved and went away, I stopped doing the Recipe, and three and a quarter years later none of the signs and symptoms of the disease have returned. That is the definition of being cured. For me, the Recipe was the roadmap to my cure.

Also, Marie, Pratima, and Betty, the other three at that time who had full recoveries doing the Recipe, had written on the blog comments that they stopped doing the Recipe the day their symptoms went away and none of them had their symptoms return.

As we wound down 2013, there were four of us who had done the Recipe to reach our cure. And hundreds of people had posted comments on the blog about reversing their Parkinson's. Even though I had stopped doing workshops at that time, 2013 felt like it had been a very good year.

I began the 2014 year with a blog post about faith. Faith was an important part of my recovery and it has continued to be an important part of my life.

In my recovery, I had faith in my Higher Power, faith in the Recipe, and faith in myself to see it through to the end. As I went through my recovery, faith grew into acceptance that whatever was happening in my life was there for a reason and surrendering the idea that anybody owed me an explanation for why things appeared in my life.

In February of 2014, these lessons were put to the test. In the late morning of Sunday, February 23, 2014, I received a phone call from my sister's fiancé (now husband) Rick regarding my father.

He said that my father was breathing, but he could not be awakened, and the ambulance was on the way to pick him up to take him to the hospital. This came as a surprise; to the best of all of our knowledge, my father had not been ill.

Approximately an hour later, the phone call told me that they were working on my father and how things would turn out would be determined in the following eight to ten hours. I asked Rick to let me know what was going on in an hour and I would decide at that time whether to go down to Miami.

Thirty minutes later, he called and said, "You need to come down now." Upon inquiry, I learned that my father's brain was bleeding and a neurologist was on the way.

I packed a suitcase and got in the car for the four-and-a-half hour drive...four and a half hours is a lot of time to come to terms with life and death.

On the life side, I was happy that we had an 80th birthday party for my father the previous summer. Also, I was happy that my father had been up to Tampa during the holidays and got to visit with Sally and me as well as our three children. And in January of 2014, our daughter, Victoria, had an event in Miami, so we made it a three-day weekend and spent time with my father.

On the death side, I realized that my mother had died on February 20, 2007. I imagined that February 20th had been a hard day for my father and maybe there was something really wrong with him and he decided not to fight it because he was ready to be with my mother. She had died five months prior to their 50th wedding anniversary.

CONTROL, ACCEPTANCE, SURRENDER
CONTROL
Whether the end result of this episode for my father was going to be life or death was out of my control. The only things in the entire situation over which I had any control were getting in the car and driving to Miami and my emotional reaction to the events of the day as they unfolded.

ACCEPTANCE
I had to accept that my father might die that day. This type of acceptance

is something I learned in my Parkinson's recovery. It is the acceptance that says, "Okay. I do not like what happened. What am I going to do about it, if in fact, there is anything I can do about it?"

SURRENDER

I had to surrender to my Higher Power that if my father died that day, not only did I have no control over the event of his death, but also that I had to accept that there was nothing I could do to change it if it occurred. This is absolute vulnerability—no control over the potential outcome of an event, and even if I did not like the outcome when it occurred, acceptance of it nonetheless with the understanding that there was nothing I could do to change it. And then the further surrender that whatever was the outcome, it was necessary in the grander scheme of the Universe, and nobody owed me an explanation.

My father had suffered a massive aneurysm. He died that night.

What helped me deal with his death were the life concepts of control, acceptance, and surrender that I had learned as part of my Parkinson's recovery. And, what put a smile on my face was thinking about my parents' spirits together again after 7 years of separation. I feel my father was ready to join my mother, and he did.

A few months later, things got very busy. My daughter, Genevieve, graduated from college in May, was planning her wedding in June, and a few days before her wedding, received a job offer in Maryland. Once again, a friendly reminder that life did not stop going forward when I had Parkinson's, and life's events did not slow down or become decidedly easier just because I had a full recovery from Parkinson's.

So, we had a wedding, which was lovely, and Sally and I have a wonderful son-in-law, Azhar. Three days after the wedding, we put the newly married couple in what was previously my mother-in-law's car, and off they went to Maryland.

Fortunately, our son Steven and his then-girlfriend, now-wife, Jenna, were living in Baltimore and offered their second bedroom to Genevieve and Azhar until they found a place of their own. And, once again, when I said "okay," and let go of control by practicing acceptance and surrender, everything kept moving forward in a very positive manner.

In the fall of 2014, something quite significant took place. A scientific study about Parkinson's came out of Copenhagen, Denmark, and it confirmed that my "blocked-dopamine, not depleted dopamine" theory of Parkinson's was correct.

It is the position of Western Medicine that the substantia nigra, basal ganglia, in the brain are dying or already dead leading to a depletion of dopamine in the brain. They say they do not know the cause of this nor can they cure it, so they seek to treat symptoms of Parkinson's with dopamine enhancement and dopamine replacement medications.

The September 16, 2014, study from Denmark is entitled, "Researchers debunk myth about Parkinson's disease," states that the dopamine is blocked because the brain triggers a stop signal, like letting go of the handle on a motorized lawn mower. It is not that the dopamine is not there, but that it is blocked from flowing correctly.

From the time I began working on my recovery, I always have taken the position that the dopamine is not depleted, only blocked, and that the dopamine faucet is turned down low. The Recipe is what helped me open my dopamine flow again.

In the introduction to the Recipe, I say:

I do not believe that the dopamine is depleted or gone. I believe that the body has been working in adrenaline mode and dopamine has taken a back seat, essentially, it has mostly closed the faucet and is not flowing at full capacity. It is why I believe the medications cause Dyskinesia—the body is being given artificial dopamine replacements that are not able to fully assimilate into the system and thus cause uncontrollable movement as opposed to controlled movement.

By listening to my body, talking to my body and examining my electrical impulses, I was able to re-open the dopamine faucet. The result was full recovery with 100%

pre-Parkinson's controlled movement.

In the Affirmations/Meditations/Prayers section of the Recipe, I say:

> The medical profession says that with Parkinson's, dopamine is depleted in one's brain and the basal ganglia controlling movement are 60–80% dead. Having lived in a Parkinson's body and thought with a Parkinson's mind, and held my firm faith with a Parkinson's soul, I can tell you they are incorrect. It is why after nearly 200 years, they are no closer to a cure than when they started. Parkinson's is an electrical problem and they are trying to fix it with chemicals. The dopamine is there, but the flow is interrupted. Adrenaline has taken over, which ultimately leads to dopamine taking a back seat. Just like anything else, after years of operating in adrenaline mode, the dopamine just turns off the faucet.

In the Denmark study, in a section of the study entitled "A thorn in the side," the researcher points out that not only was there no lack of dopamine, but that the theory of "lack of dopamine" has not been established:

> *A thorn in the side*
>
> *Scanning the brain of a patient suffering from Parkinson's disease reveals that in spite of dopamine cell death, there are no signs of a lack of dopamine—even at a comparatively late stage in the process.*
>
> *'The inability to establish a lack of dopamine until advanced cases of Parkinson's disease has been a thorn in the side of researchers for many years. On the one hand, the symptoms indicate that the stop signal is over-activated, and patients are treated accordingly with a fair degree of success. On the other hand, data prove that they are not lacking dopamine,' says Postdoc Jakob Kisbye Dreyer.*

This study came as no surprise to me as I am living proof that my dopamine was not, and is not, depleted. However, it was very exciting that there now exists scientific proof that I have been correct all along.

I was hopeful that the Denmark study would help people remain hopeful and feel empowered as they moved toward Parkinson's recovery.

As 2014 was nearing the end, I received a startling reminder of letting go of control by using acceptance and surrender as my guiding principles. Also, I received a huge reminder of the fragility of life and the importance of gratitude. During my recovery, I learned gratitude. Ultimately, near the end of my recovery, I gave gratitude every day for being alive, as life was a precious gift. I have mentioned this before, that I gave gratitude for being alive, even in a Parkinson's body. I became engrossed with deeply living my life and paying as little attention to the Parkinson's as possible. I continue my gratitude practice daily, each day fully remembering how precious and fragile is my life.

On November 19, 2014, I was driving in the car with Sally as my passenger when a person ran a light, hit the front and driver's side of our vehicle, and completely obliterated it. When our car came to a stop, smashed against the curb a few feet from going head-on into a utility pole, Sally and I gave gratitude for being alive and being conscious.

Although banged and bruised, I was able to get out of the car on my own. My precious Sally was not so fortunate. She is the strongest, bravest person I know, so when I asked how she was and she said she did not know, it was difficult for me to find the strength to be strong for her. After all those months of Sally being strong for me in my Parkinson's recovery, I needed to be strong for her that day.

As the paramedics were tending to Sally, they wanted me out of the way. I called for reinforcement, our dear friend Mary. We are grateful for Mary. She dropped her life and was at the scene within minutes. She helped me empty the car, and she provided me with good advice about the day. I went to Sally and explained that as brave as she was, she needed to get in an ambulance and go to the hospital. I would ride with Mary.

The day ended with me banged and bruised, and nothing more serious than that. Sally was banged up, had cracked and bruised ribs, and she had a broken bone in her foot and could not walk without crutches.

At the end of our evening that day, Sally and I gave a lot a gratitude for how things turned out. Things could have been worse, but they were not. We were grateful.

The accident had not been in our control; somebody else ran a light. We accepted that the accident happened, and we surrendered that not only did we have no control over it, but also that the Universe did not owe us an explanation for why it happened.

November 19, 2014, was a not-so-subtle reminder of how precious and fragile life is. Lesson learned with Parkinson's. Lesson re-learned in the car accident.

Sally got a knee-walker scooter so she could get around. She could not walk with crutches without great discomfort because of the injury to her ribs. Over the next ten weeks, her body healed her ribs and the broken bone in her foot for a full recovery.

I finished out the year by going back to Seattle and having my final workshop, but this time there was a little more to the trip than having a workshop. Sally and I wanted to explore Seattle as a potential place to move.

As a result of Sally's injuries, I made the trip without her, and I did not explore the area for future-moving purposes. However, I had a great time while I was in Seattle and the workshop went well. I wrote a post about it on December 8, 2014.

As you know, on Saturday, December 6, 2014, I continued taking my Parkinson's Recipe for Recovery on the road. The venue was a return visit to the place of my first workshop two years ago, Seattle, WA. The day was filled with recovery! Imagine: 22 of us, some with Parkinson's, some of their spouses and partners, one of their daughters, a couple of health practitioners, some from Washington, some from Oregon, and some from California, all in one place with one purpose...Parkinson's recovery!

Some of the people in attendance already knew

each other; most did not. However, there was a buzz that resonated through the Seattle Creative Arts Center because nobody in the room felt alone anymore on this journey. There we were, fully vulnerable, opening our hearts and souls to each other. You could feel the common thread of recovery being sewn throughout as we talked, and laughed, and cried, and did the Recipe exercises together.

The Seattle workshop was recovery...absolutely an atmosphere of friendship and recovery. Everybody in the room felt safe to be who they were, Parkinson's and all...it did not matter...we all were connected.

I hope all of you can take some inspiration from this group and keep working on the Recipe on your path to recovery.

At the end of Saturday, everybody at the Seattle workshop had hope, real, genuine hope, that Parkinson's recovery is attainable...and every one of them left the workshop armed with the tools to stay on their path toward recovery with the Recipe and with the firm conviction to not leave that path until they are fully recovered. They know they are worth it!

And, as we were wrapping up, some of the people who already had been doing the Recipe suddenly started encouraging the others by explaining how the Recipe was helping them. Then, a young woman who had sat quietly all day, having accompanied her mother to the workshop, announced to us that her mother had started doing the Recipe and that she had gotten her mother back. There was not a dry eye in the room. Clearly, it had been an amazing day of recovery, and there was nothing left to say.

We had an exhilarating day together at the workshop, and I left with the same warm feeling I had two years prior in Seattle and on my trip to Victoria, British Columbia, Canada. I felt at home in the Great Northwest!

When I got back home to Tampa, Sally and I began more serious discussions about moving to the northwest some day. Our immediate family situation was changing and there was a sense that it was time to make a change.

Our son, Steven, would be getting married in the fall of 2015 and was moving to Georgia. His soon-to-be-wife, Jenna, had a brother who lived in Seattle, plus Steven had mentioned that professionally he thought he might end up on the west coast one day, but who knew.

Our daughter Genevieve, who had attended university in California, had discussed ideas of moving back to the west coast at some future date. And our daughter Victoria would be beginning university in the fall of 2015 with the professional goal of being in animation.

Victoria's top choice for university was in California, and even if she went to school elsewhere, her profession would be in California. For Sally and me, all of the Universe's signs pointed west.

Sally and I decided to prepare our home to sell. Our thought process was rather simple: if Victoria went to university one hour south of our Tampa home, we would live there for four more years and then head west. If Victoria went to university in California, we would step up our home renovation plans and move west sooner.

There were many "where do we move" ideas floating around in the Shifke household as we brought 2014 to a close, but certain Parkinson's-experience lessons remained very clear: I never lost sight of how fragile life was and I continued to give gratitude every day for being alive.

As 2015 was appearing on the horizon, I did not lose site of how life was for me five years earlier. As 2010 had been appearing on the horizon, I was joyful to have put 2009 behind me. However, there was a melancholy feeling as well because it was difficult for me to look excitedly at the 2010 year ahead when I was starting that year with Parkinson's.

As I was reflecting on what it had been like in 2010 bringing in a new year already having Parkinson's, I became filled with compassion for everybody with Parkinson's. This prompted me to write a blog post on January 1, 2015, entitled "Fighting Parkinson's, and 2015…the year of compassionate choices."

Making compassionate choices on behalf of others never had been a problem for me. Unfortunately, making compassionate choices for myself had been a monumental problem for me.

However, in my post, I identified what had been two very distinct choices for me.

Option 1 was the Western Medicine philosophy: progressively degenerative disease where they did not know the cause, did not have a cure, and the prognosis was degeneration while taking medications that would provide symptomatic relief only.

Option 2 was refusal to believe the Western Medicine way.

Option 1 simply did not appeal to me. I had watched my mother's physical degeneration from Parkinson's and mental degeneration from the medications, my research told me that Parkinson's symptoms had been identified and written about in China about 5,000 years prior to James Parkinson's existence, and I did not want anybody telling me what my future would be like based upon that person's belief system and inability to offer me something to help me get better.

So even though I had not been thinking about being compassionate to myself at the time, in September of 2009 when I decided to create my own recovery program, to go on my unchartered journey, it was one of the most compassionate things I ever had done for myself.

I picked Option 2, the unknown; in part because I was dreadfully afraid of an outcome like my mother's if I had chosen Option 1, and in part because I simply refused to believe that Option 1 and its prognosis was all there would be to my life for the rest of my life.

In proceeding forward into 2015, I kept my focus on compassion, and being in my heart instead of my mind. These were very important lessons in my recovery, and they had resurfaced many times after my full recovery.

I continued writing my blog and coaching people in the Recipe, never losing sight of a very important lesson I had learned in my recovery: as human beings, people suffer. The suffering may be physical, mental, or spiritual, or a combination of two or all three of these.

As a result, whenever somebody was saying or doing something unpleasant, I looked beyond the words and actions, and felt the suffering.

I had stopped internalizing that the unpleasant words or actions had anything to do with me, and I offered compassion to the other person.

Sometimes the offer of compassion was silent, and sometimes it was a response such as, "Something seems to be bothering you, are you okay?" I had learned that a judgmental mind lashes out at unpleasant words and actions whereas a compassionate heart feels the suffering and extends compassion. It was a Parkinson's recovery lesson that is just as important today as it was when I learned it all those years ago.

In the spring of 2015, my sister Allison married her long-time partner, Rick. I already considered Rick my brother, but this made it official. It was a stupendous wedding celebration.

Also, in the spring of 2015, my daughter Victoria got into her first choice for university, and she was going to be heading to California that fall.

This got Sally and me vigorously looking at what we needed to do to finish fixing our house for sale, and where we would be moving.

We already had begun the work on the house, so we had a pretty good idea how that was going and how long it would take; the bigger task was figuring out where to move. We had been living in our Tampa home since 1993.

We started looking on the Internet at places to live in California and Washington. I had been to Seattle, Washington, a couple of times and really liked it, including the drive up I-5 to Anacortes, Bellingham, and Canada. One thing that Sally and I knew for certain is that we wanted to find a piece of property with two to five acres in a more quiet, remote area.

We had been living on a cul-de-sac in the city, and we wanted something on the opposite end of the spectrum. It did not take us long to learn how expensive it would have been to live in California, plus at the time there was a drought in California. We scratched California from the list.

As we proceeded forward, we were thinking that we would take Victoria to California for school at the beginning of September, after which we would take a week and head up to Seattle and explore Washington.

In July, we were sitting with our friend Betsy at our friend Jerry's birthday party and catching up on life. Sally knew Betsy before she knew me, and Betsy and her husband Jack had given us a wedding shower dinner party in 1987 after Sally and I had gotten engaged. We had known Betsy a long time.

She asked a simple question that changed the course of where we would be going on our September trip: "Have you looked into Oregon?"

Our answer: "No, not specifically, yet."

She told us that she had been to Oregon many times and thought we would fit in nicely. She told us about Portland and Eugene, and we decided to explore Oregon.

We started looking at Portland and Eugene, cost of living, areas to live, amenities, climate, etc. Since we had some familiarity with Seattle already, we decided to explore Portland on our trip west.

Sally remembered that our neighbors a couple of blocks away, Nancy and Carrington, had mentioned a son living near Portland. They put us in touch with their son, who put us in touch with a realtor friend of his, and we scheduled a trip to Portland to look at the area and a few homes.

At the beginning of September, we got Victoria situated in her residence hall at school, and off we went for a week in Portland. We fell in love with Portland, no doubt about it. We looked at many areas surrounding the city, and we felt comfortable that we would be able to sell our home in Tampa and find a nice home on two to five acres within thirty to forty-five minutes of downtown Portland.

I remember when Sally told the realtor in September that our plan was to go back to Tampa, finish getting our home ready to sell by March, sell it, come back and buying a home in the spring, and then move. The realtor looked at us like we were from Mars. But I understood how strong Sally is as a person, and how fully understanding of the real estate market she was. I knew that she was going to get this accomplished.

Sally had a sense of the big picture and had a plan. I said, "Okay," and I did my part, which was mostly just getting out of her way as she orchestrated the transition.

We got back to Tampa and we were elated. We had fallen in love with Portland, and we knew that if everything went as planned, we would be able to afford to move three thousand miles across the country in rather short order.

In October, we went to Atlanta for Steven and Jenna's wedding. We were so happy to have our marvelous daughter-in-law Jenna join our family. Then, back to Tampa to get the house ready to sell.

Needless to say, as we headed into the holiday season, we had a packed house for all of the holidays. Everybody knew it was going to be the last Sally-home-cooked holiday meals they would get for a while.

As I was easing into the end of the year, feeling like everything was falling into place nicely, a huge surprise grabbed me all the way from Australia. Helen, a woman I had been coaching and who had been doing the Recipe for four years and three months, had her full recovery.

I wrote about her full recovery in a blog post dated December 21, 2015. Here is an excerpt from that post:

> Helen was diagnosed with Parkinson's in the spring of 2011. When she went back for her follow up visit the following year, her neurologist noticed something amiss in addition to the Parkinson's. After much testing, it was determined that Helen had suffered two strokes in addition to her Parkinson's.
>
> Helen has worked diligently over these years, showing faith, vulnerability, strength and courage. When you look at what she has posted in comments on the blog, there is one common thread: Helen felt she would have a recovery one day and she was not going to give up on herself...ever!
>
> It is difficult to describe Helen's glow on our Skype when she explained to me her most recent visit with two specialists. Here is what they told her: There no longer are signs or symptoms of Parkinson's. Her "drop foot" is a classic symptom of the two strokes and they will work with her to improve the drop foot. However, make no mistake, there is absolutely no Parkinson's signs or symptoms in Helen.

What a way to finish the year!

As 2016 was beginning, I knew exactly what I wanted to write about on my blog. Near the end of 2015, there were a couple of mornings when I was outside with our dog, Cricket, and the Beatle's song "All You Need Is Love" started playing in my head. I took this as a sign.

I looked up the lyrics and two lines jumped off the screen:

Nothing you can do, but you can learn
How to be you in time.

That was it. I was staring at so much of my Parkinson's recovery right there. "Nothing you can do" was giving up control, accepting life as it was, and surrendering that anybody owed me an explanation for why things were happening.

"But you can learn how to be you in time" was the internal struggle to be vulnerable and not be afraid to be the real me. Essentially, learning to be the real me again.

And then the lyrics say:

It's easy.
All you need is love.

Okay. I understand the "All you need is love" part. However, it was not easy. There was nothing about my recovery that was easy. There was nothing about learning to love myself, being vulnerable, and accepting life as it was rolling out in front of me that was easy. In fact, learning to love myself was the most gut-wrenchingly difficult part of my entire recovery.

However, once I learned to love myself, it was easy. In large part it was easy because Parkinson's no longer mattered in my life. It was just there. But I had found the real me again, and that is what mattered most. My focus became being loving, compassionate, joyful, and grateful.

I knew that learning to love myself had been so instrumental in my recovery, and I knew it had been instrumental for the four others who had their full recoveries, so I quoted them when proclaiming 2016 the year of love.

Here is an excerpt of what I posted:

Marie (Cured of Parkinson's doing the Recipe): *"What? She*

sits around loving herself???? I'll tell you, I do, every chance I get."

Pratima (Cured of Parkinson's doing the Recipe): *"I am worth it. I am going to WIN."*

Betty (Cured of Parkinson's doing the Recipe): *"I can only think the mental/spiritual/emotional aspects of healing myself all fell into place."*

Helen (Cured of Parkinson's doing the Recipe): *"I looked at myself in the mirror a few days ago, not at my skin or hair, but deep into my eyes. I found someone there I respect, admire for her courage, strength and love. I felt compassion for myself and all I have experienced in life. I saw a shy, hurt, self as well. I kept looking at her and gave her love. I now am feeling a relationship and soul love for myself. I am going to keep doing this mirror looking till I am healed. Falling in love with my depth, my individuality, my soul."*

Yes, 2016 was shaping up to be the year of love. My love, Sally, and I finished getting our home ready for sale. We put it on the market on March 9, 2016, and we sold our Tampa home on March 11, two days later, with a closing date of April 20. We knew that all of the contingencies would be met by the end of the month, so we booked our flights for a week in Portland.

On Friday, April 1, we arrived in Portland, were picked up at the hotel by our realtor, Carol, and off we went. The second home we visited was everything we had hoped it would be. We had seen it on the Internet, and it was our first choice of the homes we had seen online.

We saw three homes on Friday and two on Saturday, and then we went back on Saturday for a second, more extensive, walk-through of the home we liked the most. On Sunday we made an offer, and on Tuesday we were in contract with a closing date of May 12. Fortunately, Carol was able to put us in touch with people to do the inspections, and when we left at the end of the week we had a lot to do in a very short amount of time.

Returning home to Tampa was incredible. After being gone for ten days, we had ten days until our closing of the Tampa home. There was a final walk-through scheduled for April 19, so we needed to be moved out by the 18th, have the house cleaned up from moving out, and be ready for the closing on the 20th.

As a result of me having just spent ten days of a break from coaching, my schedule was booked solid from the time we got home until the time we left. Sally had the brunt of packing and dealing with the movers.

On April 18, Cricket and I checked into the Residence Inn in downtown Tampa, as they allowed pets. I logged into the wi-fi and was able to do my Parkinson's coaching from there. Sally stayed at home and dealt with the movers. At the end of the day, she watched the movers leave with almost all of our belongings, including our car. When she arrived at the hotel, we both were exhausted.

On the 19th, Sally met with a cleaning crew to get the house ready for the walk-through, spent a lot of time with her mother, and said goodbye to other friends. Cricket and I were at the hotel. I was doing coaching, and she was keeping me company.

April 20, 2016, finally arrived. Sally and I went to the house closing to sign the papers; Cricket joined us. We had one suitcase each and a rental car. We left the closing, ate some lunch, and went to the airport. As a result of there being no direct flights from Tampa to Portland, and the fact that Cricket would be having her first plane ride, we opted to take the only direct flight from Tampa to Seattle and then drive down to Portland instead.

We flew to Seattle with Cricket in her carrier under the seat. We spent the night in Seattle, and the next day we headed to Portland, where we stayed at the Residence Inn North Harbor until we moved into our new home, one month later.

On our first evening in Portland, we went grocery shopping and bought rain gear, as it looked like it was supposed to rain in the upcoming days. Fortunately, the hotel room had a mini-kitchen, albeit without an oven, and Sally could be creative with the stovetop so that we could still eat "home-cooked" meals in the hotel room.

I will say, the thought of living in a hotel for a month was not a particularly appealing one. However, it was necessary in the process of being able to get to move into our new home.

My thought process here was quite similar to my thought process when I had Parkinson's. Living in the hotel and not worrying about the discomforts of not living in my home were necessary steps to getting into our new home. Getting into our new home was a given, a fully accepted future fact.

Doing the Recipe as part of my daily routine and not worrying about the discomfort of my symptoms were necessary steps to getting my full recovery. My full recovery was a given, a fully accepted future fact.

When I had Parkinson's, my life was not about my Parkinson's recovery. My Parkinson's recovery was something happening in my life. Life keeps moving forward whether I am participating in it or not. So while we were staying in the hotel Sally dealt with Cricket and trying to find things to do, and I proceeded forward with Parkinson's coaching from the hotel.

While we were living in the hotel, Carol from the Portland Parkinson's Alternative Healing Support Group contacted me; her husband Bill has Parkinson's. Sally and I had dinner with them the second week we were living in the hotel.

Part of our moving west was the open-mindedness of the people. And here we were, complete strangers living in a hotel, and Carol and Bill reached out to us. It is very difficult to explain how accepted we felt, as people, and as people bringing a message of Parkinson's hope and recovery.

After dinner, we walked back to their home for tea and a longer visit. I was invited to speak at the Parkinson's Group's May meeting, which was the week prior to moving into our new home. When I arrived, I was showered with beautiful plants that people had grown in their gardens; these were welcome gifts for Sally and me. I was overwhelmed.

For the first time since my Parkinson's recovery, nearly five years earlier, I felt at home. I was in an environment where I was accepted. There are no words adequate enough to describe that feeling. I am grateful for Carol,

167

Bill, and the rest of the group who came to the meeting that night.

Also at the meeting were three familiar faces of people who had driven up to Seattle to attend my December 2014 workshop. It was another feeling that I had found my home. I have been attending the meetings on a monthly basis, and this is the most amount of time I have spent in-person with a group of people who have Parkinson's. The experience has been wonderful, primarily because the people are wonderful.

Finally, on May 16, 2016, a couple of days later than expected, but all-in-all in good shape, the movers arrived with our possessions and our car. Our daughter Victoria had arrived a week early to Portland, home for summer break from university, and the three of us and Cricket moved into our new home.

From Sally's and my conversation about Portland with our friend Betsy in July of 2015, to selling our home, finding a new home 3,000 miles away, getting through all of the processes, and moving into our new home on May 16, 2016, we had just completed a ten-month whirlwind undertaking. Our new adventure in Warren, Oregon, thirty miles north of Portland, was just about to begin.

Sally's birthday is May 18, and it worked out better to celebrate at home on the 18th and out to dinner on the 19th, so Sally, Victoria, and I headed to Portland for a birthday dinner the day after Sally's birthday. We had a lovely birthday celebration, our first in Oregon.

On the way home, as we were driving up Highway 30, Victoria noticed a bald eagle flying by, and as we were about a mile from our home, we spotted our first deer. Suffice it to say, Sally is not the only one with really fond memories of her first birthday in The Great Northwest.

Here we were, 3,000 miles from Tampa, and finally situated in our new home. We could not have been happier. Seeing our first deer was undoubtedly special, but soon we learned that the deer were pretty fond of the plants on our property.

Part of our move was to get away from the city and live more with nature. We moved from a 5,500 square foot lot in Tampa to a 2.3-acre property in Warren. We are on the side of a mountain at the edge of the forest.

We realized that the deer from the forest thought it was quite inviting to come up on the property and lie down under a tree to get some shade or nibble on practically every plant we had in the yard. We learned quickly that the deer had not read the deer-resistant list of plants, some of which we had purchased for the sole purpose of being able to watch the plants grow and flower.

As soon as buds would form, whether the plant was supposed to be deer-resistant or not, the deer would clip them. The reason we are so certain that it was the deer is because we watched them do it; when somebody in the house would spot a deer, usually two or three deer at a time, everything in the house would stop, and we would just sit at the window and stare.

For somebody who spent the first fifty-five years of his life (except when away at school) as a Floridian, watching the deer was exciting. In fact, I cannot ever imagine it being not exciting. So, eat what they will, we still love seeing them. We even have been granted the pleasure of a mother deer bringing her two fawns to the property for a nibble at our plants.

Which brings me to another reason we moved to Oregon and wanted a couple of acres. We wanted to grow our own fruits and vegetables and become more self-sustaining with as small a carbon footprint as possible. The deer taught us that if you do not want them to eat something, you have to have a fence around it.

We created a vegetable garden at the back of the property. The former owner had a fenced area with three raised boxes. Once we weeded them out and cleaned them up, we put in the proper soil and started planting vegetables plants. It was late June, so we were woefully behind in the season and had to plant what was available, and unfortunately we could not begin with seeds.

The fenced vegetable garden, although tempting and accessible to the deer (if you ever have seen deer jump), there was no safe landing spot, so they left the vegetable garden alone. While I was doing Parkinson's Coaching, Sally was busy working on the vegetable garden. She has turned out to be quite the vegetable gardener.

Also, we moved at an excellent time…berry picking season. About thirty minutes from our home is Bella Organic on Sauvie Island. Sally and

Victoria went there to pick blueberries and raspberries. They did not pick blackberries, as we have about a hundred feet of wild blackberry bushes along the back section of our back yard.

On one occasion, we had dinner from the vegetables and herbs from our garden, followed by a blueberry pie dessert from blueberries that were picked earlier that day. Quite frankly, we felt like we had moved to paradise.

Another part of this adventure was our daily walks with Cricket. It is half a mile from our home to the end of our street. The walk down to the end of the street is literally downhill the whole way. The walk back is not as easy, particularly past the last few houses prior to reaching ours, where there was a substantial incline.

One of the best ways I can describe it is that when we turn our car onto our street, the outside temperature registering in the car reflects a three-degree decrease in the half mile from the corner to our house. Needless to say, that half mile walk, twice per day with the dog, has kept us in exceedingly good shape.

Also, the walk assisted us in meeting almost all of our neighbors. When you live on a street that winds up a mountain in a forest, it is not like you see your neighbors often. However, over time while walking Cricket, our neighbors stopped their cars as they passed to say hello and to introduce themselves. It did not take long to learn that we had extremely nice neighbors.

There were some other things that we learned after moving to Warren. Warren is a small town (1,700 people) with Scappoose to the south (6,700 people) and St. Helens to the north (13,000 people). Postal delivery in this more rural area does not take place at our home. Instead, there is a row of mailboxes about a quarter mile further up the mountain from our home.

One of the things that we experienced in walking up to get our mail was that if we walked a little bit beyond the mailboxes and turned around, we were staring at Mount St. Helens in Washington State. It seemed like every day we were learning new things that made us feel even better about our move to Oregon.

As we learned more about the area to which we moved, we noticed that the summer days were very long. Usually, it was light out by 5:15am, and even though the sunset occurred around 9:15pm, it was still somewhat light outside until around 10:00pm.

The sunrises and sunsets were the most spectacular we had seen.

On the Parkinson's side of things, I continued writing my blog and coaching, and there was one big change. Some people from Portland started coming up to my home for coaching in person. It was very meaningful for me to be able to teach people one-on-one in person.

I enjoy the time I spend with people doing Parkinson's coaching on the phone, on Skype, on FaceTime, and in person. It is extremely fulfilling to be doing Parkinson's coaching; I have been watching people get better from Parkinson's Disease for over seven years now.

Plus, the move west has greatly enhanced my ability to be with people with Parkinson's through in-person coaching at my home and attending the monthly Parkinson's support group meetings. The Parkinson's community here is a large group of truly delightful people, including their spouses, partners, and families who help support their efforts in recovery.

As the summer wound down and autumn began to appear on the horizon, Victoria returned to university, and the rainy season started showing up for Sally and me. Also, fewer people were able to make the drive up to our home. So, we adjusted coaching to Skype and FaceTime for most of those in Portland.

Rainy season was something new and different for Sally and me. In the summers in Tampa, we would get the afternoon deluge, sometimes inches of rain within an hour or two. In Warren, we received a misty drizzle… almost all day…almost every day.

Actually, it wasn't raining all day; it would rain for an hour or two, take a break, rain a little more, etc. By the end of October, we learned that it was the third most amount of rain for October that our area ever had seen. What we kept hearing from our neighbors was that summer was not normal, and that the early rain in October was not normal either.

However, for us, it was glorious. One thing we learned in a hurry was if you did not continue with whatever you wanted to do because it was raining, you never would leave the house. The lessons of my Parkinson's recovery fit well into these new changes.

Sally and I felt joyful as we walked Cricket down the street each day even though it was raining. We used to laugh at the drizzling, often commenting something to the effect, "Can't you try a little harder?"

The joy we felt came largely from acceptance and gratitude. We accepted that even though all of our research said it would be raining from November through February, it was raining part of almost every day in October as well.

And we gave gratitude for the beauty of nature as we watched the brown grass turn green, the autumn leaves change colors on the trees, and the entire sleepy forest come back to life with the wet autumn rain. The aroma of the freshly rained-upon pine trees is indescribable.

In my recovery, I learned that the more I could accept what was happening in my life, the less stress I would have and the more I could actually live in a grateful and joyful manner. This was a lesson for life, not just for my Parkinson's recovery.

The events of life were occurring whether I liked them or not. How I responded to the events of life substantially changed my overall wellbeing. These were difficult lessons in my recovery, but once learned, they have stayed with me and assisted me in remaining joyful.

Another thing we learned as autumn rolled out was the difference in daylight hours. It no longer was light at 5:15am. Some days, it was not light out until after 7am. And, as the season continued, it was completely dark outside by 5:30pm. This meant no more after-dinner walks for Cricket.

Since we live on a mountain in the forest, when it gets dark, it really gets dark. Plus, over the first few months of living here, we have had the occasional sighting of a coyote or two.

Our dog Cricket is all of nine pounds, hardly an appetizer for the coyotes, but, just the same, Sally would take the evening walk with Cricket generally around 3:00pm while I was doing coaching. Everything was constantly changing.

This was another valuable lesson from my Parkinson's recovery. Also, it was one of my harder lessons to learn. During my recovery, I was reading the book *Not Always So, Practicing the True Spirit of Zen*, by Shunryu Suzuki. The book is thirty-five short chapters filled with life lessons.

Each day after doing the Recipe, I read one short chapter. The lessons taught me how to sit zazen, how to begin to accept life as it rolled out in front of me, and how to not worry.

When I finished reading the book, I realized that the book and its lessons had become an important part of my morning routine. I decided to continue that routine by starting the book from the beginning and following the one-short-chapter-per-day routine I had adopted.

Little did I know that this is where the true learning would take place.

When I would re-read a chapter, it would have a completely different meaning to me than thirty-five days earlier. I was learning first-hand that even though everything seemed the same to me with life and Parkinson's, so many changes had taken place in the thirty-five days I could not remember them all.

It occurred to me that the fear and worry that consumed me during my days with Parkinson's were nothing more than illusions of the future, guess-work, vapor…they had no solid existence…the were not real. However, if I continued to live in fear and worry, then even when the things I was afraid of or worried about did not come true, it did not matter because I had lived and died them a thousand times as if they actually had taken place.

My over-thinking, adrenaline-driven mind had created this entire illusion, and I was prey to it. Sitting zazen, calming my mind, removing fear and worry from my life, and opening my heart to the opportunities that life was presenting me in the moment became a much more healthy way to live. Ultimately, this shift to a healthier way of living helped me finish my full recovery.

Just as Sally and I were getting adjusted to the autumn rain, the later sunrises and earlier sunsets, and the almost-daily incredible changes in the forest as we walked through it, winter arrived with a bang, or maybe I should say with a flurry, of snow.

Snow! As a native Floridian, I had rarely seen snow in my life. Sally was born and raised in Michigan, so she was familiar with it. The snow was absolutely breathtaking. The forest became a winter wonderland. And then the weather took a decided turn below freezing, presenting another life lesson on acceptance.

This time acceptance meant that when the snow melted a bit and the temperatures then went below freezing, we were faced with black ice. When you live on the side of a mountain at a fairly steep incline, black ice means a week without trash collection, mail, UPS and Fedex deliveries, or taking the car out of the garage. It also means special shoes and carefully walking the dog. Okay, that is how it is; I accept what is happening in my life right here, right now.

Also, it meant having to hire a driver from the airport to deliver our daughter Victoria roughly a mile from our home to a friend's house when she came home from school for winter break. We met her there with winter gear and made the trek back up to our house with her suitcase in tow.

And then more snow two days later. Victoria had seen snow in the past, but only snow on the ground. She never had seen snow falling. It was quite magical that Monday morning, as I was getting ready for my first coaching Skype of the day, to watch Sally and Victoria head outside in the fresh falling snow and start building a snowman.

What a glorious end to 2016. It had been quite the year. As 2017 was beginning, I was struck by the realization of how instrumental acceptance of what was happening in my life had become as a guiding principal.

On January 1, 2017, I wrote the following post, "Fighting Parkinson's, and 2017...the year of acceptance of your cure!" Here is the post:

> Happy 2017...wonderful year ahead for all of us! Okay, I already hear the question: How can I "accept" I will be cured? Simple. Do you want to be cured? Then decide that you are going to get what you want, and decide that you will put up with whatever you have to put up with in order to achieve what you want, and accept that you are worthy and deserving of receiving what you want...and do it! Accept that you will be cured!!!
>
> Simple enough...in theory. Difficult in practice. Why? Because Parkinson's is a symptom of your life out of balance, and until you restore balance to your life, physically, mentally, and spiritually, the symptom called Parkinson's

will remain with you as a reminder that you have more work to do.

Accepting you will be cured. Do the physical part of the Parkinson's Recipe for Recovery® and heal your organs. Do the mental part of the Recipe and calm your mind. Do the spiritual part of the Recipe and open your heart for dopamine flow, filled with love for yourself. Love yourself, embrace your essence, and accept that you will be cured! AND, do not be afraid of Parkinson's. When you love yourself, you make your Parkinson's afraid of you.

To accept that you will be cured, you need to get beyond fear, so let's take a look at that. When I had Parkinson's, my fears were in two places: 1. That the known path my mother had followed resulted in her being crippled in a wheelchair with barely any voice to speak, and that the Alzheimer's and Dementia from 20+ years on medications had rendered her mindless three years before she died; and 2. Life. Fear of not being perfect enough or having all of the right answers or making everybody else happy or being in control of everything…you know this fear.

As you can see, fear of Parkinson's was a luxury I could not afford. So what choice did I have? Decide I would cure myself and chart my own course…fearlessly!

Was my life out of balance at that point in time? Absolutely yes! (They call it Parkinson's). Is your life out of balance at this current point in time? If you have Parkinson's, then absolutely yes!

Lets take a look.

Physically out of balance (not an exhaustive list):
If you cannot stand up straight and walk like you did
    pre-Parkinson's, then physically you are out of balance.
If you are suffering from tremors (shaking), rigidity (stiffness),
    Bradykinesia (slowness), and/or fatigue, then physically

you are out of balance.

If you are suffering from constipation, urgent urination, and/or chronic indigestion, then physically you are out of balance.

Mentally out of balance (not an exhaustive list):

If you think that you need to be perfect in all things, then mentally you are out of balance.

If you think you have to control everything going on in life including, but not limited to, all the other people's happiness and feelings in general, then mentally you are out of balance.

If you cannot accept something you do not like when it is happening in the moment and you respond to it with the emotions of anger, frustration, resentment, stress, anxiety, worry, and/or fear and you are consumed by those emotions, then mentally you are out of balance.

Spiritually out of balance (not an exhaustive list):

If you love God, but you think that God does not love you, then spiritually you are out of balance.

If pre-Parkinson's and/or now you did/do things unconditionally for others, but even in your physically debilitated current Parkinson's body you are unable to fully and open-heartedly accept others unconditionally doing things for you because you do not love yourself or find yourself unworthy, then spiritually you are out of balance.

If, instead of being in the present moment of what is going on in your life, you are looking at the past with regret and guilt instead of acceptance, and you are looking at the future with fear instead of faith, then spiritually you are out of balance.

As you can see, Parkinson's is a symptom, a manifestation, of all of these imbalances in your life. Why does it manifest in such harsh physical symptoms? I will be the first one to step up and answer (admit) this one: Because if Parkinson's did not provide me physical symptoms that lasted until the day of my cure, I would not have fixed the physical, mental, and spiritual imbalances in my life. I lacked the understanding and motivation to change.

I had made adjustments in my life to my essence, my authentic self, and I had become a version of me that was not the true essence of my inner being, my soul. However, it is what worked in my life, so I thought. In my recovery, I had to admit to myself that I was out of balance in my life. Did I do it on purpose? Of course not. It happened while I was living life that way I thought life was supposed to be lived. There is no shame, no blame, no finger-pointing, no fault, no guilt in getting Parkinson's.

I knew the way I thought and felt had to change because the way I was thinking and feeling had helped me get Parkinson's. So, I decided to do what was the complete opposite of how I thought and felt...I decided with full faith and no fear that I would cure myself from an incurable disease and I would tolerate whatever it had in store for me along the way, and that I would do it day-by-day, moment-by-moment, in the present, here and now.

For me, that was anti-Howard of the Howard I had become. That is why I knew it would work. It would require me becoming the real me of who I always was in my heart and soul, but who I had covered up with the toxicities of life.

And, how did I restore balance to my life? By doing the Recipe day-by-day, moment-by-moment, staying in the present.

And, how will you restore balance to your life? By doing

the Recipe day-by-day, moment-by-moment, staying in the present.

And be patient. The journey you are on is life. When you cross the final finish line in your life, it is death. I haven't heard one person say they are in a hurry to reach the final finish line in life. Slow down, and please be patient and enjoy the journey of life.

Feel your recovery in your zest to be alive, in the joy in your heart, in your compassion for yourself and others, in your love for yourself and others. And be grateful. It changed my life the day I became grateful for being alive, even in a Parkinson's body. I cherished the breath of life; I still do. And I was grateful; I still am.

Love yourself and realize how precious you are. Accept that you will be cured. Do the Recipe. Make it happen. Be your own cure!

2017...the year of acceptance of your cure!!!
You are worth it!!!
Happy New Year 2017!

All my best,
Howard

For me, healing my Parkinson's was healing the imbalances in my life, physically, mentally, and spiritually. Accepting that my best was good enough allowed me to open my heart to all of the possibilities of life. It removed self-judgment and self-criticism, the constant would have, should have, could have subconscious nagging of my mind.

Instead, accepting that my best was good enough allowed me to be compassionate with myself, remove stress and anxiety from myself, and eliminate worry and fear from my being. The more I eliminated the negative emotions, the more my heart vessel filled with love, joy, gratitude, compassion, forgiveness, happiness, and contentment.

In my recovery from Parkinson's, I learned how to live a healthy, well-balanced life, physically, mentally, and spiritually. Whatever arrives in my life, I accept as an opportunity and a potential lesson. Does this mean that I am happy with everything that arrives in my life? Of course not.

What this means is that I simply accept what is happening without a negative emotion. Sometimes, something will show up in my life that appears unfavorable. I see it as an opportunity to exercise acceptance rather than anger. Also, it also is an opportunity to create a solution to resolve the unfavorable event.

I learned this in my recovery. If I accept what is occurring in my life without exhibiting a negative emotional response, then I am in a much better position to create a solution.

Most of the time the lesson is the same lesson I learned in my Parkinson's recovery: with strong faith in the flow of my life, and with acceptance and surrender, I can deal with anything that arrives in my life with compassion and gratitude, and without attachment, worry, or fear.

As we were heading into the second week of January of 2017, the weather report said that we were going to get one to four inches of snow. Sally and I already had done our winter preparedness shopping, but it looked like we were a little low on fruit.

After dinner, we made an assessment of the driving conditions on our street, and I decided I would make a quick drive to the local grocery store for some bananas and apples. The store is seven minutes from our home, so the round trip would have been under thirty minutes.

Everything was going smoothly until I reached the steeper incline of our street, two homes prior to reaching our home. In the thirty minutes I was gone, the street had frozen with a thin layer of ice. When the car shifted from gas to battery, I lost momentum and started heading backwards toward the ravine.

Fortunately, there was no time to panic. I stood on the brakes with both feet and turned the wheel. The car stopped. Gratitude seems like an understatement for the feelings I was having. I called Sally and told her where I was located, and she suggested knocking on the door of our neighbor, Dave, as it was in front of his home where I came to a stop.

Within minutes, not only was Dave outside helping me, but Shelby passed us in her car and came back with her husband Troy; Dave then got on the phone, and Jim and Ryan arrived for the rescue. They gave me explicit instructions, "When we get you moving, put your pedal to the floor and do not remove it until you get home."

As I was getting up the street I could hear them cheering me on and yelling to not take my foot off of the pedal. I made it home safe and sound. When I walked out of my garage, I shook their hands and thanked them profusely, promising to not take the car out of the garage for the next week based upon the weather report.

And then my neighbor Troy said to not worry about it, that we are all neighbors and this is what neighbors do for each other. He added that one day I would get the call to help another neighbor and he knew that I would respond the same way that they did. I cannot explain how welcoming it felt to hear those words, "we are all neighbors and this is what neighbors do for each other."

The following day, we got eleven to thirteen inches of snow, depending upon where on the property we measured it. For our third season in a row, our neighbors explained that this was unusual weather. Sally and I saw it as another opportunity for acceptance.

This time, when the temperature fell below freezing, it was for two weeks. Eight months earlier, we were living in Tampa, Florida, the Sunshine State. Here we were in Warren, Oregon, with a foot of snow covering every part of our property.

Two weeks of no mail, no trash collection, no UPS, no Fedex, no leaving our street unless we walked, and we loved every minute of it. One of the great advantages of my Parkinson's coaching is that I do not have to leave the house. So I did my coaching, and Sally and I hiked the mountain in the snow.

Since everybody who did not own a big truck with snow tires and/or chains was in the same situation as us, we ran into our neighbors, met many people as we hiked up another street on the other side of the mountain, and we gained a further sense of community and acceptance.

And with that sense of community came an incredible offering. Three times during the two weeks, a couple of our neighbors either called or drove up our driveway in their big vehicles to tell us they were going to the grocery store and would we like to come or could they bring us something back.

We would smile, say thanks, and let them know that we had been "hurricane" shopping prior to the snowstorm. Each year in Florida, prior to hurricane season, we would do the big "can goods, bottled water, non-perishable pantry items, etc." type of shopping in case we found ourselves without electricity and without the ability to get to a store.

At the end of the two weeks, the temperature rose, the sun came out, and one could barely tell that there had been a snowstorm at all. Sally had really pushed it the last few days to make our meals with what was left in the house, but we did well.

After I finished coaching for the day on Friday, January 20, Sally said to me, "How much is fourteen times three?" I responded, "Forty-two, why?" She said, "Because I have cooked forty-two meals in a row and I would like to go out to dinner tonight."

We had a big laugh, went out to dinner, and had a Friday night date at the grocery store. As beautiful as the snow had been, and as wonderful as it had been to hike the mountain, we were grateful for being able to get out of the house and for the green grass and trees.

A couple of weeks later, our son, Steven, and his wife, Jenna, came for a weeklong visit. We brought Victoria home from school for a three-day weekend while they were here so she could see them as well.

Prior to their arrival, Steven commented to us that even though he knew we had seen enough snow for a while, what would make the trip extra special (coming from Georgia) would be if it snowed while they were here.

Steven got his wish. On February 5, as we were preparing to hike up the mountain with Steven and Jenna, we started to get a light snow. By the time we reached the top of the mountain, we were in a downpour of huge snowflakes. We all agreed that it was one of the most beautiful things we ever had seen.

I was filled with gratitude. I had gratitude for the snow, gratitude that Steven and Jenna could enjoy it, and gratitude for the ever-changing things in life that brought me continuous awareness of how glorious an existence I was able to live once I stopped being afraid of living and once I stopped worrying about the future.

The future was February 6, another day where there was a possibility of snow. That is the day what we were supposed to drive Victoria back to the airport. As the snow started falling on the 5th, I drove our car to our friends' house, the same place where we walked to get Victoria when she came home on winter break.

And then we decided to enjoy Sunday with full acceptance that whatever weather would arrive on Monday, we would deal with it on Monday.

This is so different from how I was prior to getting Parkinson's and for most of my Parkinson's recovery. Why? Because I was filled with fear and my adrenaline-driven mind would have been in overdrive.

On Sunday the 5th, I already would have been worrying about Monday the 6th. My over-thinking mind would have been working through all of the possibilities and trying to compartmentalize the potential solutions.

For starters, I would have been non-accepting of Sunday's snowfall: "I wish it wasn't snowing because now we may not be able to drive Victoria to the airport on Monday. And if we wait too long to make a decision to call the car service, maybe they will not be able to pick her up. And if they cannot pick her up, do we tell her she will have to miss Monday afternoon's classes and do we fly her back to school on Tuesday. And what if we call the car service and pay for them to pick her up on Monday and it stops snowing Sunday night and we could have driven her to the airport. And what if, what if, what if...."

This only begins to explain what my mind did all of the time for as far back as I can remember in my life. What I realized in my recovery was that this type of adrenaline-driven mind did not allow me to be present in the moment.

So in the midst of everybody else having a delightful time enjoying the freshly falling snowflakes, I would have been elsewhere in my mind. Realistically, I know they would have felt it. They would have felt my agitation and, at some level, it would have ruined everybody else's fun day.

Acceptance of life changed all of that. Surrender to what is occurring in my life changed all of that. Being grateful for the fact that this life is a precious gift changed all of that. Acceptance, surrender, and gratitude lead to solutions and letting go of attachments to worry and fear.

On the morning of February 6, it was not snowing. I walked down to where the car was located and it was covered in ice and snow. I got inside, turned on the defrosters and waited for the ice and snow to melt before walking back home.

That morning, I had one coaching call prior to having to leave for the airport, and then I was taking the rest of the day off to spend time with Steven and Jenna. In the middle of my coaching call, I caught the snow flurries out of the corner of my eye.

When the call ended, the five of us started to make our way to the car. As we were walking down the mountain, we walked from snow flurries into drizzling rain. The elevation changed just enough in that quarter of a mile that it drizzled the rest of the way to the car, and off we went to the airport.

One of the things I learned about fear was that almost all of the time, the event of which I was fearful did not come true. However, living in fear would negatively impact my life in between the time I became fearful of the future event and the time that the future event of which I was fearful did not happen.

This was just another example of how living in the moment without fear leads to a happy ending. Though sometimes living in the moment without fear does not lead to a happy ending, it is okay. That is real life.

Once I awoke and started experiencing real life with the understanding that real life is messy, I never wanted to go back to the illusions of my mind of what life was supposed to be. I choose messy life over illusions every time.

As we made it through February, we realized that rainy season had no intention of ending. March was another cold and rainy month. As my birthday was approaching, Sally asked me if there was anything special I wanted to do to celebrate my first birthday in Oregon.

I told her that hiking the mountain seemed like an appropriate Oregonian way to celebrate my birthday. I originally had a busy day of coaching on my birthday, but with a couple of people who needed to reschedule their coaching day that week, my coaching day ended at 2:00pm.

Sally prepared a special birthday lunch and when I finished my last coaching call of the day from 1:00–2:00pm, we headed up the mountain. During the winter, a gentleman near the top of the Blaha street side of the mountain had given us permission to hike the forty acres of paths on his property to the north of his home, so that's what we did.

As I mentioned earlier, we learned that if we waited for the rain to stop before doing anything, we would find ourselves doing nothing, so we had a glorious hike in the rain.

We had the best Oregonian birthday imaginable.

When we got home and got dried off, Sally made a birthday dinner and birthday cake for me, and we had a quiet celebration. It was a spectacular day.

Our daughter Victoria finished her second year of college and came home for a few weeks beginning May 13. We were very happy to have her home and to be able to spend time planning a fun visit.

On May 14 we celebrated Mother's Day with Sally and on May 18 we had a small birthday celebration for Sally, as the bigger celebration was that upcoming weekend.

On May 20, the three of us headed down to Salem and Silverton, Oregon, for the weekend for Sally's birthday celebration at the Oregon Garden on Sunday.

On Saturday, we went to the Schreiner's Iris Garden and to the Adelman Peony Garden. It is very difficult to describe how absolutely magnificent it was to see row after row of spectacular irises at the Schreiner's Iris Garden. Each row was beautifully designed and crafted for a visual sensory experience beyond compare.

And then, just when we thought we might be underwhelmed, we arrived at the Adelman Peony Gardens and were just as awestruck as at the iris garden. What an enchanting day in Salem.

The next morning, we got an early start to head out to breakfast in Sliverton, and then off to the Oregon Garden. The Oregon Garden was breathtaking. There were different areas of trees, plants, vegetable gardens, fruit trees, and bushes, and once we started walking through the gardens, we simply did not want to leave.

One of my favorites was a fascinating area of medicinal herbs. Each had an explanation of how the herbs were used for healing. It opened up a whole new area of exploration for us. The day in the Oregon Garden could not have been nicer, cool weather, bright sunshine.

As we got in the car to get a late lunch and head home to Warren, we all felt wonderful, and Sally's "birthday weekend" had been a big success.

Two days after we arrived back home, our daughter Genevieve and her husband, Azhar, arrived from Maryland for a visit. It was very nice that this visit coincided with when Victoria was on break from school.

We had a great time with them while they were here for five days. Sally and I did our best to introduce them to some of our favorite Portland restaurants and coffee shops. Also, we enjoyed spending down time together at our home.

On Saturday, May 27, they headed back to Maryland, and on the following Saturday, June 3, Victoria headed back to California to take some summer art classes. Once again, our home was empty except for Sally and me, and Cricket, of course.

June 12 is the anniversary of my recovery. On June 12, 2017, I became seven years cured of Parkinson's. However, one week prior to that, when I got on my coaching call with Tony C., he announced to me that he had been blessed with his full recovery.

The following day, I posted on my blog, "Fighting Parkinson's, and Tony C. is symptom free." Tony was forty-six years old and had been coaching with me for two years. He did not take Parkinson's medications, but he did have a DATscan confirmation that he had Parkinson's Disease.

Tony and I had been talking every Monday for two years and it was fantastic to hear the joy in his voice as he explained how he had watched the symptoms wither away over the previous week. Needless to say, I was thrilled for him. Also, I was excited for all of the hope it would provide to those who follow my blog when they read about it the following day.

On June 12, 2017, I posted, "Fighting Parkinson's, and being cured seven years." Here is what I had to say:

For me, today is a blessed day filled with gratitude, acceptance, and surrender. It is the day I woke up seven years ago, Parkinson's gone, life back in balance...cured.

In my recovery, I learned a lot about gratitude, acceptance, and surrender. I became completely grateful for my life, even one that temporarily had a body with Parkinson's symptoms. My soul was untouched by Parkinson's, and I was grateful that my soul was in a human body. I learned to accept whatever was happening as necessary in my life and my recovery. And, I learned to surrender that nobody owed me an explanation as to why the things were happening in my life..."Okay. Apparently this is supposed to be happening or it would not be happening."

Seven years after my final surrender and awakening, cured of Parkinson's, I live my life following these lessons.

This is why Parkinson's does not come back after one is cured doing the Parkinson's Recipe for Recovery®. It is why none of the six of us cured of Parkinson's doing the Recipe does the Recipe anymore and why none of our symptoms have, or will, return. Once you learn the lessons and have your recovery, your attitude and behavior reflect the "lessons learned" and you never have to learn them again. Faith, attitude, action, progress, recovery!!! It is life back in balance.

Full acceptance and surrender of what is going on in life looks like this: "Okay! Apparently, I was supposed to get Parkinson's, so I could cure myself, so I could find my purpose, so I could serve all of you." I am grateful to all of you for your hard work and dedication in taking the path less traveled and knowing you can recover from Parkinson's. I am grateful to all of you for helping me fulfill my purpose.

I am grateful for my children, Steven, Genevieve, and Victoria. You have grown into loving, caring, beautiful adults. You make Mom and me proud everyday. I couldn't have done it without your love and support in helping me around the house and not giving up on your dad. Thank you. I love you.

And, Sally, the love of my life...what a journey it has been and continues to be. Thank you for holding me and never letting go. Thank you for holding my hand as we took our most recent leap of faith, leaping 3,000 miles from Florida to Oregon last year. What a wonderful year it has been since we moved. I love you!

Yes, today I am seven years cured of Parkinson's. You can do this too!

You are worth it!!!

All my best,
Howard

EPILOGUE

These last eight years of Parkinson's Disease and recovery from Parkinson's have been an incredible journey of life. Thank you for going on this journey with me. In the Appendices that follow, you will find my Parkinson's Daily Journal and the physical exercises from the Recipe.

Over the last seven years subsequent to curing myself from Parkinson's, I have been asked, "Why is Western Medicine not jumping all over this?" My reply has been consistent, "I do not know. You will have to ask somebody involved with Parkinson's and Western Medicine to find out."

Nearly seven years ago, I stopped trying to convince people with closed minds and closed ears that Parkinson's is curable. Instead, I have spent my time teaching people with open minds and open hearts my Parkinson's Recipe for Recovery®.

I learned in my recovery to accept what I can control and to not be attached to the rest. I accept that there are two things I can control: 1. What I am doing right now; and 2. What my emotional reactions will be to the people and events in life. I choose to react to life with acceptance, surrender, and compassion.

In these last seven years, I have been invited to speak at Parkinson's events, have provided workshops in the United States and Canada, and have been teaching people the Recipe with one-on-one coaching.

Technology allows me to talk on the phone or, via Skype and FaceTime, to sit face-to-face with people as if they are sitting across the desk from me. It does not matter where in the world they are located or what their native language is. Parkinson's has brought us together and we always find a way to communicate.

Also, as a result of our moving to Warren, I am coaching people who come up to our home from Portland for our coaching meetings.

I am grateful for all of the people with Parkinson's whom I have met; wonderful people, each and every one. Also, I am grateful that they are interested in learning the Recipe.

My life is enriched by the amount of time I spend on a daily basis with people with Parkinson's. We laugh, we cry, we talk about life, and we talk about Parkinson's. Sometimes the jokes we share lose out in the translation; the funniest part ends up being trying to explain a double meaning punch line that has no comparable double meaning translation.

Since March of 2010, I have been writing my blog with one or two posts per week.

Through the posting of comments on the blog, my readers and I have developed a worldwide community of people who are focused on living healthy lives and who are sharing their stories of how they are doing with their Parkinson's recoveries.

We are a family on the blog. These are people who want something more for their lives and their Parkinson's than what is being offered through conventional means. It is rewarding to see the courage and faith of the people I am coaching and those who are commenting on the blog.

In the future, maybe somebody involved in Western Medicine will take an interest in the Recipe and we can have a study performed as to the efficacy of the Recipe for people with Parkinson's. I would be delighted if this was to take place.

In the meantime, I am continuing to teach the Recipe to people with

Parkinson's, one person at a time. I cannot imagine doing anything else My life is blessed.

APPENDIX ONE

When I realized that I probably had Parkinson's Disease, I did a week of research and then put together what is now my Parkinson's Recipe for Recovery®. On September 28, 2009, I started doing the Recipe and also started a Parkinson's Daily Journal.

Below are excerpts from my Parkinson's Daily Journal. By mid-November, it was painfully difficult to write and even more difficult to read my writing, so I stopped writing.

Not being able to write was a blessing in disguise. When I was writing the journal, I still was in Parkinson's adrenaline-mind perfectionism mode, so I was consumed with "perfectly" journaling my symptoms and my degeneration. After I stopped writing in the journal, I stopped paying so much attention to the daily changes in my symptoms, and that assisted me in my recovery.

09/28/09. Last Tuesday, I sat down with Sally to explain that I have Parkinson's. I have tried denying this for a little while, but the internal tremors were very strong that day and no telling when they might appear as external tremors.

Sally and I have been through everything, and she is the strong one and I needed a plan.

We talked things through and agreed to explore every option and jointly make a decision.

After much research and much discussion, the plan is to move forward with a Traditional Chinese Medicine (TCM) approach. There are three main causes of Parkinson's from a TCM viewpoint:

1. Qi and Blood Deficiency, which is caused by emotional stress, anger, frustration, and resentment.
2. Phlegm-Fire Agitating Wind, which is caused by dietary considerations such as consumption of too much greasy, fried or sweet foods.
3. Kidney and Liver Wind; Deficiency, which is caused by overwork and insufficient rest which unbalances the body's natural rhythm.

The healing approach will change as the disease changes. However, the starting point is to keep a strict diet in place, perform Qigong (Chi Kung) for elevating the Qi and Blood Deficiency, elevating the Kidney and Liver Yin Deficiency, and acupressure for stimulating the brain and spinal column. [In layman's terms, here is what I was getting at: The liver was overworked and not cleaning the blood well (Blood Deficiency). As a result of the blood being deficient, it was not bringing the body the proper nutrients and oxygen, thus causing the body to be weak and fatigued (Qi, life energy, Deficiency). The physical part of the healing methodology was to heal the organs and bring the body back into balance so blood and Qi would no longer be deficient and the body again would be vibrant].

Reference Materials:

1. *The Yellow Emperor's Classic of Medicine* by Maoshing Ni, Ph.D.
2. *Chinese Health Care Secrets* by Henry B. Lin
3. *Qigong Empowerment* by Master Shou-Yu Liang
4. *Soul Mind Body Medicine* by Dr./Master Zhi Gang Sha
5. *Integrative Acupressure* by Sam McClellan
6. "Degenerative Diseases, Interpretation and Treatment with Chinese Medicine" by Subhuti Dharmananda (http://www.itmonline.org/arts/degenerative.htm)
7. *What Your Doctor May NOT Tell You About Parkinson's Disease* by Jill Marjama-Lyons, M.D.
8. *Teach Yourself Chi Kung* by Robert Parry

What I am experiencing:

1. Internal tremors when my body is at rest. When I move, they seem to go away, although it just may be that my attention is elsewhere because I am moving rather than being stationary.
2. Rigidity. My left arm is very tight in the muscles, particularly my forearm. I am in constant pain in my left arm and although it is my stronger arm as I played all sports left-handed, I have no strength. I have a hard time lifting the water pitcher and cannot squeeze the pump at the gas station.
3. Bradykinesia. My movements are slow and my balance is horrible, particularly when I first get out of bed. Example: I cannot hold my shorts and lift

one foot to step into them. I have to hold onto something, hold my shorts in one hand at floor level, step into them and finally pull them up. My walking is very slow and if I am not consciously paying careful attention, I walked hunched over while shuffling my feet. I need to use the chair arms or the table to stand from my sitting position. I need to focus before walking up the stairs holding the railing. It is painful, but I can walk up the steps. I must hold on and focus on my balance because I go backwards when I lift either leg. Sometimes I have to go one step at a time where the second leg moves up only to the step where the first leg is located and I progress a step at a time in this manner. When I turn around to go back in the other direction (regular walking, not stairs) I go in a semi-circle almost like walking around a marker.

Treatment:

1. Dietary—fruits, vegetables, whole wheat (bread, rice, barley), oatmeal. No preservatives, no alcohol, no fried foods. Focus is to dispel the Phlegm-Fire Agitating Wind. (reference: Chinese Health Care Secrets).
2. Qigong—Medical Qigong focused on elevating the Kidney and Liver. Deficiencies. Buddhist Qigong for elevating the Qi and Blood Deficiency. (reference: Qigong Empowerment).
3. Acupressure focused on the Governing Vessel, GV, and Conception Vessel, CV. (reference: Integrative Acupressure).
4. Sound, Vibration, Energy elevation, near hand-far hand healing techniques (reference: Soul Mind

Body Medicine).

5. Exercise for Qi circulation in the same channels as #3 above. (reference: Teach Yourself Chi Kung).

6. Smile more, be more patient with my situation, think before moving. Try to be a nicer person. Take each moment as it occurs and deal with it in the best possible manner. No fear allowed. Let my family know every day how much I love them.

I learned today that if I want to try to walk normally, I need to focus on standing up straight, extending my leg and getting my foot off the ground, and, swinging my arms. Apparently, as I have been hunched and shuffling my feet, my arms have stopped swinging. Consciously swinging my arms helps a lot with balance.

I learned another very important thing: when I am walking, I need to be really focused. I got the mail and on the way back up the driveway, I started looking through a magazine; the next thing I knew is that I was completely off balance and I fell down. I read an article last week where the author, a Parkinson's sufferer, said that the days of walking and chewing gum were over. I laughed. Today, I learned it wasn't funny.

* * *

09/29/09. 4:00am woke up. Last night, Sally did GV [Governing Vessel] acupressure right before bed. I slept well and do not think I moved positions the entire night. When I got out of bed, all of the muscles in my back were very tight, probably from acupressure releasing toxins.

Performed Medical Qigong for the Kidneys, elevating and strengthening, and the chui sound Qigong for kidney health. I need a break. I am a little dizzy, my legs hurt, and my kidneys feel like somebody has been punching them — apparently the Qigong is working. Performed Medical Qigong for the Liver (suggested 10 repetitions, I could do 4 only) and Xu sound for calming the liver (could do all suggested 6 repetitions).

During breakfast, I remembered the same thing that I remembered during dinner last night. When I go to eat with a fork or spoon, my arm/hand gets the food on the fork or spoon, lifts it up from the plate or bowl, and STOPS in mid-air, hovering a couple of inches above the food. I then have to think about moving it to my mouth. I have tried concentrating on the fluid motion of picking up the food and going directly to my mouth, but so far, I have not been successful. There's always lunch today...we will see.

* * *

09/30/09. Got up at 4:00am. This is my worst day so far. Hard to get off the bed and whole body is tight and aching. Hard to get dressed. Hard to get downstairs. I follow the same routine every morning—out of bed, get dressed, go downstairs, use bathroom and put on contacts, go to kitchen and turn on espresso machine. I look at the clock as the machine takes 10 minutes to warm up.

Every day the clock shows 4:04am or 4:05am. Today it showed 4:08am. I am hopeful that the slowdown is a result of the Qigong performed yesterday. I have found that releasing toxins always makes me worse before I get better. I can only hope this will be the same.

Performed the Kidney Qigong. Kidneys are aching, which is a good thing.

At 10:00am, I started feeling a little lightheaded so I ate a banana and the extra vegetables Sally set aside after she prepared our lunch. She told me they could be my "elevens-ees." They were my "second breakfast." ["elevens-ees" and "second breakfast" are Lord of the Rings references to extra meals].

* * *

10/01/09. It is October. Where has the year gone. Today, Sally suggested I reset the alarm for 4:30am. Got up, felt no better, felt no worse. No worse is a plus and I look for the pluses. Took me 8 minutes to get going to turn on the espresso machine. Oatmeal for breakfast — great breakfast again. Had a good morning of work, so feeling happy. Lunch was delicious — dumpling squash filled with sautéed onions, brown rice and wild rice. Sally really takes care of me.

Just did the kidney and liver medical Qigong. After the liver Qigong, I stand straighter and feel physically exhausted but stimulated at the same time. I get a lot of tingling inside my head and my brain aches. I feel like the Parkinson's fights me back. However, I am very patient and intend on winning.

We had Italian Wedding Soup for dinner. It was wonderful. Sally and I did the kidney and liver Qigong together. I am blessed. I do not use the word lightly. I need to do the kidney and liver Qigong to fight Parkinson's and Sally joins me in the Qigong so I won't be fighting by myself.

She does GV acupressure on me before I go to bed. I have an absolute partner in this fight. Sally is everything to me and gives me strength to do my exercises when I have no strength or desire.

I think about Steven and Genevieve and Victoria (our children) all the time. How am I going to tell them? And Dad and Mark and Allison (brother and sister), after watching Mom. And Sally's Mother and Mary and Jerry (friends).

What do I say? I do not know where to begin.

* * *

10/02/09. Got up at 4:30am again. I had noticed yesterday that the pain I have had in my left arm has replicated in my right arm. This is not good, but then again, maybe it is.

There were a couple of things different for me this morning — waking up 30 minutes later than usual and Genevieve wanted to get up at 5:15am instead of 6:00am — I got confused thinking about the difference, and for some reason, I felt pressed for time, which in hindsight is ridiculous.

I forgot to warm the bowls for the oatmeal for breakfast. Sally said it was no big deal. To me it was a huge deal—I learned, although I kind of already knew from other experiences, my brain is disorganized now. Still have clarity in my thoughts and reasoning, however, I cannot process too many different concepts simultaneously—something will go into a black hole never again to be thought of in my cognitive processes.

I am considering making checklists to make certain I remember all the steps when I am doing something like making breakfast. There are not a lot of steps, but if my mind gets distracted, I lose my place; sometimes when the confusion comes over me I just cry.

I cannot help it, it does not solve anything, and my tremors get worse until I can calm myself down. I also noticed that if I start to use my hands to help me explain a concept, my arms go wherever they want and my hands get spastic as well.

The rigidity has gone into my legs a lot. My forearms already look like I am a weightlifter (powerful looking, veins popped up to the surface); now my calves look like I have been training for a long-distance bike race. The stairs have become my biggest physical challenge. Everything else is pretty equal in its challenging nature.

I am looking forward to the weekend. Sally is taking (our daughter) Genevieve and three friends to Orlando to shop for Homecoming dresses. I am so happy for Genevieve. She is very pretty and always looks beautiful when she gets dressed up. Genevieve is doing great and we are really proud of the nice young woman she has become.

We are very proud of (our son) Steven too. He started college this year. He is a kind and compassionate young man. Even though he is 30 minutes away living in the dorm, he is doing a great job of having his college experience instead of coming home on the weekends.

I am looking forward to time with (our daughter) Victoria while Sally and Genevieve are in Orlando. She is a sweet, beautiful young lady, and as the third child, has to wait a lot for one-on-one time. Tomorrow we get one-on-one time for whatever she wants to do. It should be fun.

Sally and I took Victoria to her clarinet lesson this evening and then went to Taco Bus for butternut squash tostados—pure heaven. After we all got home, we watched Project Runway and wound down the evening. Nice way to end the week.

* * *

10/03/09. Saturday. Slept in until alarm rang at 7:00am. Sally headed to Orlando for Genevieve and friends to get homecoming dresses. I did not see any difference in how I felt getting up at 7:00am versus 4:00am.

Victoria and I are going to California Pizza Kitchen for lunch...what a treat. I love their white bean hummus. It cannot hold a candle to Sally's hummus, but it is very good and it is something I can eat in a restaurant and still eat healthy food.

Victoria and I are back home. She had a cheese pizza for lunch, and then we went to Westshore Plaza to get her new earrings. They are musical notes and she looks pretty. We stopped and picked up dog food, went to Blockbusters to rent a movie and then went back home.

Steven kept me apprised of USF's score (college football game of his college, University of South Florida, USF) via texting, and Victoria and I put on the TV and watched the 4th Quarter as USF won the game and got a 5-0 record. Steven is very excited.

Did the liver and kidney Qigong again, felt really good as it had been a long day. We had chicken and baked potatoes (I was not a vegetarian yet) for dinner. It was so good. Watched a movie with Victoria. 10:00pm and heading to bed.

* * *

10/04/09. Up at 4:00am. No difference in how I feel. Same Qigong routine. Then, lazy morning. Sally and I went grocery shopping. About ¾ of the way through the shopping, my legs felt as if I was pushing the cart through mud.

When we got home, Sally and I did the kidney and liver Qigong. This always energizes me...gives me 1-2 hours of feeling "on." I knew I needed to do it because I wanted to cut the grass. While I was "on," I cut the grass and only started to run out of steam towards the end.

Sally and I had wheat angel hair pasta with a homemade tomato sauce. What a great dinner. As the evening went on I was feeling very sluggish. We watched the movie "Earth" with Victoria, and then I started winding down.

My calves had been tight since the morning. Sally had

done GV acupressure for me in the morning, and did it again before going to sleep.

* * *

10/05/09. Up at 4:00am. Feeling the same. My knees hurt, but that is probably the result of the store and the lawn from yesterday. Victoria is home from school with a stuffy nose. I am constipated and having a rough day.

I am trying to work, but I am miserable today. Oatmeal for breakfast, drank lots of water, apple and watermelon for lunch—terrible day.

Went with Sally and Genevieve to a Duke University event at the Marriott Westshore. It was good.

Dinner was great—black beans and rice. Also, just remembered—took handwriting test today—not good.

Note to reader: The handwriting test I mentioned was to look at micrographia (I had read small handwriting was a sign of Parkinson's). There was a test I had learned about that said to take a blank sheet of paper with no lines and sign one's name again and again down the page creating one column.

A sign of Parkinson's would be a shrinking signature as one moved down the page. I gave myself this test on September 28, 2009, the day I started the Recipe, and then every week through December 21, 2009.

Also, I found a surprise when going through these handwriting samples; I must have been feeling particular well five days prior to my full recovery because after not taking this handwriting test for six months, I took it one more time on June 7, 2010.

Obviously, on June 7, 2010, I had no idea that I would be having my full recovery on June 12, 2010, but something made me take the handwriting test that day. The June 7, 2010 handwriting looks exceptionally good compared to how it had been from September through December of 2009, so I know I must have been inspired by the results.

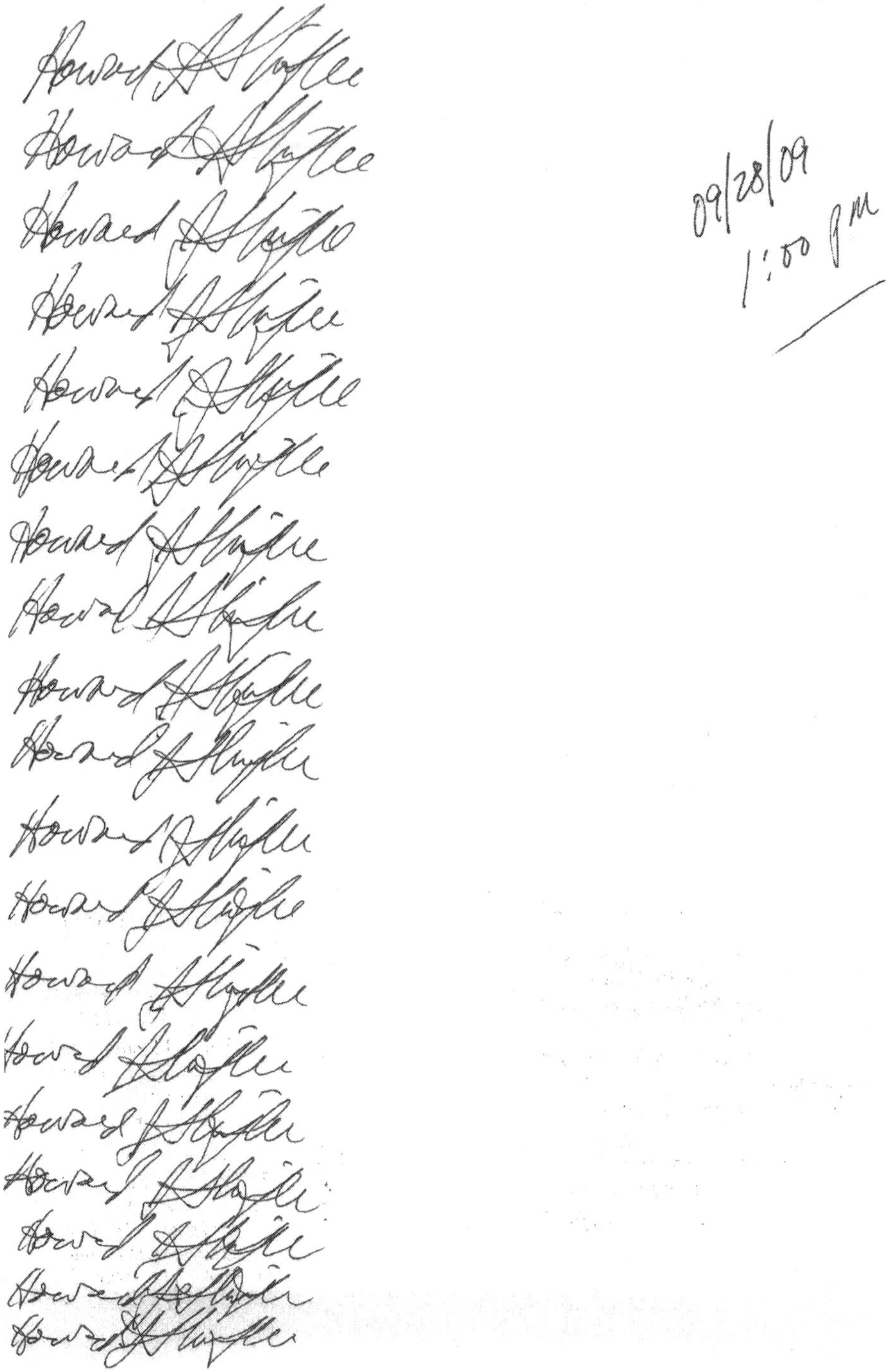
09/28/09
1:00 pm

Howard Shifke (signature, repeated many times)

10/05/09
1:35 pm HS

Howard A. Shifke (repeated signatures)

10/12/09
1:00 pm

Howard H Shifke
Howard H Shifke
Howard H Shifke
Howard H Shifke
Howard H Shifke
Howard H Shifke
Howard H Shifke
Howard H Shifke
Howard H Shifke
Howard H Shifke
Howard H Shifke
Howard H Shifke
Howard H Shifke
Howard H Shifke
Howard H Shifke
Howard H Shifke
Howard H Shifke
Howard H Shifke
Howard H Shifke
Howard H Shifke

10/19/09
1:05 pm
HS

Howard Shifke

Howard Shifke

Howard Shifke

Howard Shifke

Howard Shifke

Howard Shifke

Howard Shifke

Howard Shifke

Howard Shifke

Howard Shifke

Howard Shifke

Howard Shifke

Howard Shifke

Howard Shifke

Howard Shifke

Howard Shifke

Howard Shifke

Howard Shifke

Howard Shifke

Howard Shifke

Howard Shifke

Howard Shifke

Howard Shifke

Howard Shifke

10/26/09

1:02 pm

HS

Howard A Shifke
Howard A Shifke
Howard A Shifke
Howard A Shifke
Howard A Shifke
Howard A Shifke
Howard A Shifke
Howard A Shifke
Howard A Shifke
Howard A Shifke
Howard A Shifke
Howard A Shifke
Howard A Shifke
Howard A Shifke
Howard A Shifke
Howard A Shifke
Howard A Shifke
Howard A Shifke
Howard A Shifke
Howard A Shifke
Howard A Shifke
Howard A Shifke

11/02/09
HA
1:05pm

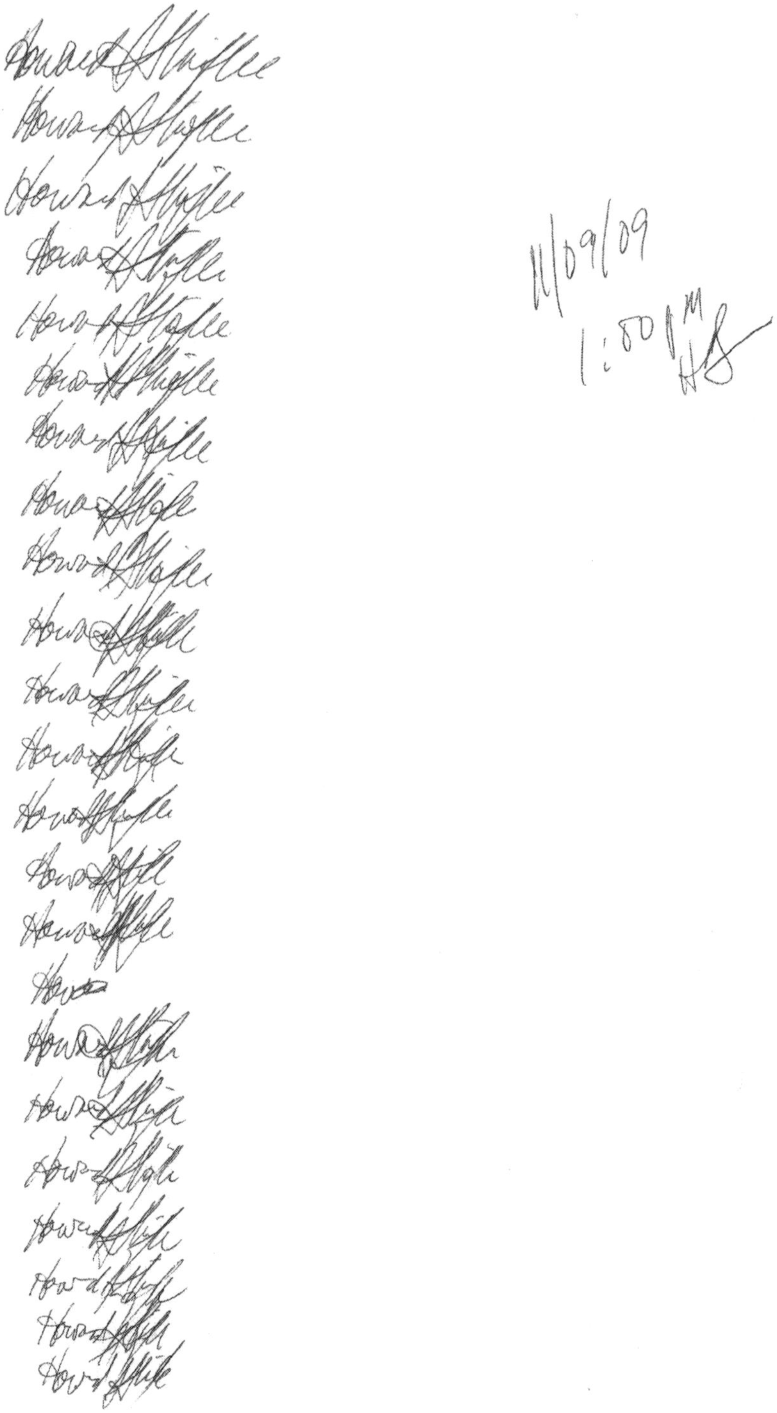
11/09/09
1:00 PM

Howard Shifke
Howard Shifke
Howard Shifke
Howard Shifke
Howard Shifke
Howard Shifke
Howard Shifke
Howard Shifke
Howard Shifke
Howard Shifke
Howard Shifke
Howard Shifke
Howard Shifke
Howard Shifke
Howard Shifke
Howard Shifke
Howard Shifke
Howard Shifke
Howard Shifke
Howard Shifke
Howard Shifke
Howard Shifke

11/16/09
1:10 pm
HS

11/23/09
1:02 pm

11/30/09

1:03 PM

1:04 pm
12/07/09

214

Howard Shifke
Howard Shifke
Howard Shifke
Howard Shifke
Howard Shifke
Howard Shifke
Howard Shifke
Howard Shifke
Howard Shifke
Howard Shifke
Howard Shifke
Howard Shifke
Howard Shifke
Howard Shifke
Howard Shifke
Howard Shifke
Howard Shifke
Howard Shifke
Howard Shifke
Howard Shifke

12/14/09 1:16pm
HS

[handwritten signatures]

12/21/09   1:15pm
HAS

Howard J Shifke
Howard J Shifke
Howard J Shifke
Howard J Shifke
Howard J Shifke
Howard J Shifke
Howard J Shifke
Howard J Shifke
Howard J Shifke
Howard J Shifke
Howard J Shifke
Howard J Shifke
Howard J Shifke
Howard J Shifke
Howard J Shifke
Howard J Shifke
Howard J Shifke

06/07/10
12:15 P
HJS

10/06/09. Up at 4:00am. Peas and carrots for breakfast. After breakfast, I talked with Sally and completely lost it and cried and cried. Some days, she must feel really miserable being with me. She held me and I felt better after we talked.

My system is more regular today. Mom would have turned 75 today. I called Dad and I think he was happy for the call.

No real change in my physical condition today—at least it is not worse today than it was yesterday.

* * *

10/07/09. Got up at 4:00am, very slow moving. Got to the kitchen at 4:09am, my record for slowness.

Today I decided to go up and down the stairs the normal way with each foot going to the next step rather than two feet on a single step before advancing. I had to hold onto the railing and use some arm strength to accomplish this, but I went up and down the stairs this way a couple of times.

My legs are tight and they ache. My knees hurt, and when I sit to rest, the tremors in my lower legs and feet are pronounced.

The St. Pete Times came late today, so I made two trips down the driveway this morning. I was surprised to find myself out of breath with a fast heartbeat after the second trip down the driveway. My body "wakes up" slowly, so I am guessing that was the problem.

* * *

10/08/09. Up at 4:00am, sore all over and slow. Got to the kitchen at 4:07am, not bad. I am moving very slowly today and need to find some energy...haven't figured that out yet.

At lunch, I did not have too much trouble getting the spoon directly up from the food to my mouth…fairly smoothly once I got it going after the freezing that took place after I picked up the food. At 3:30pm, did the kidney and liver medical Qigong, looking for some extra energy, and felt okay the rest of the afternoon.

At dinner, made it halfway through the meal before my fork started freezing and hovering above the food. At about 6:00pm, I felt like I was walking in mud and this lasted until bedtime.

* * *

10/09/09. Got to the kitchen at 4:08am. I am a little concerned today because my thighs are killing me. My calves hurt, but they have been hurting all week. My concern is rigidity setting into my legs at a greater degree than already exists. I am concerned about the effect this will have upon my ability to stand, walk, go up and down stairs. So I am going to stretch and massage my legs and see where we go.

Tonight we go to a Plant/Gaither (high school) game as Victoria will be playing in Plant's band. I did an extra set of kidney and liver Qigong in the afternoon to help with getting ready for the evening. Afternoon went okay

As we were heading to the game, I wondered how I would get into the bleachers. We sat in the front row of bleachers, great idea of Sally's. Took the stress out of the evening…it was enough of a workout getting to the stadium from the parking lot.

* * *

10/10/09. Slept in. Woke up at 6:35am. No improvement

from yesterday, but not worse either. Sally has to work from 1-4pm today, so it is not fun for her.

Genevieve went to a walk-a-thon for Alzheimer's disease. After Sally went to work, Victoria and I went to Hyde Park, got treats for Cricket (our dog), and ice cream for Victoria. I think she had a fun time.

Genevieve was invited to a hockey game in the evening, and Sally and I watched "Enchanted" with Victoria. It is a very funny movie and was a great escape for a couple of hours.

* * *

10/11/09. Slept in again. Got up around 7:30am. Very slow moving. I think it is a real Catch 22—I am supposed to get "enough" rest to heal, but when I wake up without an alarm waking me at 4:00am, I am stiff and sore worse than when getting up at 4:00am.

I got downstairs, and within a few minutes, Cricket started barking. I took her outside in the back yard and stayed there 10-15 minutes. She had gone all the way across the yard and went up the stairs near the kitchen.

Apparently, my legs were not awake enough for the steeper stairs as I could not manage them. I learn something new every day. I am looking forward to the day when I learn something I can do again as opposed to my normal day of learning a new limitation.

After lunch, Sally and I had a date — we went to the grocery store. I cherish every moment I have with Sally— the drive in the car, the walking through the store, the drive home, the comfort of her being the last thing I see before I go to bed and the first thing I see when I wake up in the morning.

Parkinson's Disease is a pain to have, but it pales in

comparison to the blessings I have in my life.

* * *

10/12/09. Monday again. Up at 4:00am…slow. Got to the kitchen at 4:08am. I had woken up in the middle of the night as I felt like something was crawling on my back.

I got out of bed to use the bathroom and felt as if bugs were crawling all over me. Just remembering this makes me cringe. My legs hurt a lot and my back is tight, very, very tight. I noticed the internal tremors very much this morning as well.

It is the end of the day, and I am worn out, but I am looking forward to what tomorrow may bring.

* * *

10/13/09. Tuesday. Up at 4:00am. Slow again. Got to the kitchen at 4:09am, unbelievable. Sally and I discussed Dr. Sha and some of the things he has to offer.

I remember typing up a Mandarin Chinese number chant for the brain, and I found it. I did it this morning and my entire head vibrated. I will do it for 5 minutes at least three times a day and see if it helps. It was energizing.

Lunch was great—since nobody is around, I try really hard to get past the freeze that occurs when I pick up any food with the utensil. No luck…it moves to my mouth very slowly in about 6-8 independent movements.

I tried left-handed and thought my bones would crack before I could get my food to my mouth. How disappointing. Did the kidney and liver Qigong today just like every other day.

Sally and I discussed other things from Dr. Sha's Soul Mind Body Medicine book. I will implement them.

* * *

10/14/09. Up at 4:00am. Slow, same, no big deal. I will see Steven today, so I am smiling. I went up to USF to see him. He had an hour to kill, so we went to his dorm room and just hung out. I miss him, but I am very happy he is in college and seems to be doing incredibly well.

Genevieve is a high school junior this year and Victoria is a middle schooler...time has really flown by. I get to see them every day, so I am smiling about that, too.

It was an interesting day. I had the feeling a couple of times that Steven was going to ask me if anything was wrong with me. It was just the look on his face and the feeling it had given me.

I have terrible tremors this evening and I am going to bed early—what a mess.

* * *

10/15/09. 4:00am up and at 'em, ha, ha. Started the day by dropping my espresso cup on the kitchen floor. Tile is very unforgiving. Oh, well, I need to pay more attention to what I am doing.

Today is the last day of the 20th year that Sally and I have been married. Every day I love Sally more than the day before. She is my one constant in this ever-changing world.

Once again, I will look at her tomorrow and wish her happy anniversary, and wish there was more I could do for her.

I had black beans and brown rice for lunch. Two hours after lunch I had tremors like last night, bad, bad tremors, and could not sit up.

I discussed this with Sally—maybe the toxin cleansing I

am giving my kidneys with the black beans is releasing into my system before leaving. **NO** black beans tomorrow—let's see what happens.

* * *

10/16/09. Up at 4:00am…slow, slow, slow, oh, well. Happy 21st Anniversary!

The nicest thing happened. Victoria, even though she realized she would be alone at home, insisted that Sally and I go out to dinner for our anniversary. We are going to Pho Quyen for Noodles/Noodle Bowls, whatever. Happy Anniversary.

Sally and I did not go to Pho Quyen. The weather was really bad. We went to a new place on Gandy called Luigi's. It was wonderful and we had a happy anniversary dinner out.

Quite frankly, if all I did for our anniversary was sit on the couch and hold Sally's hand, I would be very happy.

* * *

10/17/09. 4:00am, here we go. Steven came home today for the weekend. Tomorrow we will tell the children about my Parkinson's. Not really looking forward to that.

Sally made kettle corn and we had movie night. Great way to spend a Saturday evening with the family.

* * *

10/18/09. 4:00am, cold morning, slow moving. At 10:00am we had the family meeting to tell the children about my Parkinson's Disease. It went as well as could be expected, and then life goes on—we have a busy household.

* * *

10/19/09. 4:00am. Monday, oh boy! It is cold today, 48 degrees. Yesterday evening my kidneys and lower back began to hurt. I think it was the lentils doing a cleansing.

As I was reading about lentils and kidneys, many articles referred to lentils as being used to relieve constipation. Of course, I am having the pleasure of constipation today, go figure. This is very discouraging.

However, I refuse to accept that I cannot get better. Maintaining where I am today is not the future I envision... we will see.

* * *

10/20/09. Up at 4:00am. Slow and stiff, so what's new. I am constipated today. It is strange to be 48 years old and the highlight of my day potentially could be that I am not constipated...how sad is that.

Stairs have been very hard today — my legs are very tight and hurt a lot. I feel unsteady when I walk. I definitely need to get that figured out as soon as possible!

* * *

10/22/09. OMG. Tuesday evening, 10/20, I had a gallstone attack! Cannot describe the pain, chills, sweats, I do not know how Sally could stand to take care of me through this ordeal. The pain began at 6:00pm.

At 12:45am on 10/21, the stone finished passing through the duct and the pain went down in half...fell asleep. Woke up at 2:00am, made my way downstairs and had a glass of water, 8oz.

Within seconds, I broke out in a sweat and got chills, so

went up to bedroom...headed straight for the bathroom and threw up. Fortunately, all I had for dinner was broth with noodles. Five minutes later, threw up again.

Sally said this was good because the articles she had read about passing a gallstone said that after the gallstone successfully passed, I should throw up—I've always been an over-achiever—threw up again in the morning, 10/21, after a glass of water and a cup of peppermint tea.

Sally told me that I was in so much agony during the ordeal, that she had spared me the news that I would be "throwing up" after I successfully passed the stone.

Sally got me propped up on the bed and gave me a small glass of Gatorade...it stayed down. I had slept 1.25 hours in the previous 28 hours and fell asleep sitting up. Sally came home from work at lunchtime and woke me, gave me another glass of Gatorade, and I went back to sleep.

I woke up a little after 4:00pm, had a little more Gatorade, took a shower (which wore me out), and went back to bed. Woke up at 7:45pm, stayed up until 10:30pm and went back to bed.

On 10/22/09, up at 4:00am and VERY, VERY slow. Got to the kitchen at 4:12am, my new world record of slowness. At 9:30am, I started an email response that took me 30 minutes to write. It exhausted me and I went back to bed from 10:05am until 11:50am.

I read an article about post-gallstone-passing care, and it mentioned about staying on clear liquids for a couple of days—I will do whatever they say not to have that happen again.

I spent some time reviewing the Large Intestine channel and acupressure points because, even though I was having a gallstone attack and ultimately threw up, periodically during the ordeal, I headed to the bathroom for bowel movements...7 times, and I passed probably 10 feet or more of stools. That is a lot to just be hanging out in my large intestine.

I learned something important for me. A major point on the Large Intestine channel, LI 12, is the exact spot where I have had terrible pain with rigidity. Maybe the rigidity is squeezing the life out of a section of the Large Intestine channel and maybe that is why constipation is a common symptom of Parkinson's.

I did acupressure in the LI channel and it was interesting—every single point on the LI channel ached, my internal tremors went crazy, and I could barely move my fingers (I could not make a fist) for about 20 minutes.

* * *

10/23/09. Up at 4:00am. Still slow from interesting previous couple of days. I slept through Wednesday and skipped my Qigong on Thursday as I wanted to give my body a little time to recuperate.

* * *

10/24/09. Slept in until 6:00am. Sometimes I feel I need to be up at 4:00am even on Saturday so I can learn more just sitting in the quiet of the morning before anybody else wakes up.

Seems like a no win...I need the rest, but I need to get better, too!

Took Victoria to her clarinet lesson, which we now will have on Saturday's at 10am.

Around the house, I am noticing that there are things I no longer can do and other things I need help to do. It seems so odd—"things I no longer can do"—things I hope to do again some day, but need help with in the meantime. I remain forever hopeful.

Sally had to work a half-day today. I do not know how she does it all, and now with my additional burden…I just don't know.

* * *

10/25/09. Up at 4:00am. Today, for the first time it occurred to me that internal tremors probably burn calories. I will research this tomorrow.

We told Sally's Mother about my Parkinson's tonight. She seems okay, or at least put on a good face once we went over all of the facts and our plan of attack.

* * *

10/26/09. Up at 4:00am. It is Monday and I wish it was the weekend. I am hoping for a good week, but quite frankly, I am physically and mentally exhausted.

Mary (our friend) loaned us a book about Jin Shin Jyutsu and I started reading it yesterday. It appears to be an amazing Japanese art of energy balance that may add a new dimension to my road to health.

I wish I felt better mentally, and I will continue to work on that. It is harder than the physical part.

Sally and I went grocery shopping in the evening. It was good for me to be walking, but again, it felt like walking in the mud.

* * *

10/27/16. Up at 3:27am and couldn't go back to sleep… our little secret! Stayed in bed until 4:00am when the alarm went off. Spent the 33 minutes stretching my body so as to not wake Sally. Out of bed at 4:00am.

Even with the stretching, still did not make it to the kitchen until 4:08am. Learning more about Jin Shin Jyutsu. It holds a lot of answers, so I remain excited.

My lower back and my trunk all around on sides...NOT GOOD, too tight — very painful. It wears me out to walk across the room. At 2:30pm, did the following really slowly to get the pain to go away: Medical Qigong for Kidneys and for Liver, Near Hand Far Hand (both types), Brain Vibration Chanting, Jin Shin Jyutsu jumper-cabling.

No luck. I felt energized at the end of my hour+ long session, but no change in back and trunk pain and stiffness. I am hopeful that it is just from yesterday's grocery shopping.

* * *

10/28/09. 3:42am up, can't go back to sleep. Alarm goes off at 4:00am, out of bed. Pain and stiffness in back and trunk still there. Back and trunk loosened up a bit after hot shower.

Last night, the pain and stiffness finally wore me down. I took a hot bath at 8:45pm and went to bed. How sad is that? Pretty pitiful.

Learned many new things from Jin Shin Jyutsu book. I wonder if part of why I feel the energy is a result of the tremors. My goal in this regard is to recondition the tremors' energy to improve my motor skills.

* * *

10/29/09. OMG! The alarm went off at 4:00am and didn't wake me until 4:01...I was really sleeping hard. Yahoo! I am so happy. Slow as always, but no back or trunk pain. Got to kitchen at 4:08am.

Did Jin Shin Jyutsu jumper cabling and my tremors raged—I felt vibrations throughout my body. What an experience.

Okay, I have had it with the constipation—enough is enough. It is absolutely depressing to sit multiple times during the day for 20 or 25 minutes and maybe get results 50% of the time...and then have to vigorously push to get those results.

Today I learned something new...apparently, I have been walking and going up and down the stairs with my feet/legs in terrible positions. I imagine they have compensated for lack of balance. When walking, my left foot is approximately 60% left of center and my right foot is approximately 45% right of center.

I forced my feet to point forward and attempted to walk...this is the terrible part...I could barely walk, and walking came with lots of pain. I am back at square one learning how to walk again.

One day, I will write in this journal that I learned something new about my physical abilities and motor skills and that it is a good thing—that day is not today!

* * *

10/30/09. Up at 4:00am. Nothing new to report on the health end of things.

Steven is spending the weekend after his football game tonight. Genevieve has Homecoming tonight. I hope she has fun and I hope she has a great overnight at Dana's.

Tomorrow is Halloween. Victoria has big plans and will be Corpse Bride. The rest of us will go to Mary and Jerry's (good friends) and hand out candy. They get a lot of trick-or-treaters. It is always fun.

* * *

10/31/09. Up at 4:00am Happy Halloween.

I received the Tai Chi video and book that I had ordered. I watched the video and it seems nearly impossible in my current state to do any of it.

The book shows simplified Tai Chi postures and breathing. However, when I look at the stylized postures and movement, the feet, the legs, the stand on one leg, the turning, the squatting...OMG...they look like climbing a mountain in difficulty. Certainly, nothing I can do like I am now.

I will stick to what I am doing. Time will tell. I have learned to not be in a hurry for anything.

* * *

11/01/09. Sunday. Steven has been here this weekend, and it has been nice. I think he needed a break from the campus.

Mary and Jerry's was a lot of fun for Halloween. At one point, there were a lot of people and there was a lot of commotion...I don't know why, but commotion wears me out physically even though I am just sitting in a chair.

Victoria was the Corpse Bride last night. She looked great and had fun. The previous night, Genevieve had Homecoming, and she looked beautiful and very grown up.

I am dragging today. Maybe it is because tonight I will be telling dad about Parkinson's. Not looking forward to that. Told dad about Parkinson's and he gave me Marcie's number at Dr. Sanchez-Ramos' office. I will call tomorrow.

* * *

11/02/09. Up at 4:00am. Slow as usual. It is Monday and I am hoping for a good week.

I called Marcie and I am scheduled to see Dr. Sanchez-Ramos on January 28, 2010. I let dad know and he did not seem happy, but what can you do.

Long day—constipation is making me crazy. I hope I will get some relief soon. I ate a plum and 20 black grapes with lunch and a gala apple with dinner. No relief. I hope tomorrow will be better.

Oh yeah, I forgot. Marcie called and I have a neurologist's appointment on Thursday, 11/05/09, at 2pm. Dad must have a lot of influence at the doctor's office or I just had good timing with a cancellation.

* * *

11/03/09. Up at 4:00am. Slow like always, no more, no less. Made poached eggs and grapefruit sectioned for breakfast. Sally was happily surprised.

It is nice to be able to give her a happy surprise for a change. Sally is my world!

Pushing along through the day. No major changes in any regard today. Most days go pretty much the same.

* * *

11/04/09. Up at 4:00am. Feel sluggish, so what's new?

If I had the money, I would go to Albuquerque to see Dr. Marjama-Lyons, then to Scottsdale to see Mary Burmeister, then to San Francisco to see Dr. Sha, then to Canada to see Master Liang. Apparently, I am hallucinating without even taking the drugs…just a little stab at humor.

* * *

11/05/09. Up at 4:00am. Snail's pace. Got to the kitchen at 4:09am. Yuck. Today should be interesting. I have a 2pm appointment at Mom's doctor, Dr. Sanchez-Ramos.

I will need to leave at 12:45pm to be there when they want me there at 1:30pm. I guess there is a lot of paperwork to fill out even though they took all of my personal info and health insurance info two days ago.

Life is very hard on Sally with my Parkinson's. I wish I could do more to ease her burdens...getting better is step #1, and I am focused on that!

I am too wiped out from the day to write. See 11/06/09 for rest of what occurred today.

* * *

11/06/09. Up at 4am. Still slow, not surprised. Yesterday continued: Had my appointment with Dr. Sanchez-Ramos. Kate, who turns out to be his wife, writes for their newsletter, and she was in there and took notes.

Yes, I received my official diagnosis of Parkinson's Disease...no big surprise there. Also, the appointment went better than expected. I explained to Dr. Sanchez-Ramos what I had been doing and he did not pressure me to take medications.

After the appointment, I talked to Dad, Sally's Mother, my sister Allison, and my brother Mark. Of course, Sally and the children, but that's a given. I explained to them that I am an open book, will answer all questions, and we all can take it from there.

Also, now that I officially have a diagnosis from a Parkinson's specialist, when I beat this and become symptom free, maybe the information will be able to help others. What a useful purpose I will have served.

* * *

11/07/09. Up at 4:00am. Had a lot of things on my mind regarding re-wiring my nervous system. I needed quiet time to read, reflect, and to experiment with mobility.

Did a couple of tests. First, held onto the counter and lifted right leg at knee, like marching, 4 times. Did the same with left leg. Slow, but okay with each individually.

Then, tried to alternate "marching." As my right foot touched the floor and I began to lift my left leg, my right leg began to tremble, my right leg collapsed at the knee, and my left leg began uncontrollable tremoring and tightening and locking only an inch or two off of the floor.

This reminded me of the test Dr. Sanchez-Ramos gave me where I held my left arm straight forward and he had me tap my right thigh with my right hand (I was sitting on the exam table, legs dangling over the side). At his office, my left arm started shaking violently.

I starting thinking that maybe I need to start training my limbs one at a time because of the negative impact each has when I try to exercise or move them together. I decided to do more standing (Standing and Balance from the Recipe outlined in Part Two of this book) to build internal energy. I put my back against the wall to hold the balance of my body while I stood (this time arms at side) for 5 minutes. I shook during the second half of the five minutes.

* * *

11/08/09. Slept in 6:35am, slow. Sally and I are going to the movie Fourth Kind with Steven. It will be nice to get out of the house and see Steven up at the college. Movie was very good and very intellectual.

* * *

11/09/09. Up at 4:00am. Start of a new week; this is exciting.

Had a good day doing my routine. About 8:00pm my upper back hurt, by 9:00pm my kidneys were in pain. Generally, pain is good. Toxins put up a fight when they are being cleaned.

* * *

11/10/09. Up at 4:00am. Slow and in pain, but feeling a bit lighter and a little straighter in my spine. By 10:00am, feeling like any other day…hunched forward and shuffling… my Parkinson's normal.

My arms and legs are feeling weak. I have severe rigidity in my thighs, which is worse than it has been, and I have regular rigidity in my arms.

Oh well, tomorrow we will see how all this plays out.

* * *

11/11/09. Up at 4:00am. Slow, slow, slow. Got to the kitchen at 4:10am. Legs are very wobbly, but this might just be the effect of yesterday; we will see as the day progresses. The girls are out of school today for Veteran's Day and Sally slept in an extra 1/2 hour — good for her — she really needs the rest.

I was doing fair today, but at 1:00pm I hit the wall and needed to go to sleep for an hour. I need to find more energy, so I am going to focus on my Medical Qigong exercises. They are exhausting and exhilarating, go figure.

* * *

11/12/09. Up at 4:00am. Seems cooler this morning, no real difference in how I feel. We had an apple salad for breakfast. Interestingly, I spent the morning trying to think of something different for breakfast and all I could come up with was an apple salad. When I woke Sally and asked her what she wanted for breakfast, she said, "How about an apple salad?" Great minds think alike, haha.

The day has gotten cooler and at 9:30am I switched from shorts to jeans. I noticed that my legs do not like this cooler, damper weather. They are fighting me. Regular walking (if you can call it that) has been difficult today. Balance is off and knees are wobbly, calves and thighs are tight and not working in conjunction. Long day; really wore me out.

* * *

11/13/09. Up at 4:00am. COLD! Moving very slowly. Got to the kitchen at 4:10am. Legs are very tight. I am starting to learn better how much extra energy it takes to get around.

Generally, when I am walking, I do not sense that I am having to exert myself any more than I ever had to exert myself to walk before Parkinson's. However, today is in the mid-50's and when I got back inside from getting the newspapers, I was out of breath and the tremors were raging throughout my body, particularly in my calves and thighs.

I am still quite puzzled how they can be raging like that and you cannot see any unusual shaking in my outward appearance.

* * *

11/14/09. Up at 4:00am. Took Victoria to her clarinet

lesson and brought Steven his bike. In the afternoon, I cut the grass.

It was cool out, but it still wore me out. However, the yard looks nice.

Sally, Victoria, and I watched 27 Dresses. It was a cute movie.

* * *

11/15/09. Up at 4:00am. Very slow. Think it was cutting grass yesterday. Got to kitchen at 4:14am. I believe that is my new world record for slowness.

I had a hard day today. Very slow, lots of pain. Very dizzy. I am going to blame it on cutting the grass yesterday and see how I feel tomorrow.

* * *

11/16/09. Up at 4:00am. Slow moving. Got to kitchen at 4:09am. I feel like my body is heavy. No lightness in my movement. Low energy took its toll today.

At 8:00pm, had to go to sleep. With my usual wake up time of 4:00am tomorrow, that will be 8 hours in bed. I either will feel refreshed or not be able to move...no control over that, we will see tomorrow.

* * *

11/17/09. Up at 4:00am. Eight hours in bed. Got up a few times to use the bathroom, but no problem going back to sleep.

I feel rested and stiff...slow moving, but the weighted feeling of yesterday is gone. Got to the kitchen at 4:09am. Expecting a great day today.

APPENDIX TWO

In Part Two of this book, I presented my Parkinson's Recipe for Recovery. I pulled out the physical part of the Recipe and placed it in this Appendix. I will present the "Ingredients" of the Recipe and then proceed forward with the physical part as I did it.

INGREDIENTS
(Discussed in detail below list; the times listed are the approximate amount of time it took me to perform these ingredients):

Exercise: Medical Qigong for the Liver. (15 minutes in morning and 15 minutes in evening)
Exercise: Medical Qigong for the Kidneys. (10 minutes in morning and 10 minutes in evening)
Exercise: Qigong for Clearing Liver Wind. (5 minutes in the morning)
Exercise: Neck exercises. (5 minutes in the morning)

Exercise: Standing and Balance. (5 minutes in the morning)

Exercise: Awareness of Neural (electrical) Impulses. (15 minutes in the morning)

Exercise: Near hand–far hand Exercise for Kidney and Brain. (10 minutes in the afternoon)

Acupressure for Tremors: Governing Vessel, GV2-20. (5 minutes in the evening)

Jin Shin Jyutsu for Balancing Energy Flows. (12 minutes in the morning)

Brain Vibration Chanting. (5 minutes each of morning, afternoon and evening)

Sitting Zazen. (10 minutes in the morning)

Vegetarian diet.

Yin Tui Na (Forceless Spontaneous Release). (30 minutes in the evening for 5 days)

Mediations, affirmations, prayers. (Varied throughout the day)

MEDICAL QIGONG FOR THE LIVER

1. Held my hands in front of my navel like holding a small ball.
2. Slowly raised my hands to slightly above eye level.
3. Lowered each hand to chest at lowest level of ribs directly in line straight down from nipples.
4. While pressing my palms against my ribs, rotated my hands six times in one direction and then six times in the other direction. Leaving my palms where they were, I alternated bending toward the sides four times to each side.
5. Lowered my palms to lowest point on ribs on each side of the body directly in line straight down from armpits.
6. While pressing my palms against my ribs, rotated my hands six times in one direction and then six times in the other direction. Overlapped my hands against my body just below the belly button, alternated bending forward and backwards four times each.
7. Put my hands on my knees, traced the bone down front of

each leg. When reaching ankle, I lifted my hands and pointed my fingers at my toes. Then, I straightened back up.

8. Repeated 1 through 7 sequence 10 times.

I slowly worked my way up to ten repetitions, stopping before ten if necessary so as not to over-do it. My body told me when to stop, and eventually I achieved ten repetitions. A little background will help with the explanation of this Medical Qigong. According to the Chinese body clock, each organ is at its peak of functioning in a two-hour window of time during the day. The gallbladder is from 11pm until 1am and the liver is from 1am until 3am. So from 11pm until 3am, my liver and gallbladder were at their peak of cleaning toxins from my body. This was a good time to be at rest.

Here is what I felt was occurring:

1. *Held my hands in front of my navel like holding a small ball.* The reason for beginning this way was to create an internal focus and an intention to heal; I was grounding myself in the moment.

2. *Slowly raised my hands to slightly above eye level.* When I brought my hands in front of my navel like holding a small ball and then raised them slightly above eye level, my focus was directed inward; my intention was directed toward the Qigong, and I was solidly grounded in the exercise.

3. *Lowered each hand to my chest at lowest level of ribs directly in line straight down from nipples.* This was to get in me in the correct position to stimulate the liver meridian.

4. *While pressing my palms against my ribs, I rotated my hands six times in one direction and then six times in the other direction. Leaving my palms where they were, alternated bending toward the sides four times to each side.* The point I was pressing and rubbing was Liver Meridian point 14. My feeling was that I was stimulating this point as a way to say, "Wake up. I know it is not between 1am and 3am, but I am toxic with this Parkinson's, and I want to strengthen you and have you assist

me with another cleansing of toxins. Thank you."

Then, doing the circles was to generate energy in the liver meridian. I often had a difficult time pressing and massaging in circles, so I stimulated this point by either lowering my hand quickly and hitting the points with my palms, or rubbing my hands up and down or side to side, or even pressing with my fingertips.

When bending to the right, I was stretching and pulling and then releasing the liver meridian that was running up the inside of my left leg. When bending to the left, I was stretching and pulling and then releasing the liver meridian that was running up the inside of my right leg. This strengthened the meridian, strengthened my liver, and assisted in opening up blockages in the meridian. Sometimes this would cause my tremors to increase. However, my view of this was that as I was creating more energy flow in the meridian, and it was causing tremors to increase because the energy (electricity) was hitting blockages.

5. *Lowered my palms to lowest point on ribs on each side of the body directly in line straight down from my armpits.* This was to get in me in the correct position to stimulate the gallbladder meridian.

6. *While pressing my palms against my ribs, I rotated my hands six times in one direction and then six times in the other direction. Then I overlapped my hands against my body just below the belly button, alternated bending forward and backwards four times each.* The point I was pressing and rubbing was Gallbladder Meridian point 25. My feeling was that I was stimulating this point as a way to say, "Wake up. I know it is not between 11pm and 1am, but I am toxic with this Parkinson's, and I want to strengthen you and have you assist me with another cleansing of toxins. Thank you." Then, doing the circles was to generate energy in the gallbladder meridian. I often had a difficult time pressing and massaging in circles, so I

stimulated this point by either lowering my hand quickly and hitting the point with my palm, or rubbing my hands up and down or side to side, or even pressing with my fingertips.

When bending forward, I was stretching and pulling and then releasing the part of the gallbladder meridian that was running up my legs. When bending backwards, I would have been stretching and pulling and then releasing the part of the gallbladder meridian that was running up the sides and front of my body; however, my balance was poor, and I could not bend backwards. The idea of this Medical Qigong was to strengthen the meridian, strengthen my gallbladder, and assist in opening up blockages in the meridian. Sometimes this would cause my tremors to increase. However, my view of this was that as I was creating more energy flow in the meridian, it was causing tremors to increase because the energy (electricity) was hitting blockages. Also, although my balance was poor and I could not bend backwards...I still had a full recovery.

7. *Put my hands on my knees, traced the bone down front of each leg. When reaching ankle, I lifted my hands and pointed my fingers at my toes. Then, I straightened back up.* Looking at a liver meridian graphic would show that I was helping push energy down the meridian to remove blockages—I was tracing Liver Meridian points 7–4 before lifting my hands and pointing at my toes. This assisted in clearing blockages.

8. *Repeated 1 through 7 sequence 10 times.* As explained earlier, it took a while for me to work up to 10, but I got there.

There were some very valuable lessons I needed to learn in doing the Medical Qigong and working on my Parkinson's recovery, particularly when it came to my ability, or inability, to perform a certain exercise as it was written. I had to learn to do my best with the understanding that my best was good enough and that I needed to be kind to myself on this issue.

When I had Parkinson's, my balance was so poor that my center of balance was somewhere behind my heels. I hunched forward to not fall backwards. In the second half of Medical Qigong for Liver, where I was supposed to bend backwards, I could not even stand straight up, so I bent forwards and stood up as far as I could without losing my balance. It was my best, and it was good enough. In the end, I fully recovered.

When I had Parkinson's, the near hand–far hand exercises (explained on p. 267) became unbearably painful after a couple of weeks doing them as they appear in the Recipe, which required holding my hands away from my body. So I sat in a chair, put my hands on my kidneys (lower back, either side of the spine), and I did the first one that way. I then took one hand out and put it on top of my head and did the second one that way. It was the best I could do and my best was good enough. In the end, I fully recovered.

Ultimately, I learned that to be able to look at myself and accept that my best was good enough, I first had to learn to be kind to myself.

I looked at it like this: If I hired a contractor to remodel my kitchen and he provided me a list of tools and materials, I would buy the tools and materials, provide them to the contractor, and leave him alone to do the remodeling. If I stood there and tried to tell him how to do his job, nothing good would come from that. I hired him because he was the professional, and I needed to have trust and faith that he would do the remodel properly. I treated my body the same way.

I was providing my body the tools and materials to do the remodel. I had to refrain from trying to tell my body how to do it. When the contractor breaks through the drywall to get to the old plumbing to yank it out so the new plumbing can be put in place, if I was standing there and cringing and losing faith that he knew what he was doing because he just smashed a hole in my kitchen wall, and as a result I was to question his professionalism and abilities, the remodel would be a disaster.

Such was the same with my body. If I provided my body the tools and materials to support my recovery (the Recipe), and then I was to question my body's ability to take those tools and materials and heal me because I felt some pain or stiffness or I shook more, essentially questioning my body's professionalism and abilities, the remodel (my recovery) would not have taken place.

I needed to not lose trust and faith because of symptoms "feeling or looking worse" as this often was nothing more than a sign that I had increased my energy flow and that my body was healing itself. I would imagine that if the drywall in the kitchen had feelings, it would be shaking and feeling a lot of pain when getting hit by the sledgehammer. However, the remodel cannot take place without getting through the drywall to fix the plumbing. My recovery could not take place without breaking through the blockages and cleaning the toxins out of my body.

MEDICAL QIGONG SOUND FOR CALMING THE LIVER

1. Stood with my feet shoulder-width apart and eyes closed.
2. Placed my hands overlapping over the Dantian. The Dantian is an energy center inside the body located approximately one inch below the navel and two inches inward inside the body.
3. On the inhale, visualized energy rising up the liver meridian (beginning at inside of my big toe, came across foot and went above the inside ankle bone, up the inside of the leg to the groin, across to the outside of the ribs).
4. On the exhale, opened my eyes and while pulling in the abdomen, squeezed my anus and let out the Xu sound (it is pronounced Shuuu Yiii).
5. Repeated for a total of 6 inhalations and 6 exhalations.

Here is what I felt was occurring:
1. *Stood with feet shoulder-width apart and eyes closed.* This put me in a position of balance. Eyes closed, focus turned inward.
2. *Placed my hands overlapping over the Dantian. The Dantian is an energy center about one inch below the navel and two inches inward from there inside the body.* This created a concentration of energy, and my intention was focused inward.
3. *On the inhale, visualized my energy rising up the liver meridian. I would begin the visualization at inside of big toe, come across*

foot and go above the inside ankle bone, up the inside of the leg to the groin, across to the outside of the ribs. In Medical Qigong for the Liver, I stirred up a lot of toxins, and in the final movement of each repetition, I pushed energy down the liver meridian. Here, I was helping calm the liver by bringing energy slowly and smoothly back up the meridian, simultaneously up each leg and through the groin to the ribs, ending at the same point where I began Medical Qigong for the Liver, Liver Meridian point 14.

4. *On the exhale, I open my eyes and while pulling in my abdomen, squeezed my anus and let out the Xu sound (it is pronounced Shuuu Yiii).* Here, there was a shift in intention and energy flow. Opening my eyes brought my intention outward. Pulling in the abdomen and squeezing the anus forced the energy to flow upward and through the liver. The Shuuu Yiii sound was a vibration combination that was soothing to the liver. Any residual toxins flowed outward on my exhale, clearing and calming the liver.

5. *Repeated for a total of 6 inhalations and 6 exhalations.* That is what it took to calm my liver.

When doing visualization, I liked to picture something I knew the mechanics of in the physical world. For this visualization, on the inhale, I visualized pulling liquid up a straw running up the inside of my legs simultaneously, through the groin to the ribs. I then pictured it turning into vapor as I pushed out my exhale.

MEDICAL QIGONG FOR THE KIDNEYS
ELEVATING

1. Stood with my feet shoulder-width apart.
2. Placed my hands overlapping over the Dantian.
3. Took a deep inhale.
4. On the exhale, squeezed my anus and visualized pumping energy from my kidneys to my brain.

5. Repeated for a total of 20 inhalations and 20 exhalations.

Here is what I felt was occurring:

1. *Stood with feet shoulder-width apart.* This was centering myself.
2. *Placed hands overlapping over the Dantian.* This created a concentration of energy, and my intention was focused inward.
3. *Took a deep inhale.* This opened up my body and started feeding fresh oxygen throughout my body.
4. *On the exhale, squeezed my anus and visualized pumping energy from my kidneys to my brain.* This helped me move more energy to my low-energy Parkinson's brain.

   In Traditional Chinese Medicine, the kidneys are viewed as the storehouse of innate energy, or jing. The jing in the kidneys is brought up to the brain and converted to life energy, or qi. With Parkinson's, there is low brain energy, so this Qigong exercise assisted my kidneys in bringing energy to my brain. Squeezing the anus helped direct energy in an upward direction toward the brain. The visualization assisted my kidneys in moving the energy up to my brain as the kidneys are situated on either side of the spine in the lower back area.

   Moreover, fear negatively impacts the kidneys...as I healed my kidneys, I released fear...as I released fear, I healed my kidneys.
5. *Repeated for a total of 20 inhalations and 20 exhalations.* My brain was low on energy, so this is what it took.

STRENGTHENING

1. Sat in a chair and slid toward the front, back straight and feet flat on the ground.
2. Put my palms lightly on my thighs.
3. Inhaled and visualized the inhale filling the Dantian.

4. Exhaled and squeezed my anus while visualizing the energy going from the Dantian to the coccyx to the Mingmen (approximately the 4th vertebrae). Once it reached the Mingmen, I visualized bringing the energy around my waist on both sides to my navel).

5. Repeated for a total of 10 inhalations and 10 exhalations.

Here is what I felt was occurring:

1. *Sat in a chair and slid toward the front, back straight and feet flat on the ground.* This got me centered and grounded for the Qigong.

2. *Put my palms lightly on my thighs.* This kept my body in a stationary position so the energy movement was concentrated around the kidneys with little or no external movement.

3. *Inhaled and visualized the inhale filling my Dantian.* This was to build internal energy to best strengthen my kidneys.

4. *Exhaled and squeezed my anus while visualizing the energy going from the Dantian to the coccyx to the Mingmen (approximately your 4th vertebrae). Once it reached the Mingmen, I brought it around my waist on both sides to my navel.* This was challenging, but it absolutely was worth the effort. I wanted to use my kidneys to energize my brain and bring more qi energy to my body. However, my kidneys were low on energy as well with Parkinson's, so I had to strengthen my kidneys to assist them in helping me get more energy to my brain. I found it difficult to visualize the three movements on a single exhale, so I improvised.

    I did my single exhale with three separate pushes of air back-to-back, and I visualized each of the three movements with a push of air. On the exhale, push 1 saw the energy going down and backwards from my Dantian to my coccyx (tailbone); push 2 saw the energy moving straight up my spine from the coccyx to the Mingmen (4th vertebrae); push 3 saw the energy separating around my waist from my Mingmen to my navel. By then, I really needed another inhale, and the process started all over again.

I understood from looking at the kidneys' location that they were in my lower back on either side of my spine; this exercise was strengthening my kidneys because my exhale energy movements encapsulated my kidneys with circulating energy.

5. *Repeated for a total of 10 inhalations and 10 exhalations.* My kidneys were weak, so this is what it took.

MEDICAL QIGONG SOUND FOR KIDNEY HEALTH

1. Stood with feet shoulder-width apart.
2. Brought the backs of my hands across my kidneys and around to the front so that the backs of my hands were facing each other in front of my navel.
3. Raised the arms up in this position until the backs of the hands reached chin level.
4. Rotated my elbows down so the palms were facing each other like holding a small ball in front of the chin.
5. Exhaled and squatted down while saying Chui. (pronounced chew).
6. Stood back up out of the squatting position.
7. Repeated for a total of 6 inhalations and 6 exhalations.

Here is what I felt was occurring:

1. *Stood with feet shoulder-width apart.* I was centering myself.
2. *Brought the backs of my hands across my kidneys and around to the front so that the backs of my hands were facing each other in front of the navel.* I was gently stroking my kidneys and saying, "Hello kidneys, wake up, and let's get ready for an energy boost."
3. *Raised my arms up in this position until the backs of my hands reached chin level.* This was a physical lifting of my energy.
4. *Rotated my elbows down so my palms were facing each other like*

holding a small ball in front of my chin. I was centering my thoughts and intention, and bringing myself inward.

5. *Exhaled and squatted down while saying Chui. (pronounced chew).* The squatting stimulated Kidney Meridian point 1, also known as the "bubbling springs." This is a very powerful energy center in the body. The Chui sound calmed and soothed my kidneys.

6. *Stood back up out of the squatting position.* The squatting (number 5) stimulated Kidney Meridian point 1 and activated energy from Kidney Meridian point 1. When I stood back up, the energy moved from Kidney Meridian point 1 up the kidney meridian for kidney health and more energy for me.

7. *Repeated for a total of 6 inhalations and 6 exhalations.* This is what it took.

Another thing I did for my kidneys was drink more water. Lower back pain with Parkinson's generally meant kidney pain from not drinking enough water. I suffered from urgent urination and multiple trips to the bathroom to empty my bladder in the middle of the night. It may seem counter-intuitive for me to have drunk more water when I was going to the bathroom so much already, but drinking more water solved this issue.

The frequent urination and multiple nighttime bathroom visits were because I was too toxic, and my kidneys were telling my bladder "get this toxic liquid out of the body NOW!!!" Drinking more water diluted the situation and solved the problem.

QIGONG FOR CLEARING LIVER WIND

This was a sitting form of Qigong exercise. It was for strengthening my liver and clearing internal pathogenic Liver Wind.

1. I sat upright with legs crossed. For the days when sitting on the floor was not possible, this step was accomplished by sitting in a chair: I sat forward in a chair with my back straight and feet on the floor pointing forward, and then

performed the other parts of this exercise.

2. My palms faced toward my Dantian (below my navel) and my hands were placed so my fingers were loosely interlocked only as far as the first knuckle.

3. I twisted my body to the left and to the right 15 times in each direction.

4. Then, I fully interlocked my fingers and turned my hands facing away so I was looking at the backs of my hands and interlocked fingers.

5. I pushed my hands out and up (to just above eye level) 8 times.

6. I chomped my teeth together and then swallowed the saliva.

7. I finished by meditating quietly.

I viewed Parkinson's from the perspective of Traditional Chinese Medicine. My liver was in a weakened state and was unable to clean toxins from my body properly. As a result of being in this weakened state, my liver became invaded by wind…wind makes things shake…tremors. This Qigong helped to clear "liver wind."

Here is what I felt was occurring:

1. *I sat upright with legs crossed.* For the days when sitting on the floor was not possible, this also was accomplished by sitting in a chair: I sat forward in a chair with my back straight and feet on the floor pointing forward, and then performed the other parts of this exercise. What I was accomplishing here was keeping my lower body stationary.

2. *My palms faced toward my Dantian (below my navel) and my hands were placed so my fingers were loosely interlocked only as far as the first knuckle.* This focused my energy inward and centered me. The lightly interlocked fingers assist me in twisting my body as a whole unit.

3. *I twisted my body to the left and to the right 15 times in each direction.* This twisting in each direction was the functional equivalent of twisting my liver in the same way one would

wring out a towel.

4. *Then, I fully interlocked my fingers and turned my hands facing away so I was looking at the backs of my hands and interlocked fingers.* This created a solid unit for performing the next step in this Qigong.

5. *I pushed hands out and up (to just above eye level) 8 times.* After wringing out a towel (my liver), I needed to pull and stretch it back to its original shape and form. That is what I was doing here (4 and 5 combined).

6. *I chomped my teeth together and then swallowed the saliva.* As I was "wringing the wind" out of my liver, toxins would flow down and up, so my mouth would have excess saliva. Chomping my teeth and then swallowing sent the toxins down for elimination.

7. *I meditated quietly.* I had given my liver quite a workout. Meditating quietly for a short while calmed my system. I accomplished this by closing my eyes and doing ten long inhales and exhales.

This Qigong exercise was not something I started doing right away as part of my daily recovery routine. However, it was something that I found to be quite powerful.

In April of 2010, seven months into doing the Recipe, I posted on my blog about Clearing Liver Wind. Here are excerpts from that post:

> This needs a little background; I will be as brief as possible. In my Chinese Medicine books and research, Parkinson's is described succinctly as internal pathogenic Liver Wind. In short, the liver is not functioning well, and "wind" causes things to shake and tremble, i.e., internal tremors.
>
> Last month, I reviewed *The Yellow Emperor's Classic of Medicine.* Subsequent to explaining how the Heaven and Earth and all of the elements of nature as well as the seasons relate to one's health, the Yellow Emperor's physician then

explains a course of events and health issues (many of which I began experiencing in 2009) that lead to "Finally, when autumn arrives it is likely to be particularly harsh, and rapid decline in nature would be obvious. At this time, one's liver is particularly vulnerable to illness." Page 259. When autumn arrived in 2009, I began having internal tremors.

For about 7 months, I have been doing daily QiGong for liver deficiencies. Two weeks ago, I came across the first Chinese Medicine book I had read. It is called *The Complete Illustrated Guide to Chinese Medicine*, by Tom Williams. I found a sitting form of QiGong exercise that Mr. Williams refers to as "Form 3 of the Sitting Form Brocade Exercises." It is for strengthening the liver and clearing internal pathogenic Liver Wind. On page 201 of the book, it states: "Sit upright with legs crossed. The palms should be held inward toward the Dantian (step 1). Turn the trunk to the left and to the right 15 times (step 2). Interlock the fingers and turn the hands to face away from the body; push outward eight times (step 3). Strike the teeth and swallow the saliva. Finish by meditating quietly."

My breakthrough—this exercise makes me sweat (about the only time I have broken a sweat since November is every morning for the last two weeks when I have performed this exercise). Also, while meditating for a couple of minutes after the exercise, I have no tremors. It is the only time I am sitting still and experiencing no tremors. It's a start.

In late November of 2009, I had lost feeling in my skin. I was in the shower one morning and called out to Sally to ask if she had a problem with getting enough hot water that morning. She took one look at me and screamed for me to get out of the shower, that I was scalding myself.

I complied and asked her how it was possible; the water did not even seem hot to me. She had me look over my shoulder and my entire back, buttocks, and legs were very bright red. It was then that I realized that I could feel nothing when it touched my skin. And as somebody who had been a profuse perspirer in life, I simply stopped sweating.

By then, I had reached a level of acceptance that my Parkinson's symptoms were going to be unusual, so my panic button about symptoms had a lot of flexibility. This threw me off. It did not throw me off that I was getting worse or not going to have a recovery, but it startled me to the point of thinking too much about why it was happening.

Finally, to pacify myself, I decided that I was doing such a good job at cleaning toxins that they had come to the surface and clogged my skin, thus rendering me without feeling in my skin. This explanation, albeit seemingly ridiculous, was good enough for me to let go of the skin issue and move forward in my recovery.

I will say that over the following six or seven months, I would receive notifications from Sally or our children that my leg was bleeding or I had five mosquitoes on my ankle...just the subtle reminders that even though I could not feel what was happening to my skin did not mean that things were not happening.

If you can only imagine the elation I felt when completing Clearing Liver Wind and breaking out in a sweat followed by a short period of no tremors. Just remembering it still makes me feel great.

STANDING AND BALANCE

That's all I did...stand. It is a very powerful exercise because it opens meridians, lubricates joints, and gets balance back where it should be. As a result of being unable to stand straight without falling over backwards, I modified my standing as follows:

1. I put my back against a wall where I could be looking at a clock.
2. My feet were shoulder width apart and pointing forward.
3. I bent my knees a little as if squatting to sit on the edge of a stool, squeezed my anus once, and released.
4. I held arms in front of my body as if holding a beach ball against my chest, with my hands at eye level and palms facing my abdomen.

252

5. My shoulders and elbows were as relaxed as possible.

6. My mouth was closed, my teeth closed but not clenched, and tip of my tongue was resting against the roof of the mouth directly behind the middle two top teeth.

7. I inhaled deeply through my nose into my diaphragm.

8. I exhaled fully through my nose.

9. I started standing for two minutes. Gradually, I worked my way up to five minutes.

There were two main purposes for Standing and Balance. First, the liver and kidneys Qigong exercises had stirred up a lot of toxins. Standing and Balance held my body in a stationary position so the toxins could settle downward and be eliminated from my body. I thought of the Qigong exercises like shaking up a snow globe, and Standing and Balance as putting it down on the table to let all of the snow settle down to the bottom.

Second, by just standing, I was allowing my body to search out blockages in my meridians and open up again its own natural energy passageways. By standing in a stationary position, I was not interfering with my body healing me.

Here is what I felt was occurring:

1. *I put my back against a wall where I could be looking at a clock.* This is a modification of standard standing. Normally, standing is performed without leaning on a wall. However, my balance was so poor that I would have been unable to do the standing without leaning on a wall.

2. *My feet were shoulder width apart and pointing forward.* This was the beginning of getting myself centered and balanced.

3. *I bent my knees a little as if squatting to sit on the edge of a stool, squeezed my anus once, and released.* The bend in the knees allowed for smooth energy flow. The squeezing and releasing of the anus once was to "close" the orifice so energy would circulate inside my body and not escape.

4. *I held arms in front of my body as if holding a beach ball against my chest, with my hands at eye level and palms facing*

my abdomen. This put a relaxed roundness in my shoulders, elbows, and wrists for better energy flow.

5. *My shoulders and elbows were as relaxed as possible.* By situating my arms in this way, I was positioning the parts of the meridians that flowed up and down my arms to my hands into a better position for smooth-flowing energy. With Parkinson's, I found that the tightness in my shoulders pinched the meridians and interrupted smooth-flowing energy. Here, I was releasing and relaxing the meridians so they could flow more freely to open blockages.

6. *My mouth was closed, my teeth closed but not clenched, and tip of my tongue was resting against the roof of the mouth directly behind the middle two top teeth.* The purpose here was to have a good flow of energy by not clenching my teeth. The purpose of the tongue placement was to connect and keep a smooth flow of the microcosmic orbit of the Conception Vessel and Governing Vessel.

7. *I inhaled deeply through the nose into diaphragm.* This allowed for maximum oxygen to enter the body (more on this below).

8. *I exhaled fully through the nose.* This allowed toxins to leave, and it allowed me to keep my tongue in place on the exhale.

9. *I started standing for two minutes. Gradually, I worked my way up to five minutes.* This was a challenge, but I saw the increased Standing time as a sign along the way that I was getting better.

As mentioned earlier, I had been doing a brocade of Qigong exercises for ten years prior to getting Parkinson's. I knew that Qigong by itself would not cure Parkinson's. Clearly, it had not even stopped me from getting Parkinson's. Since the Qigong I had been doing for ten years had not stopped me from getting Parkinson's, I put it to the side. That is why the Qigong in the Recipe is Medical Qigong. It was there to heal my organs.

However, I made one exception. I knew how important and powerful Standing and Balance was! It is the only Qigong I had been doing for those ten years that is in the Recipe.

Here are some additional things I did to assist me with Standing and Balance:

1. I PRACTICED DEEP BREATHING.

Breathing is a complicated issue. I know to some it seems simple… breathing is an involuntary action without which we would die. So allow me to rephrase: Parkinson's breathing was a complicated issue.

Shallow Parkinson's breathing did not bring enough oxygen into my body. This exacerbated a number of unfavorable things, including fatigue and constipation. Deep belly breathing, or diaphragm breathing, brought a large amount of additional oxygen into my body. My energy level would increase because my cells were nourished by an amount of oxygen much greater than they had been receiving.

From a Traditional Chinese Medicine perspective, the organs work as organ systems with a yin (passive) and a yang (active) organ; the lungs and large intestine form an organ system. Regarding breathing, I looked to the lungs (yin), but I also looked to see how the large intestine (yang) was doing in the organ system. Also, this system impacts the skin and is associated with the emotion of grief. As mentioned above, my skin was clogged.

I was a Parkinson's sufferer who faced the issue of constipation. This was a large intestine issue that could negatively impact the lungs, the skin and the emotional balance regarding grief. I know it did with me. Deep breathing was difficult, and so was the emotion of grief.

I was quite grateful for the things Sally and our children were doing to assist me. However, it still was very difficult to have Parkinson's and not grieve over daily misgivings. That was a constant battle for me in the beginning. Along the way in my recovery, it caused me to refocus my energy on keeping faith and moving forward.

Just because I understood that anger, frustration, fear, worry, and grief all were detrimental to recovery did not mean that these little demons did not show up to play every day. That is where faith played a big part. Faith overtook these demons.

Circling back around to breathing, I started with the basics: breathe in, breathe out. Repeat. I describe below a method I utilized to assist with bringing in the most amount of oxygen possible.

I would lie on the floor on my back with my knees bent and feet flat on the floor. This would lower the small of my back to the floor. I placed one hand on my chest and one on my navel. I inhaled slowly to see which hand would rise. When it was my navel hand, I knew I was breathing into my diaphragm and I was then in good shape for deep breathing exercises. With Parkinson's, my rigidity fought this deep breathing, so I had to learn to be patient and to practice.

Once I mastered diaphragm breathing, I did the following breathing exercise:

1. Inhale deeply for a count of 4.
2. Hold breath for a count of 4.
3. Exhale for a count of 4.
4. Hold breath for a count of 4.

I would do this set of breathing four times in a row, and it helped with the breathing issues I was facing with Parkinson's.

2. I FOUGHT THE FEAR OF NEW TREMORS AND MORE PAIN WHILE DOING STANDING AND BALANCE.

In my recovery, I viewed a new pain in an area where I had not been feeling anything as a message that said my electrical impulses were getting to an area where they had been blocked from reaching before. This was a good thing. It meant progress. I felt the same way about increasing tremors.

Recovery from Parkinson's took a lot of faith. It required looking at what was often viewed as getting worse, e.g. temporary increase in pain or tremors, and actually knowing that what was taking place was progress in getting better.

When I would feel pain in an area where I had been feeling nothing, I was thrilled because it meant my nerves were not dead. It meant they just had not been getting enough impulses to the area for me to be able to feel anything. Pain was a welcomed thing for me because it meant my nerves were alive; if they were dead, I would have been feeling nothing, not even pain.

My Parkinson's brain did not create enough impulses to go through my entire body in a normal manner, so the Parkinson's symptoms appeared to move around or increase as I would feel a new pain or increased tremors in different places.

As I increased my brain energy and the electrical impulses flowing in my body through Standing and Balance Qigong and Brain Vibration Chanting, more impulses were generated and got sent throughout my body. As these electrical impulses reached areas of blockages in my energy flow, and as I was fighting to break open the blockages, I would feel some new pain and I would experience some increased tremors. Once I would break through those blockages, the pain would subside a bit and the tremors would lessen a bit.

NECK EXERCISES
TURNING HEAD TO SIDES
1. I sat up straight and slowly turned my head to the right.
2. Slowly turned my head to face forward again.
3. Slowly turned my head to the left.
4. Slowly turned my head to face forward again.
5. Repeated this 10 times to each side.

TILTING HEAD FORWARD AND BACK
1. I slowly tilted my head forward with my chin moving down toward my chest.
2. Slowly brought my head up to face forward again.
3. Slowly tilted my head back.
4. Slowly brought my head up to face forward again.
5. Repeated this 10 times forward and 10 times back.

TILTING HEAD TO SIDES
1. I slowly tilted my head to the right side as if trying to place my right ear on my right shoulder.

2. Slowly brought my head back to face forward again.
3. Slowly tilted my head to the left side as if trying to place the left ear on the left shoulder.
4. Slowly brought my head back to face forward again.
5. Repeated this 10 times to each side.

If my neck was particularly stiff and I could not perform any of these movements as written, I would use my hands to assist my head and neck in doing the exercises. However, I would only do the movements slightly so as to not strain my already stiff neck. After I would do this with the assistance of my hands for a number of days, the tightness would loosen up a little, and I would be able to do these neck exercises without using my hands.

I saw the neck exercises as something very important for tremors and energy flow in the body. Tremors occur from blockages in the electrical system. The Parkinson's brain is sending weak impulses and the impulses are trying to get through passages squeezed tightly by the rigidity, thus resulting in shaking.

A tight, stiff neck negatively impacted the ability for electricity (the neural impulses) to be delivered correctly to my body. The rigidity was literally squeezing the life out of the neural impulses...and out of me...it made me slow, unsteady, and fatigued.

This produced a large amount of pain. It occurred to me that in order to feel pain, it had to be the nerve endings themselves that were sending the "I'm experiencing pain" message to the brain.

If I was just sitting around watching TV and felt pain from my rigidity, it made sense to me that my ridiculously tight muscles were squeezing down so hard on my nerves that my nerves were sending an "I'm experiencing pain" message to my brain.

This squeezing caused blockages in the energy flowing throughout my body and these blockages negatively impacted my movement and caused me pain. To make matters worse, my dopamine faucet was nearly turned off, so I was getting very little assistance from my dopamine.

In taking a careful look at the gallbladder meridian, I saw that there were 40 points in my head (20 per side). Blockages at GB20, GB21, and

GB22 (running from the base of my skull on either side, down my neck, through my shoulders, and around the front of my chest) caused a host of issues, from headaches from energy not being released from the 40 points in my head, to a stiff and locked neck and shoulders from a poor flow from GB20 to GB21, to tremors in my arms and hands from poor flow from GB20 through GB22.

Having a looser and more flexible neck helped with many things in life, including reduction of tremors, improved balance, and looking backwards when backing up the car. Also, it helped with opening up the first line of electricity blockages in my body and thus assisted in my Parkinson's recovery overall.

Further, here is a comparison I noticed regarding the neck exercises and other exercises in the Recipe:

1. The "Turning Head to Sides" neck exercise was the identical movement for the neck that is achieved for the trunk when doing Clearing Liver Wind Qigong.
2. The "Tilting Head Forward and Back" neck exercise was the identical movement for the neck that is achieved for the trunk in the second half of Medical Qigong for Liver.
3. The "Tilting Head to Sides" neck exercise was the identical movement for the neck that is achieved for the trunk in the first half of Medical Qigong for Liver.

These movements for the neck and trunk loosen the passageways for the body's electricity to flow and for the neural impulses to have the best possibility of getting where they need to go carrying the messages from the brain.

AWARENESS OF NEURAL (ELECTRICAL) IMPULSES AND BRAIN VIBRATION CHANTING

I did the Brain Vibration Chanting to increase the energy in my brain. Also, I did slow-moving exercises to learn where the impulses were going inside my body, and then I combined the two ideas and visualized the streamlined impulses so each side of my brain eventually was retrained to control the same side of the body rather than the opposite side.

BRAIN VIBRATION CHANTING

I would sit up straight, take a deep inhale, and then repeat the following chant as fast as possible for five minutes (each time my breath ran out, I would pause, take another deep inhale, and begin the chanting again):

ling yow chee chee chee—joe ling bah

ling yow chee chee chee—joe ar ar sih sih

NOTE: sih sounds like sit without the "t"

I had leaned this chant from Dr. and Master Zhi Gang Sha. I knew my Parkinson's brain was low on energy, so I put Brain Vibration Chanting into the Recipe to increase the vibrational energy in my brain. These are Mandarin Chinese numbers arranged in a sequence to increase brain vibrations. I did this chanting for 5 minutes, three times per day.

AWARENESS OF NEURAL (ELECTRICAL) IMPULSES

1. While standing still, I slowly lifted my right arm up to my side and then lowered it; I did this four times. Then, I closed my eyes to if I could feel the impulses. I drew a crude outline of an individual and marked where I felt the impulses, e.g. right side of neck, left knee, etc.
2. I repeated the entire part 1 of the exercise with my left arm.
3. While holding onto my countertop in the kitchen, I slowly lifted my right knee (as if marching) and then lowered my foot to the floor; I did this four times. Then, I closed my eyes and see if I could feel the impulses. I drew a crude outline of an individual and marked where I felt the impulses, e.g. right side of neck, left knee, etc.
4. I repeated the entire part 3 sequence with left knee.

When I first did the awareness of neural impulses, each time I moved a limb, I then closed my eyes and the only impulses I felt were on the opposite side of my body.

Once I got used to doing these two processes, I combined them. After I performed Brain Vibration Chanting, as I felt my brain vibrating, I visualized the energy (electrical impulses) from the right side of my brain going down the right side of my body all the way to my right foot. Once I could visualize a smooth flow of energy, then I did the same thing for the left side of my brain vibrating all the way down the left side of my body to my left foot.

Over time, when I performed the Awareness exercise above, I felt impulses only on the side of the body where I was moving an individual limb. This took time to accomplish, so I had to learn to be patient.

Here is why I did these processes. On the day I received my diagnosis, my neurologist put me through a large number of physical tests. Some of the tests he had me perform included repetitive motion on one side of the body, which each time setting off rigid, often painful, and then uncontrolled movement on the other side of the body.

When I asked what was going on, my neurologist explained that with Parkinson's, there is often a mix-up in the cross over of right brain controlling the left side of the body and left brain controlling the right side of the body.

The following morning, I decided that I needed to feel where the electrical impulses in my body were going so I could work to control them. I remembered when I was young having learned about people who had a brain injury to one side of their brain leaving the opposite side of their body paralyzed, and that these people eventually were able to move their entire body. This told me that the non-injured part of their brain was able to move the same side of the body it was on, which at the time was paralyzed.

I felt that if I could retrain my brain to move the side of the body it was on, then I would not suffer from the crossover issues experienced at the neurologist's office.

As expressed earlier, after getting my brain to vibrate, I visualized energy going from the right side of my brain to the right side of my body only, and then the same with the left side.

When doing visualization, I liked to picture something I knew the mechanics of in the physical world. For this visualization, I visualized the right side of my brain filled up with oil, and then strings going down my body. The oil slowly went down the strings to the right side of my neck, through my right shoulder, all the way down to my right hand, then down the strings from my neck through the right side of my torso, eventually reaching my right foot. When my entire right side was "full," I shifted to the left side and repeated the entire visualization down the left side.

NEAR HAND–FAR HAND EXERCISE FOR KIDNEY AND BRAIN

PART 1

1. I placed both of the hands behind the body with palms facing toward the Snow Mountain area. The Snow Mountain area is an energy center much like the Dantian. It located inside the body by going up to the fourth vertebra and then forward two inches inside the body.

2. Said, "Dear soul, mind, and body of my Snow Mountain area, I love you, you have the power to boost the energy going to my brain, you have the power to heal me. Do a good job. Thank you."

3. Chanted jiu, which is pronounced joe, for 5 minutes while visualizing snow melting at the top of the Snow Mountain area, bringing energy to the brain.

PART 2

1. Placed one hand with palm facing the kidney and the other hand overhead with palm facing the top of the head.

2. Said, "Dear soul, mind, and body of my brain, I love you, you have the power to heal yourself, you have the power to heal me. Do a good job. Thank you."

3. Chanted jiu-yi, pronounced joe-ee, for 5 minutes while visualizing bright energy flowing from your kidneys to your brain. (I had read to not do this part if I had high blood pressure, a brain tumor, or brain cancer, but I did not have any of those things so I felt it was safe to do).

Near hand–far hand healing was another healing modality I had learned from Dr. and Master Zhi Gang Sha years prior to having Parkinson's. I had intended to do this near hand–far hand when I started doing the Recipe, but I forgot about it for a few days. It was in the early afternoon one day when I remembered about it, so I did it then. The boost of energy I received for the remainder of the afternoon was incredible, so I left this part of the Recipe as something to do in the afternoon.

Here are the things I needed to know to perform this healing:

1. *Snow Mountain area.* I counted upward from the coccyx, my tailbone, to my fourth vertebrae and then moved forward about two inches inside my body to locate the Snow Mountain area.
2. *Placement of my hands.* After a couple of weeks, I no longer could stand and hold my hands away from my body, so I sat down and placed my palms on my kidneys (lower back, sides of spine). For Part 2, I removed one hand and placed my palm directly on my head instead of holding it overhead.
3. *The saying of "dear soul, mind, and body..."* was to center me and to declare my intention to my body and the Universe.

ACUPRESSURE FOR TREMORS: GOVERNING VESSEL, GV2-20

In my acupressure book, they recommended Governing Vessel Meridian acupressure for tremors beginning at the coccyx and going up the spine all the way to the midpoint at the top of the head. The Governing Vessel Meridian is longer than the section of GV2–GV20, but that section was recommended for Parkinson's.

My tremors were terrible, and they were particularly worse when I would lie in bed trying to fall asleep at night. Every night, Sally performed this acupressure on me and it was a most incredible thing. As she was performing the acupressure, I felt electrical charges from my spine go down my legs to my feet and toes, and I felt electrical charges move across my back, arms, neck, and head.

The tremors would cease to exist momentarily and I would go to sleep within a minute or two. Most mornings, I would awake in the same position in which I had been lying when I fell asleep. I slept soundly, and except for the occasional night when I woke up needing to use the bathroom, I slept through the night with no problems.

Occasionally during the day when I was home by myself and wanted tremor relief, and I would endeavor to do this acupressure myself. I was able to reach back and massage GV2–5 and GV15–20. To activate the other points, I would lie on the floor and slowly roll my spine from side to side for a couple of minutes. I felt satisfied that I activated GV6–14 this way, particularly when I would get a little relief from my tremors.

JIN SHIN JYUTSU FOR BALANCING ENERGY FLOWS

Jumper cabling is lightly holding a finger with the curled fingers of the other hand. Jumper cabling my palms and fingers in the following sequence was to open my energy meridians:

    a. Placed palm to palm with fingers extended as if in prayer.
    b. Jumper cabled thumb.
    c. Jumper cabled ring finger.
    d. Jumper cabled middle finger.
    e. Jumper cabled index finger.
    f. Jumper cabled pinky.

Jumper cabled a.—f. for 2 minutes each.

As noted above, the jumper cabling was placing a finger in the cupped fingers of the other hand, not the palm. Each of the fingers relates to an organ system, so in doing the jumper cabling, I was providing low voltage electricity to my meridians and organ systems as follows:

    a. *Palm to Palm*: Total body energizer.
    b. *Thumb*: stomach and spleen.
    c. *Ring finger*: lungs and large intestine.
    d. *Middle finger*: liver and gallbladder.
    e. *Index finger*: kidneys and bladder.
    f. *Pinky*: heart and small intestine.

The jumper cabling was a very useful thing to do. Since the electricity was flowing from the command center, my brain, down to my body through the meridians, this was a way to send energy back up through the meridians to open energy blockages from the other side.

YIN TUI NA (FORCELESS SPONTANEOUS RELEASE)

Forceless Spontaneous Release (FSR) is a special way of holding the Parkinson's patient's foot to heal the stomach meridian. I had read about it from the Parkinson's Recovery Project website and downloads. I studied this until I understood what was to be accomplished, and then Sally and I worked on this together because I needed somebody to hold my foot.

Essentially, I lied down with my legs straight and toes pointed toward the ceiling. Sally held my right foot with one hand across the top and one hand across the bottom, lightly holding my foot between her hands. Neither of us concentrated on Qi flow or me getting better. I silently performed meditations and gratitude affirmations, and Sally performed her own silent meditations.

This was a small part of the Recipe (total of 2.5 hours, or 30 minutes per day for 5 days), particularly when compared to everything else in the Recipe (performed daily for nine months). I had read about success with this method for getting the stomach meridian flowing in the correct direction, so it is the method I used. I felt an energy release in my leg on one of the days, so I felt I had derived a benefit, which is why it is listed in the Recipe. Had I felt there was a stomach meridian backward flow issue when I started the Recipe, I would have performed stomach meridian acupressure on myself instead of Yin Tua Na, or FSR.

VEGETARIAN DIET

I have maintained a vegetarian diet since January of 2010, as I feel healthier doing so. Below is a reprint of my blog entry when I had Parkinson's explaining why I started a vegetarian diet.

I am on a vegetarian diet by necessity, not choice. Except

for occasional eggs and some butter, it is a vegan diet. This decision has been quite a process to organize and figure out, but Sally has been magnificent in preparing exceptional vegetarian meals.

One of the symptoms of Parkinson's is constipation. In my view, constipation is a four-letter word. I learned the hard way that animal protein stays in my system too long and I had to give it up. It then took a couple of months of healthy eating and high fiber to get this issue under control.

I am eating whole grains, brown rice, lots of fruits and vegetables, all kinds of beans, barley, chickpeas and lentils, and this is a diet that agrees with me and my condition 100%. Sally's friend Mary gave Sally an Indian cookbook years ago and Sally has been preparing many Indian dishes that are delicious.

Recently, we discovered a vegetarian cookbook by Madhur Jaffrey, the author of the Indian cookbook, and it has 650 vegetarian recipes from various countries around the world. It has opened my eyes to all of the possibilities of a healthy vegetarian diet. Also, many of the meals have a mix of flavors in the spices; sweet, sour, bitter, salty, and tangy, and these various flavors help different organs for better digestion.

Fiber is now more important than ever, and I discovered Fiber One cereal, the original one with 14 grams of fiber in 1/2 cup. To maintain my weight, that is, not lose any more than the 35 pounds already lost, I have to eat three main meals and two mini-meals in-between a day. Fiber One with a banana and soymilk is my morning mini-meal. It is tasty enough and it helps in keeping my large intestine functioning properly.

As mentioned earlier, animal protein took a lot of energy to digest, especially when compared to vegetable protein, and it stayed in my body a long time, which caused my large intestine to slow down or shut down, and toxins to go back into my system.

I was spending so much time doing the physical part of the Recipe to increase my energy and remove toxins from my body, that I did not want my food intake to cause me constipation and fatigue. It made the choice to switch to a vegetarian diet easier.

Sally and I have continued our vegetarianism, and we are very healthy.

Which brings me to a quote from Margaret Mead:

"It is easier to change a man's religion than to change his diet."

I wanted to get rid of my constipation and improve my recovery so much that I was willing to change my diet. It helped me immensely.

Printed in Great Britain
by Amazon